THE MAN
IN THE
MIRROR

TO SADEGH

THE MAN IN THE MIRROR

A TRUE INSIDE STORY OF REVOLUTION, LOVE AND TREACHERY IN IRAN

CAROLE JEROME

UNWIN

HYMAN

LONDON SYDNEY WELLINGTON

First published in Great Britain by Unwin Hyman, an imprint of
Unwin Hyman Limited, 1988

Published in Canada by Key Porter Books

UNWIN HYMAN LIMITED
15/17 Broadwick Street, London W1V 1FP

Allen & Unwin Australia Pty Ltd
8 Napier Street, North Sydney, NSW 2060, Australia

Allen & Unwin New Zealand Ltd with the Port Nicholson Press
60 Cambridge Terrace, Wellington, New Zealand

British Library Cataloguing in Publication Data

Jerome, Carole
    The man in the mirror: a true inside story of
revolution, love and treachery in Iran.
1. Iran – Politics and government – 1941–1979
I. Title
955'.053'0924   DS318
ISBN: 0-04-440168-X

Printed in Great Britain by
Biddles Ltd, Guildford, Surrey

CONTENTS

A GUIDE TO KEY FIGURES

Albala, Nuri   Paris lawyer, of Turkish Moroccan descent, friend of Sadegh and Christian Bourguet, with whom differences grew over his membership in the French Communist Party.

Ali   Adopted son and first adherent of the Prophet Mohammad, married to the Prophet's daughter Fatima. He is the first martyr of the Shia, or "partisans of Ali" who split from the Sunni over the succession of Ali to the leadership of Islam after the Prophet. Ali was assassinated.

AMAL   The Lebanese Shia political and military organization led by Mousa Sadr then Nabbih Berri.

Amiralai, Shamseddine   Member of the National Front, appointed ambassador to France after the revolution. Always politically hostile to Ghotbzadeh, he was further incensed by Jerome's presence at embassy dinner in Paris.

Arafat, Yasser leader of Fatah, largest group in the PLO, long a political contact of Ghotbzadeh's, especially in Lebanon.

Assad, Hafez & Rifaat   President of Syria. He and his ruthless brother Rifaat were friends of Ghotbzadeh's long before they came to power, their main point in common with him being hostility to Qaddafi.

Bahktiar, Shahpour   National Front member appointed as a last ditch compromise Prime Minister by the Shah.

Bani Sadr, Abolhassan   Sadegh's longtime cohort and rival in the revolutionary movement. Elected first President of the new Islamic Republic.

Bazargan, Mehdi   Professor of thermodynamics and leader of the Liberation Movement of Iran (Nehzat e Azadi) the religious group within the National Front. Became first Prime Minister of the new Islamic Republic, appointed by Khomeini.

Beheshti, Ayatollah   The formidable leader of the clerical party, the IRP (Islamic Republic Party). Known as The Trick Fox to Iranians, as Ayatollah Kissinger to Jerome.

Berri, Nabbih leader of AMAL, the "moderate" Shia organization in Lebanon and longtime friend of Sadegh (moderate only as compared to extreme Hezbollah Shia fundamentalists).

Bourguet, Christian   Sadegh's longtime friend from Paris days one of the three "French lawyers".

Chamran, Mustafa   Early mentor of Ghotbzadeh in America in Iranian student movement, who later became key figure in AMAL in Lebanon, then Minister of Defense in Iran after revolution. A moderate.

Chayet, Claude   Emissary of the French Foreign Ministry to see Khomeini in Neauphle, and to meet Ghotbzadeh.

Cheron, Francois   Sadegh's longtime friend, partner of Christian Bourguet.

Farhang, Mansour   A moderate close to Bani Sadr who was named first Ambassador to the United Nations after the revolution.

Farsi, Djalalodin   An Iranian Prof. Moriarty, a powerful figure in the shadows, Sadegh's nemesis along with Nabawi and Reyshahri. An ally of the PLO and Qaddafi and of the clerics behind Khamenei, and a behind the scenes figure in ongoing repression.

Fatemi, Ali a fellow student revolutionary in America.

Fedayeen political formation of a mixed bag of leftists, some quasi-religious.

Habibi, Hassan mild-mannered friend of Sadegh and Bani Sadr in Paris days, later joined mullahs and became Minister of Justice. Nicknamed the Slippery Sweetmeat for his opportunism.

Hezb'ollah   Party of God, the organized/spontaneous thugs of the IRP, in Iran. In Lebanon, refers to related group of extremists backed by Khamenei, Montazeri.

Hoveyda, Fereidoun   Once Shah's ambassador to the U.N. his brother Amir Abbas was Prime Minister left in prison by the Shah as a sop to the revolutionaries.

Hussain   The other great Shia martyr, grandson of the first, Ali. Killed by the rival Sunni leader Yazid.

I.R.P.   Islamic Republic Party. The clerical party founded by Beheshti, Khamenei Montazeri, Rafsanjani.

Khalkhali, Ayatollah   Judge Blood. The fat cleric who ran the first revolutionary courts and began the Terror.

Khamenei, Hojatoleslam   Arch conservative of the IRP and President of Iran after Bani Sadr.

Mortal enemy of Ghotbzadeh, known as The One Armed Man after injury in a bomb attack (Hojatoleslam is a religious title, lower in rank than Ayatollah).

Khodapanahi, Karim Paris friend of Sadegh's who later joined forces with the mullahs of the IRP, allied especially with Rafsanjani. Working in the Prime Minister's Office he became known as the Beria of Iran.

Khoeiniha, Mohammed Moussavi the bespectacled young mullah who led the Students in the embassy. Not an Ayatollah, though sometimes called so. An extreme cleric with pro-Marxist views.

Khomeini, Ahmad Khomeini's younger son, The Little K.

Khomeini, Mustafa Khomeini's elder son, died in Iraq.

Kiannouri, Nourredin head of the Tudeh, the Iranian Communist Party (pro-Soviet).

Ladjevardi, Assaddollah Teheran prosecutor, ally of Rafsanjani, who ordered Ghotbzadeh's arrest.

Lahidji, Karim Sadegh's longtime friend, a lifelong fighter for human rights in Iran under both the Shah and Khomeini.

L.M.I. Liberation Movement of Iran (Nehzat e Azadi). The theological group within the National Front led by Bazargan and Taleghani, of which Sadegh was a member.

Mahdavi, Mehdi young mullah who worked with Ghotbzadeh in final years. Executed.

Mohammad The Prophet, founder of the moslem faith.

Montazeri Ayatollah Senior cleric and designated successor to Khomeini. Known as the Tomcat, a bit dim, but formidable. Arch conservative, though later made noises against some censorship, he remained an avid exponent of spreading the revolution throughout Islam.

Mossadegh, Mohammed Prime Minister under the Shah ousted in the British-American coup 1953.

Mousa Sadr, Imam Religious leader of the Lebanese Shia, revered by Ghotbzadeh. Far more tolerant and liberal than Khomeini. Disappeared on a visit to Qaddafi in Libya in 1978, but is still considered head of AMAL in Lebanon.

Moussavi, Mir Hossein cousin of Khamenei, Prime Minister of Iran an extremist who often clashes with Khamenei.

Mudjehedeen the ultra dogmatic Islamic-leftist political and guerrilla organization, led by Massoud Radjavi, who fled into exile, taking Bani Sadr. Later split with Bani Sadr and went with his forces to Iraq.

Nabawi, Behzad Manipulator of the hostage negotiations within the Prime Minister's Office. A onetime Tudeh member and ally of Farsi in partnership with the clerics of the IRP. Mortal enemy of Sadegh.

National Front The democratic opposition party led originally by Mossadegh under the Shah, which under his successors became the political backbone of the revolutionary movement.

Radjavi, Massoud leader of the leftist-Islamic Mudjehedeen.

Rafsanjani, Hojatoleslam The Shark. Speaker of Parliament but in effect the most powerful cleric after Khomeini. Rival for Supremacy with Khamenei. Less personal hatred for Ghotbzadeh than Khamenei, but a lethal political enemy, of all the moderates.

Rajai, Mohammad Ali dim schoolteacher who became Prime Minister after bomb at IRP headquarters.

Revco The Council of the Revolution. Appointed by Khomeini to direct the revolution after his return to Iran. Included Ghotbzadeh, Bani Sadr, Habibi, Beheshti, Rafsanjani and other mortal enemies.

Reyshahri, Mohammed The Revolutionary Prosecutor and ally of Rafsanjani who presided over Ghotbzadeh's "trial", engineered his execution, and was subsequently promoted by Khomeini.

Tabatabai, Sadegh Sadegh's longtime friend, nephew of Mousa Sadr. His sister married Ahmad Khomeini, and Tabatabai joined forces with Ahmad; he too abandoned Ghotbzadeh to work with the clerics.

Taleghani, Ayatollah religious leader of the L.M.I., adopted by the Mudjehedeen too. Perhaps most revered of all Iranian clerics, a true moderate who fought extremists in the mosque. Died mysteriously in 1979.

Tudeh The Soviet Iranian Communist Party.

Vallette, Bertrand one of the three French lawyers, Sadegh's devoted friend.

Yazdi, Ibrahim longtime friend of Sadegh and Bani Sadr from student days, whom they later distrusted even more than they did each other. Remained in Iran with Bazargan.

INTRODUCTION

This book is about Sadegh Ghotbzadeh, who became foreign minister of Iran under Ayatollah Khomeini. As one of the main spokesmen of the Iranian revolution of 1978/79 and as a central figure during the American hostage crisis that began in November 1979, he became a nightly visitor in North American living rooms. He fascinated and infuriated. He was perceived in the West as a lone business suit in a welter of turbans, as an enigmatic enemy, and perhaps even as a friend. First and foremost this is the story of the revolution as he lived it. It is also about my love for him and his for me, a brief meeting of two worlds that re-created my life.

I have not set out to whitewash Sadegh, but to paint as true a portrait of him as I can. In this way, I hope I can open the doors for others that he opened for me, and help them discover the utter darkness and the exquisite light of Iran.

What has happened in Iran — and, indeed, what will happen in Iran — cannot be understood by fragmented news stories viewed on the days when it is the priority news item. To understand Iran and Iran's role in the Middle East, it is necessary to understand the events that brought it to the world's attention. It is necessary to see and hear the story behind the camera, the story beyond the neat parameters of the television screen. I believe this can be done through the story of one of the leaders of the Iranian revolution. Sadegh's long struggle — his hopes, his dreams, his crushed ideals and ultimately his death — reveals the tragedy of a nation, just as the story of our love reveals the human beings behind the history. That is my chief reason for writing as I have: great events cannot be divorced from the people who make them.

This book does not pretend to cover all aspects of the Iranian revolution of 1978/79 or the events that followed. Other works such as Michael Fischer's *Iran: from Religious Dispute to Revolution* must be read for a deeper and more expert look at the complex theological conflict over the philosophy of Islam practiced by the Ayatollah Khomeini, or for a delineation of Ali Shariati's sociology. The memoirs of Hamilton Jordan, William Sullivan and others give details of the American drama. I have gratefully based parts of this book on their books and interviews with them.

There are also questions about the roles played by the United States, the Soviet Union, Israel, Libya and the Palestine Liberation Organization in the revolution and the hostage crisis that followed. I do not claim to have all the answers. Where I do not have the answers, I simply raise the questions.

In following Sadegh's trail, though, I believe I am able to offer important new information and insights into, for instance, the links between Lebanon and the Iranian factions, elements at the root of terror and hostage seizures.

The portrait given here of the inside of the revolution and the regime now in power in Iran should also cast an interesting light on the affair that became known as Iranscam, or the Iran-Contra Affair. When men associated with the Reagan administration were found to have been supplying arms to Iran, they said they were for better or worse trying to support moderate elements they had contacted in Iran through Israeli sources. It is clear from the information in this book that the moderates are dead or in exile, or, like Bazargan, in no position to arrange arms deals. It has also become clear that the Americans in question were in fact dealing with Rafsanjani, allies of his in the Prime Minister's office, and agents such as Sadegh Tabatabai. It is also clear in this book that these men are not moderate in any sense of the word, but are ruthless, treacherous and are at the heart of the oppressive regime in power. It has always been unclear how supplies of arms to maintain a war with Iraq — that all real moderates want ended — was to help "moderates."

The Israelis are well aware of all this, and made it clear to the Americans involved that Israel of course has other interests in keeping the war going. Former national security advisor Robert McFarlane testified to this.

McFarlane has said it all degenerated into an arms for hostages deal. But again looking at the portrait in this book, I ask instead if it was not partly as well a cynical decision to work with hardline extremists of the islamic regime who were perceived to be the anti-communist faction. To me, this is one of the most serious questions to be answered in the affair.

A word about pronunciation and spelling. It's actually quite simple. The Persian (Farsi) names and words are simply pronounced

more or less phonetically, syllable by syllable, without much change
in emphasis. "Rafsanjani" is exactly as it looks: raf san jan i.
"Beheshti" is just be-hesh-ti with soft e sounds. Breaking them
down by syllables is the easiest way on first encounter. The four Ks
might be confusing, but not if you look at them this way:
Khomeini: Kho may nee (Kh is a gutteral K)
Khamenei: Kha men ay ee (don't mix him up with Khomeini)
Khalkhali: Khal khal ee (usually referred to as Judge Blood)
Khoeini'a: Kho ay nee a (admittedly a bit difficult)

Unfortunately the most difficult of all to get right is Sadegh's
name. To pronounce it truly is almost impossible for westerners.
But a reasonable approximation is:
Sadegh: sa-deg   Ghotbzadeh: Gobe za day

All Arab and Persian words are transliterated into the Roman
alphabet. There are many transliteration systems, thus it is possible to spell the name of Mohammad, the Prophet: Mohammad,
Mohammed, Muhammed, Muhammad, or Mohamet. Furthermore,
Persian transliterates differently than Arabic. Persian proper names
have been spelled in their most common form so that Mohammad
Reza Pahlavi, the Shah of Iran's first name is spelled Mohammad
while Mohammed the Prophet retains the common Arabic transliteration and is spelled, Mohammed. Other common Arabic words
have been spelled in the way most familiar to North American
readers, for example Koran rather than Qoran. Sources used to
determine common spellings were Webster's *Ninth New Collegiate
Dictionary*, *The World Almanac*, and the *New York Times Index* (though
all three of these sources are not necessarily in agreement).

The situation in Iran has necessitated my dissembling somewhat
to protect some people mentioned in this book. Names such as
"Alef" and "Shin" were taken from the Persian alphabet and used
to replace real names. For further obfuscation, these two individuals
are a composite of several actual people. By the same token, I have
given fictional names to several journalists who return to Iran often
or are permanently assigned to the Middle East.

Many of the people I mention in this book — Mehdi Bazargan,
for instance — deserve fuller treatments than I have been able to
give them, but unfortunately I cannot return to Iran to interview
them or record their versions of events.

On the basis of information given me by participants, I have
reconstructed many scenes and conversations that I did not witness.
For example, Sadegh's conversations with Khomeini are based on

Sadegh's own descriptions of them as he told them to Christian Bourguet, François Cheron, Bertrand Valette and me.

The dialogue I report is as accurate as I can make it. I cannot, of course, ensure that these exact words were spoken, but in all cases, I have made certain that the dialogue agrees with the known facts and with the spirit of the events and the personalities of the people. In the case of my own conversations with Sadegh, I can vouch for their authenticity. Our conversations are engraved in my mind.

The "French lawyers" each gave many years of their lives to Sadegh and many hours to this book.

I owe much to Janet, Dennis and Winston, and to Paula, Paul and Sam at the New York Times Syndication Sales Corporation.

I cannot name all those who have helped, but they know my undying gratitude. My family and friends have given long-suffering support.

My thanks is this book. It is for Sadegh, for them and for those who wish to know and understand, for better or worse.

PART ONE

FLIGHT TO IRAN

1

The slender spires of the minarets and kashis of the shrine rose into the hot June skies over the holy city of Qom. Patterned in mosaic with diamond and scale shapes, they looked like jeweled serpents. In their center, the golden dome was an echo of the sun beating down on the crowd that day in 1963.

They listened to a darkly intense man in robes of black crowned by the black sun of a turban.

Ayatollah Ruhollah Khomeini was attacking the Shah. He lashed out at the monarch for making American soldiers in Iran immune from Iranian law, and for giving the vote and military service to women.

"Your daughters will be sleeping in the barracks!" he thundered. Khomeini knew how to reach them.

The soldiers came for him on June 5. Dark and expressionless, he went with them to prison.

And the holy city erupted in violence. Opposite the shrine, religious students burst from the cool tranquility of the archways and courtyards of the madresseh school, and were met by armed police. Screams were heard as young mullahs were thrown over the parapets into the dry riverbed below.

To the north in Teheran, gunshots tore the crowds who demonstrated outside the great bazaar. It was the same in other cities of the nation. After three days, thousands were dead.

For the mosque, the revolution was on.

The young man in exile in the West lived in a world that knew nothing of all this. But he knew. His dark Iranian eyes smouldered, fixed on the future. The revolution was on for him, too.

The voice on the phone was irritatingly smooth and practiced, the tones of an unctuous con man. It was the first time I'd spoken with Sadegh Ghotbzadeh, and I had no desire to meet this Middle Eastern snake-oil salesman, but I had to for my work. It was the summer of 1978. We arranged a rendezvous, but another assignment interfered, and I canceled the interview with relief.

In the weeks that followed, this Ghotbzadeh person phoned from time to time to inform me of the latest press release from his group,

جنبش آزادی ایران

the Liberation Movement of Iran, or to try to get some publicity for
their cause. I was still wary of the smooth talker with the drawling
accent. When he called early in September to tell me that Libya's
Muammar Qaddafi had kidnapped an important Iranian-Lebanese
religious leader, I groaned in despair. Yet another anti-Qaddafi paranoid, I thought. Heaven preserve me from the Middle East! In the
years to come, I regretted many times that I did not follow up the
story, but I had no idea then how important the story was, or that
it would affect my personal life forever.

As bureau producer for the Canadian Broadcasting Corporation
in Paris in the late 1970s, I was responsible for overseeing all CBC
English network production out of that city. I acted as field producer
for TV and as a backup reporter for TV and radio news. At the
same time, I was on call for radio and current affairs programs for
everything from basic research to full documentary reporting. I
worked with CBC's senior correspondent, Joe Schlesinger, along
with a production assistant and a two-member television camera
crew. The remainder of the staff at the bureau—some twenty in all
—worked for the CBC French network. Our territory was Western
and Eastern Europe, which on occasion included the Soviet Union.
We shared this journalistic impossibility with the CBC's London
bureau. The Paris bureau offered the scope of reporting I enjoyed
—everything from NATO to the Paris Opéra.

I had come to the Paris bureau of the CBC in 1974 when I was
twenty-six. Europe, especially Paris, suited me. I loved the culture
and the language, which I had begun learning in elementary school
as part of an educational experiment. All my roots were European
and British.

In my twelve years as a reporter, I had studiously avoided covering stories on the Middle East, loathing the confusion of religious
violence from Mecca to Jerusalem. Though reared a nominal Pro-
testant, I believed in no God or church myself, and I wanted no
part of people butchering each other for Christ, Allah or Yahweh.

By 1978 it was impossible to avoid Middle Eastern politics. It had
been exported to Europe and had become the business of the Paris
bureau. Throughout 1978 there had been protests in capitals around
the world and at the United Nations against Iran's dictatorial leader,
Shah Mohammad Reza Pahlavi, and his family, and accusations
that Sazmane Ettalaat va Amniyat Keshvar (SAVAK), the Shah's
infamous secret police, the State Organization for Security and
Information, was violating the human rights of Iranians.

Iran was a geopolitically important country because of its oil, its friendly relations with Israel and the United States and its position as a non-Arab, Moslem country bordering on the Soviet Union. Iran received vast quantities of American aid, had a large well-trained army and was considered a bulwark against communism in the Middle East.

In August, the Paris bureau was asked to do a report on SAVAK operations in Europe. In our "Iran" file, I found the name "S. Ghotbzadeh" with the note "speaks English and French." S. Ghotbzadeh was known as a leader and spokesman for the Liberation Movement of Iran (LMI), the anti-Shah movement in exile.

I phoned him to arrange a meeting so we could discuss SAVAK. When that was postponed I went happily back to a story on terrorists of Quebec's FLQ in exile in Paris.

My blissful ignorance of the Middle East was not to last. On October 6, 1978, the boiling cauldron of Middle Eastern politics arrived in France in the person of Ayatollah Ruhollah Khomeini. Coverage of this powerful Iranian holy man fell to the Paris bureau. Once again I called Sadegh Ghotbzadeh to arrange an interview with him on the Ayatollah's call to revolution.

He arrived for our interview precisely on time. From the moment he entered, he dominated the room. Tall and massive, with black hair and soft eyes, he looked like an elegant bear in a light cashmere coat. He seemed amiable yet somehow dangerous. He was not handsome in any conventional sense, but there was something magnetic about him. The dark eyes seemed to hold secrets, the wide mouth was almost too generous. His physical characteristics so blended with his personality that I imagined his slightly flattened nose had been shaped by his daily confrontations with life. Even his speech, slightly slurred on some sounds, precise on others, reinforced the impression of an unsharpened knife.

S. Ghotbzadeh was definitely not what I expected. I was intrigued by his intensity, his appearance and his manner. For forty minutes he expounded on the history of Iran's exploitation by England, Russia and the United States, on the activities of SAVAK, the Shah's police, on royal corruption and on the necessity of harmonizing politics and religion in an Islamic culture.

"Can you describe the mechanics of a 'democratic Islamic republic'? How would the constitution, parliament and legal system work?" I asked.

"The details will be worked out in accordance with Islamic law."

''Medieval Islamic law?''

''No, no. Islam is an evolving progressive force,'' he assured me as we finished off the interview.

It was after six o'clock. As I closed the office, Sadegh invited me to a nearby café to talk. I wanted to be with him and to get to know more about the revolution. I had listened to many Third World revolutionaries, and Sadegh's rhetoric was different. He didn't use the hackneyed phrases of the left, and his logic was exotic and peculiarly Middle Eastern. Besides, the journalist in me encouraged the cultivation of this important contact.

In this way I rationalized my misgivings. The Middle East was all new to me and I could learn about it from this man.

We sat at one of the absurd little white wrought-iron tables at the Berkeley Café. He ordered tea and I ordered a hot rum grog. I asked him about a story in *Newsweek* that suggested he was a Soviet communist Libyan agent. The article, by Arnaud de Borchgrave, said that French intelligence sources reported that Ghotbzadeh had ''direct connections with the heads of the Communist party in France and Italy, and that he works closely with the Libyan Secret Service.''

Sadegh categorically denied being an agent, dismissing the rumors as the sort of nonsense one could expect under the circumstances. ''We in the Middle East are conditioned by foreign interference. We don't believe in ourselves. We don't believe we can have a revolution on our own because we never have. In the Middle East, it always has to be a foreign plot. That kind of conditioning produces the mentality responsible for the rumors,'' he explained.

As I listened to him, I lost my desire to go home. His face was a mobile mask, open and closed, open and closed. I studied him. Sadegh Ghotbzadeh was not a professional politician. When he talked about what he wanted for Iran, it sounded like a new design, a vision. Right or wrong, this revolutionary seemed very much in charge of himself. I could not imagine him marching to anyone's drum but his own. If he had any dealings with the Soviets or the Libyans, it seemed far more likely that they were the ones being had, not he.

We talked at length that first night. ''The Shah's an idiot,'' Sadegh observed. ''He thought he was untouchable. He thought he could take Iran back to the days of the Persian empire — the pre-Islamic empire,'' he explained to me. In my childhood, the Shah of Iran had glittered as the ultimate exotic royal. And the Iranian before me dismissed him as an idiot.

Sadegh explained that he had grown up hating the Shah, yet his was not red-faced anger. He had cool contempt for the monarch, as if he were disdaining a worm. I learned later that this elaborate nonchalance was a trademark, and a deceptive trademark at that. Sadegh Ghotbzadeh hated and loved with passion, but both emotions were veiled and masked.

"The pre-Islamic empire." I pondered his words. Because I did not yet grasp the depth of Islam, or understand the impact of the Shah's so-called reforms, I did not yet realize that those changes — reforms we in the West had been led to believe were progressive — were one of the major reasons for the unrest. I thought that the revolution was largely based on a hatred for SAVAK, the police, and for the Shah's wasteful economic policies. I did not yet fathom the power of Islam or understand that the mosque — a term that is used as we use the term "the Church" — was at war with the Shah on the one hand and internally divided on the other.

Sadegh seemed to me to be "Western". He wore a three-piece suit and spoke a colloquial English. But I was also dimly aware of the vast cultural differences that separated us as we talked in the café.

Several hours later, I said good night to Sadegh and left the café. As I walked home up the Champs Elysées, I felt confused, haunted by the mixed emotions I had felt all evening and wary of involvements. But when at the café Sadegh had asked me to meet him the next day at Khomeini's headquarters, I readily agreed. Tomorrow I would go to Neauphle le Château to see this Ayatollah Ruhollah Khomeini for myself.

* * *

Only the bare facts of Khomeini's life were known to the press when the man in the black robes arrived in France. Khomeini, I read, was born in 1902 at Khomeyn in central Iran. His father and grandfather were ayatollahs. Educated in Islamic schools, he went to live in the Holy City of Qom, south of Teheran. Khomeini was fiery and outspoken as well as devout and scholarly. He produced some twenty-one books in addition to many religious articles, writing not only on Islam, but on political issues and how they related to the faith. Within the mosque, Khomeini became a powerful figure; outside the mosque many were drawn to him as a spiritual leader. In 1962 he was arrested for criticizing the Shah, but he was released because of his position and large following. When he continued his criticisms, he was banished from Iran in 1964. From 1964 till October 1978, Najaf in Iraq served as his base. Fulminating even more against the Shah, Khomeini continued to call for riots, revolution, sacrifice and martyrdom in Iran. As Khomeini raged, his following grew. The Shah, alarmed and angered by Khomeini's call to arms, sought to make a deal with Iraq. Iran had been providing military aid to the Kurds, a fiercely independent group seeking self-government for their territory, in the corner of Iraq bordering on Iran and Turkey. The Shah offered to stop backing the Kurds if Iraq would silence Khomeini and prevent him from smuggling recordings of his speeches into Iran. A deal was struck, and Khomeini was asked to leave Iraq. Khomeini arrived in France and established headquarters at Neauphle le Château, a hitherto unremarkable village on the outskirts of Paris. There, he caused a daily tempest as hundreds of devout followers, security police and the world press converged to hear his obscure pronouncements.

*   *   *

Neauphle le Château had the picturesque charm of all other French villages I had ever seen. But its quaint normality was an illusion, like the drawing room Alice found in *Through the Looking-Glass,* "just the same as our drawing room, only things go the other way." The houses had dormered and shuttered windows and red roofs, and were surrounded by low stone walls. Its main street was paved, but there were no sidewalks, and a rural air prevailed.

It was a gray fall day, and the trees on the hillsides had begun to lose their leaves. I parked my car behind dozens of others that lined the hill above the Ayatollah's house and stepped into another world. As I walked toward Khomeini's cordoned-off compound, it began to drizzle. I walked faster, pulling a scarf over my head.

The compound consisted of two unprepossessing white houses that faced each other across the main road at the bottom of the hill. Iranians from all over Europe stood three deep, waiting to see the Ayatollah, who daily strolled from one house to the other to conduct prayers under a blue-and-white striped tent in the backyard.

My feeling grew that I had stumbled into an unreal world. Mullahs, Iranian holy men, strolled the streets and greeted the press. They wore long gray coats and over them, long black cloaks. Most had white turbans, all had beards. Crowds of Iranian devotees surged against the rope barrier and the gendarmes who protected the Ayatollah's route, while hundreds of reporters from Europe, America, South America and Japan jockeyed for position.

I showed my press credentials to the guards at the gate and was allowed inside the yard. A mullah came up to me.

"I'm a reporter for CBC radio," I announced, and introduced myself.

With a formal nod, he asked, "Have you seen what the Shah has done? Come with me."

I was escorted into the garage of one of the houses to take my turn talking to one of the victims of SAVAK's torture chambers. The man I spoke with was pathetic, old and tired. Great scarred gouges on his legs and feet showed where the wire whips had sung against his skin. He shakily and fearfully recounted his story. A simple man, he had made a simple remark about the Shah, and consequently been arrested and, to his bewilderment, been accused of being a communist. I felt pain for the old man's sufferings, but his was not the story I had come for. There was already ample documentation of SAVAK's cruelty; the Shah himself admitted that people had been tortured. Under pressure from U.S. President Jimmy Carter, Amnesty International and the press, the Shah was belatedly trying to curb this abuse, but without much success. The Shah no longer had control over his own monster, SAVAK, and certainly in those autumn days of 1978 he had no control over the monster at the gate, Khomeini.

Leaving the old man, I returned outside in time to watch Khomeini emerge from one house and walk slowly across the street toward the tent that served as a mosque. The crowd broke into cheers of "Allah-o-Akbar." Some dropped to their knees, others tried to take pictures, while still others either held their children over the cordon toward Khomeini, or they themselves leaned out in a vain attempt to touch his robes.

As the black-robed Khomeini approached I watched him intently. His facial expression betrayed no emotion, and his eyes seemed like black holes. I had a sudden sense of foreboding, a feeling that I was looking into the face of evil. I tried to dismiss my intuition. Perhaps it was his long, straight, white beard, strangely black, arched eyebrows and dark robes that brought Mephistopheles to mind? But no. I have seen other old, bearded men in black, and the lines in their faces have betrayed a lifetime of smiles and laughter, or a lifetime of self-denial and bitterness. This man betrayed nothing. It was the absence of all emotion that made him fearsome. Nor did he respond to the adoring crowd, some of whom had traveled thousands of miles to catch a glimpse of him.

The horror I felt at that moment remained. My fear never lessened nor did my opinion of Khomeini change over the years, despite my feelings for Sadegh and all his assurances.

As I pushed myself forward to follow the procession into the tent, another young mullah wearing a long, dark robe and a turban stopped me and commanded me to follow him. He took me to a small room in the back of the tiny house behind the tent. Inside were a dozen or so Iranian women, their faces hidden by blue or black veils, readying themselves for prayers. In that instant I angrily understood: women were not allowed in the main tent.

The Iranian women smiled and made room for me. I knelt down, but as they did not seem to expect me to pray, I stopped short of pretense. When prayers were over I stayed and talked with them. One of the women translated for me, but my questions about the dubious status they had here in veils and in seclusion were met with a total lack of comprehension. "This is the better way," I was told. "The presence of women disturbs men. This way both are peaceful."

Exasperated and angry, I left to join the other reporters in the garden. As I left, I took a quick look into the room across the hall. It was filled with recording equipment and there was a telephone in a tiny cubicle. I imagined this was the place where the now famous cassettes of Khomeini's messages to the people of Iran were recorded. The cassettes, smuggled into Iran and played in the mosques and in the bazaar, were a call to sacrifice and martyrdom. Later, I would learn how literally Iranians believed in revolution through death in the cause of Islam.

Outside, the relative silence that had prevailed before prayers gave way to louder shouts of praise as the crowd again pushed and shoved to get closer to Khomeini. Ignoring the zeal of his followers, Khomeini walked slowly back to his quarters. Hundreds of disciples crowded around shouting, "*Allah-o-Akbar.*" Cameramen and reporters jostled for space and I recorded the noise on my tape recorder. Again, Khomeini's expression never changed. He might have been alone in the desert with a god of stone.

On the edge of the crowd I saw Sadegh and I walked up to him. "Mr. Ghotbzadeh," I said formally, "if you go back to Iran, will Khomeini rule?" I again turned on my tape recorder.

"No. The people will rule. We will vote and elect our own government. Khomeini is a spiritual guide."

I asked a few more questions and recorded his answers. Then he suggested I meet him that evening at the Closerie des Lilas, a restaurant in Montparnasse. He would be there early with friends and would wait for me to join him later.

On the way back to Paris I considered his invitation. I wanted to see him again, but I was wary of the elegant bear to whom I felt so attracted. At Neauphle, my dislike of organized religion had surfaced, and the fact that Sadegh gave his allegiance to this forbidding old priest troubled me. Still, Sadegh seemed so Western, and when he discussed Islam he discussed it in the abstract. . . . My thoughts were again confused.

In the end I did not go to the Closerie that night. Instead, I wrote and recorded my story for CBC radio. My story only slightly masked my foreboding: "Though he may not look it, shuffling across the road from his small house here to the blue-and-white striped tent that serves as a makeshift mosque for his followers, the Ayatollah is part of a long tradition of warrior priests of Islam, leaders like the Mahdi, whose bloody Moslem revolt in the Sudan ended in victory and the death of General 'Chinese' Gordon and his men at Khartoum in the last century."

* * *

The next day there was more violence in the streets of Teheran. The newsdesk in Toronto wanted background stories and more on the Ayatollah and his plans. So I was sent back to Neauphle.

"Where were you last night? I waited," Sadegh said accusingly the moment he saw me.

I apologized, mumbling I had to work late.

He shook his head and suddenly said, "Pull your scarf on!"

I glared. Female reporters were expected to wear humble hair-hiding headscarves within the precincts. We all looked like Russian peasants. The matter of the scarf had not arisen yesterday because it was raining, and my head had been covered for practical reasons. Today I had strung my scarf around my neck as a gesture, and I could not bring myself to cover my self-respect in alien shame.

Sadegh again whispered savagely for me to pull on my scarf.

"Don't tell me you believe that a woman should keep her head covered?"

Sadegh grew agitated. "Just put it on, please. All we need are reports getting back to Teheran that Khomeini and his men are surrounded by flagrant Western women."

The implication froze me, but to avoid what seemed to be imminent expulsion by an approaching mullah, I pulled the scarf partway over my head.

"Meet me for dinner at the Closerie," he urged.

I agreed, temporarily suppressing my anger over the scarf.

* * *

La Closerie des Lilas is one of the fine old Paris brasserie restaurants of literary fame. Small brass plaques identify seats warmed by Ernest Hemingway's, Oscar Wilde's, André Gide's and lesser derrières. The rich dark wood and glowing red and gold lamps are redolent of past intrigues and good times. This, I learned, was Sadegh's favorite haunt.

We sat side by side on a banquette. As we ate, he told me more about his life, about his ideas, about Iran and about Islam. My anger over the incident with the scarf started to recede until I had forgotten all about it.

Sadegh conversed with me as a professional equal. He did not listen to me merely as a cover for flirtatious contempt. When he said that conservative measures were necessary until the revolutionaries were in control of the conservatives at home, I believed him. He told me men and women would be free and equal and I believed that too. What I had seen at Neauphle made me uneasy, but I believed Sadegh was genuine. Still, the journalist in me probed. While Sadegh dwelled on what would happen, I asked, always, "How?"

Sadegh spoke again of his youth in Teheran. "They arrested me once," he said offhandedly.

I remembered the old man at Neauphle. "What happened?"

He shrugged. "They dumped me in a room at the police station and they asked if I was a communist." After they had interrogated him they let him go. But his family understood the warning. His father promptly arranged for Sadegh to leave the country.

"I went to study in America. Did I tell you about that? I even went to university in Nelson, British Columbia." Sadegh's eyes brightened. "That was a good time. I like Canada. You can take me there again someday."

Canada at that moment seemed as irrelevant as Mars. Nelson, B.C.? How had the Iranian revolution gestated in Nelson, B.C.? I understood even less what it was to be Sadegh Ghotbzadeh. To me Sadegh seemed quintessentially secular, urbane and stylish —

the antithesis of the robed priest of Islam. I had a great deal to learn of the worldliness of the mullahs, and of Sadegh's concealed piety. But he never talked of his own faith, only of Islam as a concept and so I assumed it was only a concept to him, an element of political life. I could not have been more wrong.

We left the warm glow of the crowded restaurant and went through the old revolving wooden doors into the cold night and onto the Boulevard Montparnasse. Walking along the wide sidewalk towards the lights of the Dôme, the Sélect and all the other famous old cafés and bars, we talked of life in Paris for expatriots. Sadegh was fond of the beautiful old city, he was even fond of some of Paris's exasperating citizenry.

"You must meet Christian Bourguet," Sadegh said. "He's a lawyer, a friend of mine. He can give you a lot of background. He and his partners have offices just back there." Sadegh pointed back toward the Luxembourg Gardens.

"Good. I need to know more."

"You ask better questions than most journalists," he said, referring to my interview with him.

"There's no need to say that. I know I'm a neophyte." I didn't want to explain that I had always avoided the Middle East — in some ways still wanted to avoid it.

"I like talking to you."

He turned to face me. Suddenly he pulled me into his arms and kissed me so hard it hurt.

"Not like that," I protested as I pulled back.

"No? How then?" he asked, with a slightly wounded, bewildered look.

"Gently. I'm not going anywhere."

I didn't know it then, but in that moment he showed me a Sadegh few were ever allowed to see, the one who listened with his heart and who heard. He kissed me again, gently, beautifully, passionately. And I was terrified. To this man, I was vulnerable.

Most of the men I met were in awe of my profession. They were either impressed with or afraid of the image of the journalist. This man was neither impressed nor afraid. He was strong and he had his own goals. He was intelligent and, I was surprised to see, sensitive. He challenged me, something I was not used to experiencing. And there was a physical attraction as well, one I could not deny. Yet we fought and would go on fighting. He continued to frame his dream for Iran, and I kept asking how, and later pleaded no.

2

During 1978 the revolution had developed momentum while the West slept. The dead of each demonstration were the fuel of the next as Moslems commemorated the seventh day, fortieth day and year after death. Killings and mass arrests were answered by still more strikes and protests.

Then Ramadan began on August 5. Normally a month of fasting and religious observance, Ramadan signaled heightened protest. Religious leaders were arrested and demonstrators began to return police gunfire. On August 19 the revolution was further galvanized by the tragedy at Abadan: four hundred people were burned alive in the Rex Cinema, and word spread that the police had prevented rescue attempts. At the mass funeral the people shouted, "Death to the Shah!"

Unrest increased exponentially as religious leaders made more demands. They called for the closing of casinos, the shutting down of the Ministry for Women's Affairs and the lifting of censorship. More died in protests. In vain the Shah made concessions, which William Sullivan, the American ambassador called "feeding the crocodiles."

Returning from home leave in the United States, Sullivan requested an audience with the Shah. Consulate political officers throughout Iran had been reporting on the extent of the disturbances, and the Americans were finally becoming concerned. Sullivan had also heard rumors that the Shah was ill. Both matters warranted investigation.

When the Shah greeted Sullivan in his beautifully appointed office in the Niavaran Palace he was tanned, appeared healthy and at first seemed relaxed.

The two men commented on their respective vacations, then Sullivan began to talk of the political situation in Iran. The Shah grew first grim and reticent, finally lapsing into a moody silence.

When Sullivan prodded, the Shah angrily launched into a ten-minute harangue. He listed each of the marches, demonstrations and strikes that had taken place, concluding, "It's not just students. It's industrial workers, members of religious factions, even the Shi'a *ulema* [the body of mullahs] and the leading merchants of the bazaar. It's widespread, like the outbreak of a sudden rash. This cannot be the amateur work of a spontaneous opposition. All the evidence indicates sophisticated planning." The Shah turned to face Sullivan. "And I have decided that it must all be the result of foreign intrigue. What bothers me is that this intrigue is far beyond the capabilities of the KGB. It must therefore involve the British and the American CIA."

Sullivan was speechless. The tanned, healthy-looking Shah seemed suddenly undone, nervous and deeply paranoid. How could he possibly think the CIA had turned on him?

The Shah hardly paused; the words poured forth. "I can understand the British being involved. Some of them never forgave me for nationalizing the oil industry. And I listen to the BBC. They're always broadcasting critical reports on Iran, parroting Khomeini and interviewing the opposition. But I don't understand why the CIA has suddenly turned against me. What have I done to deserve this sort of action from the United States? Or has the United States reached some grand plan with the Soviet Union to divide up Iran?"

Sullivan was astounded. Patiently, he tried to reassure the distressed monarch that he had U.S. support. He went on to tell the Shah what the Americans knew of the demonstrations and those who planned them.

The Shah seemed surprised that the Americans knew as much as they did. Sullivan, on the other hand, was rueful. The authorities had precious few sources of information, and practically no intelligence on what was happening inside the mosques. The Americans had rejected the reports of their own best field officers, who rang warning bells like Cassandra on the walls of Troy. Instead, Washington had relied almost exclusively on the inaccurate and self-serving reports of SAVAK.

"Where do the demonstrators get the money?" the Shah asked.

"We don't know," Sullivan replied, feeling inadequate. "But to the best of our knowledge, it comes from the bazaars."

The Shah was incredulous. He believed Iran's powerful network of small businessmen — the *bazaaris* — supported him.

The ambassador suggested the monarch investigate the *bazaaris'* current loyalties. He knew the Shah lived in a dream world, isolated from the people. As Sullivan was leaving, he noticed his host was limping. The Shah explained that he had twisted his leg water-skiing. Sullivan left, wondering about the rumors of the Shah's ill health and pondering the monarch's paranoid conclusions that friends had turned against him. The ambassador wired Washington urging the president to reassure the Shah, and he decided to establish some contacts with the opposition himself.

On September 7 half a million people marched peacefully through a middle-class section of Teheran to the parliament buildings, carrying pictures of Khomeini and calling for Islamic government. The soldiers, under new orders from the Shah, made no move. The next day, Friday, several thousand people gathered in Jaleh Square to repeat the message. When ordered to disperse, male students in the crowd sat down and bared their chests. The troops opened fire on the crowd. Some claimed that they had themselves been fired upon first. The massacre was appalling. Young women in the front ranks were cut down while foreign journalists looked on in horror. About five hundred were dead by the end of Teheran's Black Friday.

The Shah's government immediately cracked down on protesters while President Jimmy Carter declared his support for the embattled monarch.

It was after Black Friday at Jaleh Square that the tide of violence turned. Before, the demonstrators had been passive victims. Now rampaging mobs began to take to the streets. In more and more incidents, foreign businesses and Iran's banks were bombed or burned. There was looting and lynching. Some of the revolutionaries were thugs whose savagery foreshadowed the horrors to come. The major demonstrations were still non-violent but there was a dark undercurrent in them now.

The cycle of demonstrations continued. In Washington the confusion became greater. Iran had been considered one of America's most stable allies. In Iran the Shah made more concessions to try to quell the unrest. He had the casinos closed, and the country reverted to the Moslem calendar. He dismantled the women's ministry. But the protests continued. He then authorized a new code of business conduct for the royal family, but only after most of its members had left the country.

Iranian ambassador Ardeshir Zahedi arrived from Washington to announce that the Carter administration advised the sovereign he was "fully at liberty" to act against the rebellion. But the Shah vacillated. He wanted Washington to shoulder the full responsibility for ordering massive physical represssion.

On November 5, the Shah appointed General Gholem Reza Azhari chief of staff, in place of Sharif Emami, who had resigned. As Iran collapsed around him, the Shah gave a lavish party for 120 international bankers.

A few days later Prime Minister Amir Hoveyda was thrown into jail with fifteen other scapegoats. He had served the Shah faithfully for fifteen years. And from Paris, Ayatollah Khomeini urged Iranians on. He urged them to martyr themselves for the Islamic revolution. On November 10, thirty-five thousand oil workers went on strike. On November 12 the National Front, one of Iran's largest opposition parties, called a general strike. In a pathetic attempt to defuse the revolution's religious fervor, Farah, the Shah's wife, made a pilgrimage to the graves of Ali and Hussain, the original Shi'a martyrs. The people jeered. The Shah, who had previously ordered SAVAK to release some high-profile political prisoners, ordered the release of more. But it was too late: Muharram was approaching.

Muharram is a period of atonement not unlike Yom Kippur or Ash Wednesday, though it lasts longer. It is central to the Shi'a faith, for during the days of Muharram the Shi'a, who are literally "the partisans of Ali," mourn their two most important martyrs: Ali, the son-in-law of Mohammad the Prophet, and Hussain, Ali's son. When Mohammad died, wars were fought over the succession or caliphate. The vast majority of Arabs chose to follow the preeminent Arab Ummayid family and their successors, and called themselves the Sunni. The Persians, although forced into Islam by Arab conquest, insisted Ali was the rightful successor to the Prophet and they became the most fanatical "partisans of Ali" or Shi'a. Ali could not hold the caliphate though, and he was assassinated at the doors of the mosque of Kufa, now Najaf, by a fanatic who resented his capitulation to the Sunni pretender.

When Ali's son Hussain marched to Kufa to lead a revolt, he and his family were hacked to pieces by the soldiers of the caliph Yazid. The anguished howls of the Shi'a are heard to this day. Muharram is a time of powerful religious fervor that might well be dreaded in a country already in the throes of violence and on the verge of anarchy. Ashura is the tenth day of Muharram, and on this day the Shi'a pray, fast and self-flagellate as they relive the death of Hussain.

Sullivan cabled Washington. He suggested that if the Shah fell and Khomeini took over, all was not lost. His assessment was that the new government would be staunchly anti-Soviet and that Khomeini would remain a Gandhi-like figure. The main drawback was that Iran would become anti-Israeli. "Thinking the unthinkable," he called it.

In Washington, national security advisor Zbigniew Brzezinski reacted to Sullivan's cable with angry scorn. He thought a military coup was the only possible way to keep the Shah on his throne, and that was exactly what he advised his president to consider. He wanted Carter at least to make strong statements supporting the Shah. President Carter decided to think about the alternatives.

not backing the Shah.

3

Outside, a chill winter wind chased leaves down the sidewalks and through the parks. Inside, Sadegh and I talked in the dark wood-paneled bar of the Closerie. It was five o'clock and the Closerie was full of habitués reliving their day, or trying to forget it.

"We never really believed it would happen in our lifetimes," Sadegh confided. He was speaking of the revolution.

"*Monsieur.*" A waiter bent toward Sadegh and motioned him toward the phone.

"I'll be back," he said unnecessarily as he unfolded his large frame from the chair.

I watched as he pushed through the crowd at the bar and disappeared. He was often called to the telephone by a waiter or by the owner herself. She seemed glad to let the big Iranian use the Closerie as his headquarters, since Sadegh's new notoriety added to the luster of the storied establishment. I smiled to myself. Sadegh seemed to take a childlike delight in the role he found himself playing. "You like this, don't you? Rushing about in the eye of the storm?" I had once needled him. He laughed in response. "Sure, why not? All these years no one would listen. And now all the reporters are begging for time." The pointedness of his reply had not been lost on me.

"I thought you were another Middle East lunatic fixated on Qaddafi. Listen, you wouldn't believe the number of calls we get from maladjusted citizens with visions of glory — or at least a vision of being interviewed. If I followed them all up, I could open a home for crazies. In your case, I could kick myself. Yours was the one in a hundred calls I should have followed up."

Sadegh had smiled. "Never mind. *Le Monde* wouldn't see me either."

I took a sip of wine. "Now I feel better." If Eric Rouleau, of the famed French daily, had missed the boat, I could be forgiven.

The conversation had given me pause. With few exceptions, the Western press had been slow to notice the events unfolding in Iran.

Instead, we had been seduced by the Iranian monarch, a powerful ally who was dragging Iran out of the mists of time and into the twentieth century. I remembered vividly a *National Geographic* story that featured the tall, distinguished monarch as he crowned himself on October 26, 1967, placing the heavy jeweled crown on his own head as he sat on the Peacock Throne in the priceless gold and gemstone heart of the Niavaran Palace.

The coronation and the Shah's personal life caught America's romantic imagination. First there had been Princess Fawzia of Egypt, who left in a confusion of royal press releases and rumors of her mate's infidelity. Then the West fell in love with her successor, Soraya, a regal beauty who resembled the film star Sophia Loren. When she too was divorced, we were told it was for her failure to produce an heir. Then came Farah, another exotic lovely who married in a froth of Parisian lace and was then crowned empress at the Shah's side. None of us paid any attention to the old prelate in exile. Few reporters in Iran had ever heard of Khomeini.

The stories about the Iranian royal family were the stuff of romantic novels and fairy tales. But for Sadegh and his friends, they were nauseating. While the courtiers snacked on caviar, Sadegh's friends were being routed by SAVAK.

I looked up from my drink and saw Sadegh coming back across the room.

''I have to leave,'' he said without preamble.

I nodded, resigned. Interruptions like this had become routine. ''I'll see you later tonight.''

I lived on the rue Pergolese next to the Maison du Québec. It was a wonderful little flat, well worth the six-flight walk up to it. It was old-fashioned and very French, with high dormer windows opening onto a long, narrow balcony. Its interior walls were covered with feathered gray wallpaper and trimmed with white. In each room there was a marble fireplace surmounted by gilt-framed mirrors. The furniture was less impressive, an assortment I had collected at flea markets in Paris.

At two in the morning Sadegh knocked on the door of my flat. When I opened the door, he stood there on the threshold, cold, wet, exhausted, but looming larger than ever in his heavy coat and rakish astrakhan hat.

He kissed my cheek and took off his coat and hat. I poured the hot tea I'd kept ready, and we drank in silence. It was the comfortable silence of routine.

"It's going to happen, isn't it?" I said, sipping my tea.

"It looks like it. But we're not ready yet. It's happening too fast."

"What about Khomeini? I still don't understand why you have chosen him. He's so cold."

"You don't know him. He has a good heart."

"He has no heart."

There was a flash in Sadegh's dark eyes. "Look, he's a human being, too. You should see him sometimes. Today after prayers he came back into the house and dropped his turban in the corner and said, 'Boy, am I glad that's over!' He hates that media circus out there. You'll see. He doesn't want the limelight."

I retreated, bowing to Sadegh's years of experience. I hated my cowardice.

But I would not and could not turn our few moments together into a polemic. Instead, I tried to think only of the man with me. I tried to understand him by burrowing close to him, by enfolding myself in his warmth and energy. But as he held me, I grew afraid and withdrew, frightened of something in him I could not name; I felt we were like snake and mongoose, and unsure which was which.

It never occurred to me that Sadegh might feel the same wariness of me. He seemed utterly self-assured, self-contained, invulnerable. He was not an ordinary man. He was a leader of a seismic revolution about to overthrow the legendary Shah of Iran.

As anticipated, Muharram, which began on December 1, 1978, brought the revolution new momentum. Thousands of Iranians poured into the streets. They were wrapped in symbolic white shrouds as a tribute to the dead martyrs. Their eerie shrouds were a declaration of their willingness to die for the Islamic revolution. To die for the faith is to become a martyr oneself; it is the perfect death and will lead immediately to the afterlife paradise promised by the Koran. The demonstration was not a demonstration of acceptance, but rather indicated the desire for martyrdom. The thousands of demonstrators surged back and forth, a sea of ghostly white bodies, like resurrected forms of the long dead come back to haunt the living. Terrified, the Shah's soldiers fired. White bodies crumpled and fell to the ground. Red blood covered their white shrouds.

On Ashura, the tenth day of Muharram, the day of the death of Hussain by the swords of Yazid, there was a massive march in defiance of martial law. Millions streamed into Teheran and flowed down Shahreza Avenue into the enormous square where the

Shahyad monument rose so splendidly. In 1971, the Shah had had the great fluted column on gracefully curved supports built to honor twenty-five hundred years of monarchy. Now the people moved around the monument shouting, "Death to the Shah! Death to the American cur!" "With Allah's help we will kill the impious traitor. Victory is near!" Laborers, teachers, shopkeepers, bazaar merchants, women in western dress and women enclosed in the black folds of the *chador*, children and clerics in green, black and white turbans all shouted in unison, "Death to the Shah!"

The American government was thrown into confusion by these events. Jimmy Carter simply did not understand what was happening in Iran. Where had it all come from? There had been no hint of it in the assessments he had received. On December 7 he had decided to make a statement. "The decision in Iran," he said, "belongs to the Iranian people."

Brzezinski was horrified and, as diplomatically as possible, he said so. On December 12, Carter made a speech reiterating America's unswerving support for the Shah.

Sullivan, on the other hand, wanted to make a deal with Khomeini and Bazargan. Brzezinski rose in angry contempt. He said Sullivan's suggestions were irresponsible lunacy. He wanted Carter to give the green light for a military coup.

Sullivan and Brzezinski argued back and forth while the situation in Iran continued to deteriorate. The queen mother left for Los Angeles, and on the first of January, Shahpour Bakhtiar, the newly appointed prime minister, announced the Shah would leave the country once the new government was formed. Bakhtiar was his last concession, a member of the opposition National Front appointed to calm the storm.

"A vacation . . . ," stammered the Shah to the crush of reporters at Niayaran. "That is, if possible . . . to rest a bit . . ."

In 1953 the Shah had also taken a vacation. At that time the CIA had carried out a coup and, after a short time, allowed the Shah to come back once again fully in control. There would be no coup this time.

* * *

That night Sadegh was in a fine mood. We met at the Closerie. "It's hard to believe it's actually happening," he said as he poured my wine.

"I can't imagine how you feel. It must be a bit frightening," I reflected.

"A bit! We're stunned."

I smiled. He didn't really look stunned. "No wine for you, I assume."

"No thanks."

Sadegh never drank alcohol, though he prided himself on being something of a wine connoisseur when ordering for friends. He never made a show of the fact that he didn't drink, nor did he insist that others follow his example. It wasn't simply that he was Moslem; he abstained because he just didn't want to drink. Sometimes he would smoke a cigarette or, more often, a pipe. He seemed to enjoy the ritual of tamping down the tobacco, patiently lighting it, then sitting back to appreciate the pungent smoke.

"I'll have my usual," he said happily to the waiter. "Lamb for the lady."

I knew he liked the familiarity of this place. He liked saying, "my usual" and knowing the waiter knew exactly what was meant. I turned to face him more directly. As usual we were sitting continental style, side by side at the banquette.

"You know I'm no admirer of the Shah's regime, but I'm a bit vague on what happens next," I said.

"It's like a new beginning. You can't imagine what it's been like. All those years — I wish you knew Iran, then you would understand."

Sadegh's love for his beautiful Iran was catching. I already longed to go there.

"I want to show you," he said animatedly. "Make them send you back with us when we go. That'll be some trip!"

"I'll try. It's up to head office. And you're right. I can't understand because I don't know Iran. Or Islam. I only know you. And even you are a mystery to me in a lot of ways. I must be out of my mind being here with you."

"Why?" he asked, genuinely at a loss. "I'm not so strange. After all, I used to live in Canada." He grinned.

"I know. But your world is so far away from mine. Besides, that's not what I meant. I'm supposed to be a reporter. I feel as if I'm consorting with the enemy."

"I'm not the enemy!"

"Only a KGB agent, according to the rumors," I teased.

He laughed. "Don't forget that I'm probably a Libyan agent, too. I'm very busy." He signaled the waiter for coffee.

I basked in Sadegh's presence. At the same time I was ill at ease, unsure of my ground. He must have many womenfriends, I told myself. So what was I doing wrapping myself in passion for him? Moreover, he belongs to another world, and to a revolution as well. I sighed. But then, I had lots of menfriends, though my feeling for him was deeper than for others. And his revolution was my job.

I had watched Sadegh deal abruptly with his cronies. Even though I was accustomed in my work and my life to assertive men, he was different. No matter how fond he was of me, he would remain just that little touch beyond my reach, true to his own imperatives. Never would I be able to walk over him, as I had been able to walk over others. Prostrate devotion repelled me, but Sadegh's affection was given head-on. And to me that was irresistible. From my own fortress, I loved him in return.

As I lay beside him that night, the walls and distances crumbled and vanished. I felt as close to him as the air.

4

Day after day I joined the milling reporters at Neauphle le Château. Sadegh and two others, Abolhassan Bani Sadr and Ibrahim Yazdi, formed a kind of *magi*—a trio of wise men—around the Ayatollah. Because they had had Western education, they translated Khomeini's daily pronouncements into either French or English. They took turns in the spotlight and the media ignored the powerful figures in turbans who came and went in the shadows. What no one knew then was that the Ayatollah's men—Sadegh, Bani Sadr and Yazdi—also took turns writing the Imam's speeches.

I watched them with both concern and amusement. These three were made for television. They provided endless spectacle—in our own language. But almost always Yazdi's English translation differed wildly from Bani Sadr's French, and the next day Sadegh would say something completely different in both languages. Khomeini emerged from Bani Sadr's nervous lips as an apostle of social democracy; from Yazdi's he sprang forward as an inexorable force of Islamic destiny and democratic will; from Sadegh's mouth he was an ambiguous apostle of life, liberty and hellfire. Reporters scratched their heads, understanding at least that here there was no unity.

In Iran, people amused by the spectacle began to refer to Bani Sadr, Yazdi and Ghotbzadeh collectively as BYGH, an acronym that spelled the Persian word for fool. But I was more disturbed than amused as the rumors began to fly that soon the Ayatollah would return to Iran.

"Sadegh!" I accosted him in the yard at Neauphle le Château. "What is going on here? Have you people really agreed on what happens at the other end?"

He shrugged and made a gesture of nonchalance. "It will get sorted out. Have you seen Christian Bourguet and the others yet?"

"No, not yet. I'm going there this afternoon."

"Be sure you do. He can explain a lot."

Another reporter tugged at his sleeve. Sadegh motioned him away. "Then meet me at the Closerie, okay?"

"I'll be late," I told him.

"I'll wait." He moved away to return to the importunate press. I headed back to Paris to see the lawyers.

I parked my car and walked toward the offices on the Avenue de l'Observatoire next to the Closerie. The offices fronted on a small treed area that shielded them from traffic. The afternoon light filtered through the leaves onto the pale stone of the elegant old buildings.

Inside, the elegance was faded and worn. A battered antique lamp cast soft shadows on colorless wallpaper and a faded old tapestry. Traditional French doors led to each of the lawyers' offices. Behind the doors, the offices were furnished in a comfortable mixture of old and new. Mirrors hung over marble fireplace mantels and antique desks were piled with files and books.

I met Bertrand Vallette first. Bertrand was small and crippled, a man who overcame his handicap with brusque efficiency. He settled me in a comfortable chair opposite his desk. I asked about Sadegh and the revolution. In his deep, intense voice Bertrand told me about Sadegh's lifelong battle, about his hatred of the Shah and of the necessity of incorporating the mosque into the opposition movement. The mosque, he explained, was seen by the Iranians as the only force that could unite the disparate elements of the opposition against the powerful royal machine.

We also talked about Khomeini. It was clear that Bertrand harbored grave doubts, though he said nothing direct. When he spoke of Sadegh, it was equally clear that he was devoted to him. His face softened and he smiled with enormous pride as he spoke of his friend's role.

It was much later that I met the other two lawyers, Christian Bourguet and François Cheron. Bourguet was tall, slim and well dressed, but surprisingly for a reputable French lawyer he wore his beard long. His soft words issued through a haze of pipe smoke. Cheron, by contrast, was a stocky man with sandy blond hair, an attractive moon face and a ready laugh. He had a less serious outlook on life than Bourguet.

These amiable Frenchmen finally cast light for me on the Iranian confusion at Neauphle. Over long hours in their cluttered offices they told me of their years with Sadegh and his cohorts and of the unending rivalry among the Iranians. As close as they were ideologically, Sadegh and Bani Sadr were personally incompatible. And both of them distrusted Yazdi. No wonder BYGH was so bewildering.

As the French government tried to come to grips with the Iranian revolution, Sadegh found himself, after twenty years in the wilderness, being consulted by those in power.

When the French Foreign Ministry summoned Ghotbzadeh, his lawyer friends on the Avenue de l'Observatoire were in an agony of apprehension. Sadegh usually expressed himself in blunt and inelegant French that would hardly impress the infinitely shockable gentlemen of the Quai.

The French Foreign Ministry is housed in an ornate building that started life as a nobleman's palace. Situated on the Quai d'Orsay, on the banks of the Seine, the ministry is usually called the Quai d'Orsay, or, more simply, the Quai.

Bertrand Vallette and François Cheron accompanied Sadegh to his meeting with Claude Chayet, chief of Consular Affairs, a tall, slim, elegant veteran of the French Resistance during the Second World War.

To the lawyers' surprise, Sadegh rose to the occasion, speaking clearly and eloquently for more than two hours with Chayet. He talked of Iranian history, royal corruption, the need to rule in harmony with Islam, how Khomeini would return to the mosque when his mission was accomplished: a new Iran still friendly with the West.

Chayet was impressed. He decided Ghotbzadeh would be in the upper echelons of that new Iran, a rational man with whom the French could deal. Khomeini, though, filled Chayet with misgivings.

Chayet made the tedious journey to Neauphle le Château many times to discover the nature of the disquieting phenomenon in his backyard. Not that Khomeini had entered France illegally. Any Iranian with a valid passport was allowed a French tourist visa good for three months. But Khomeini's speeches and his following in Iran were of interest to the French government, which had relations with the Shah as well as with moderate Arab states whose leaders were distressed with the Ayatollah's call to martyrdom and revolution.

On Chayet's first visit, Khomeini at first seemed rather like the pope. Then he suddenly exploded in a furious attack on the Shah, calling him an "agent of evil."

Chayet was troubled, but the Shah had told the French government he preferred they keep the Ayatollah rather than expel him. At least in France Khomeini could be kept under wraps, whereas if he went to a country in the Middle East, who knew what might happen?

But the French had now decided to do something about Khomeini despite the Shah's wishes. Khomeini's calls for civil disobedience against martial law curfews in Iran went beyond even France's flexible rules concerning political refugees.

In early January, Chayet went again to Neauphle to warn Khomeini that if he wanted to stay in France past January 4, the limit of his three-month tourist visa, he had to make a formal request. Otherwise, France would be obliged to force him to leave.

Without looking up, Khomeini replied that France could do as it wished.

Chayet requested another meeting with Ghotbzadeh. A lunch was set for one o'clock on January 4 at the Closerie. On this occasion, Chayet was accompanied by two other high officials of the Quai. They sat like a tribunal on one side of the large table, facing Ghotbzadeh and all three lawyers, Bourguet, Cheron and Vallette.

This time the French wanted specifics on how government in Iran would be structured if the revolution triumphed. Would Bakhtiar stay? The replies were precise. Ghotbzadeh explained the historical split between Bakhtiar and the Islamic-oriented group within the National Front, and told the French there was no question of Bakhtiar remaining. None. Khomeini had refused even to meet with Bakhtiar when he proposed a visit. Khomeini demanded Bakhtiar resign from government first.

Ghotbzadeh's analysis was relayed to French president Valery Giscard d'Estaing, who was on his way to meet Jimmy Carter at the four-power summit in Guadeloupe. When Carter and the French president met, Giscard d'Estaing was able to give him a full picture of Khomeini.

Then the American president made one of the most astounding of his many turnabouts: Jimmy Carter sent a message to Khomeini. He entrusted it to the French president, who empowered Claude Chayet to deliver it to the Ayatollah in Neauphle.

Chayet squatted in the flowered room before the old cleric, as Ghotbzadeh, on his right, remained to translate.

"I have a message from American president Jimmy Carter."

Khomeini remained expressionless.

Chayet cleared his throat. "He says to tell you that the United States will not oppose any new government in Iran as long as representative elections are held."

Khomeini said nothing.

"We in the French government are concerned about the safety of religious minorities and about such people as Amir Abbas Hoveyda, if you come to power." Hoveyda had been prime minister of Iran. The Shah had sacrificed him to try to end the riots, and Hoveyda languished in jail.

Khomeini stirred and raised his hand. Then he began to speak in a monotone. Sadegh translated, "But, my dear sir, I have fought to put an end to the regime that tortures, terrorizes, spills the blood of opponents. Do you think I would take over only to put on the same boots?"

Chayet took this as some assurance that there would not be a bloodbath in Iran. He conveyed the Ayatollah's reply to the president of the United States.

* * *

The French lawyers were utterly dismayed by Khomeini in the flesh. And as each day passed, they grew more disturbed and more bewildered by Sadegh's pious reverence for the stern old Ayatollah. They were only slightly mollified by Khomeini's apparent faith in Sadegh's political judgment.

One day they discovered a slight quirk in the man from Qom. Sadegh announced that he had to pick up some cologne for Khomeini. "He likes the Christian Dior stuff, Eau Sauvage," Sadegh told Cheron, who hooted in laughter.

"Khomeini? Christian Dior?" Cheron managed to sputter.

Sadegh was defensive. "Well, why not? There's no law against smelling nice. You know Khomeini's wife Batol?"

"Not personally," Cheron answered.

"She spends most of her time in Paris shopping for Dior dresses," Sadegh revealed.

"I didn't think the budget ran to things like that. She must be very elegant under her *chador*. It seems a waste."

"She is," Sadegh replied. Then, for Cheron's edification, he launched into a defense of the *chador*.

* * *

It was late in the day. I left the lawyers, and thanked them, but our long conversation had raised more questions for me than it had answered. Later, at home, I asked Sadegh about the *chador*.

"I just don't understand the veil," I confessed.

Sadegh lay back on the couch in my apartment and let out a deep sigh.

"Why," I persisted nervously, "should women wear scarves and huddle in back rooms? What happens later if you allow such rules in the beginning?" To me a revolution should be a revolution. It should move forward, not backward. The *chador* was all wrong. It made me angry on a personal level and it made me suspicious on an intellectual level. Even Bani Sadr said he believed a woman's hair gave off libidinous rays. But what really bothered me was that, in my view, the *chador* was a symbol of the almost universal oppression of women by religion. Sadegh's Islam, it seemed, was no different.

Sadegh sighed again. I agonized inside. All day he was under fire from the press and various political factions. He came to me for solace and love. I hated probing, but what I saw terrified me. I was in favor of overthrowing the Shah and SAVAK, but what then? Here, before me, was the one man I thought could tell me anything I needed or wanted to know, but I was loath to antagonize him or disturb him in any way.

My self-inflicted prohibitions bewildered me. I was rarely intimidated by anyone, but with Sadegh I felt like a rabbit who had disturbed a sleeping bear. The bear did not roar or strike, all he needed to do was open one eye and I dithered.

"Relax," he urged. "You don't know Iran or understand the mullahs. We have to go slowly, we can't make the same mistake the Shah made and do everything overnight. Look, do I put you in a *chador*? I trust you and talk to you as I do to any of the men I know. In fact, I talk to you more. Trust me, it will be all right."

"I know *you're* not in favour of the *chador* or the trappings of fundamentalism, but what about Khomeini?"

"He offers us a new kind of society with a real religious base," Sadegh answered.

"Khomeini will be going home soon," I said, as I turned out the light.

"Within the week," Sadegh answered.

I wasn't surprised by his words. Nor was I comforted when he added, as he almost always did, "It's too soon."

Then I drifted off to sleep. I was in a large open space. Unfamiliar, shadowy beings came toward me in a swirling haze and impelled me forward, gently but inexorably guiding me according to their will. The ground seemed insubstantial as I stepped forward. Suddenly, I stopped in horror.

The ground ahead of me was honeycombed with hundreds of open graves, dug so closely together that the walls of earth between them were only a few inches wide.

"Be careful," said one of the strangers as we stepped into the honeycomb. And as we balanced precariously on the narrow walls I could see below, in the open graves, ghastly, twisted bones and screaming faces in the first decay of death. They screamed and I screamed. But no sound issued as we moved relentlessly forward over the accusing dead. Beyond us rose a small mound, the object of our journey. On it was a strange and powerful symbol. We walked painfully towards it through the hellish bones, but it remained forever beyond us.

I woke up shivering and moved closer to Sadegh, pushing the nightmare out of my mind.

On January 16, 1979, the Shah and his empress left Iran "on vacation." They stopped in Egypt on their way to America.

When Khomeini heard the news, he emitted a satisfied grunt.

"Shah mat!" he spat. "Checkmate!" The king is finished.

5

January 30, 1979. There were two worlds: one inside the big blue Peugeot, one outside. Outside, the subtle glow of the Champs Elysées seemed unreal as we drove slowly past the elegant shops and expensive cinemas. Le Drugstore, more garish and glaring than the rest, seemed even more illusory. Le Drugstore — a Franco-American hybrid — an alien glimmering in the shadow of the Arc de Triomphe, that symbol of the republic of liberty, equality, fraternity and Bonaparte. Le Drugstore, in the shadow of the emperor's conquests, of Austerlitz and Iena, of the devastation of Borodino, and defeat in the Russian snows. Le Drugstore, where the inheritors of French history and culture sucked on sodas. Every day for years I had passed these stores and gazed into their windows, but that night I saw them differently. I saw them as if they were in a dream.

The Peugeot rumbled on towards Place de la Concorde, with Sadegh at the wheel.

"Are any of us going to come out of this alive?" I asked matter-of-factly. Outside, a carefree world. Inside, the reality of my question.

"Who knows?" Sadegh replied in his languorous, negligent way. "Maybe, maybe not."

The plane that would carry the revolutionary leaders home to Iran was leaving the next night. For days rumors and hot tips had burned the newswires:

"The plane goes at dawn tomorrow!"

"It's already left! They took off from the other airport!"

"It's going tonight at midnight!"

Nerves stretched as the historic moment was delayed, confirmed and then postponed again. The world waited to hear that Ayatollah Khomeini was in fact winging his way towards whatever strange destiny he and Iran had prepared for each other. Newsrooms panicked as wire-service machines clanged urgent reports of departure. "No," I had assured my newsdesk, "it hasn't gone. It isn't going tonight."

The man beside me in the Peugeot knew when the plane was leaving. We would both be on it tomorrow night.

We were both tired, possessed of the kind of weariness that temporarily buries apprehension and overtakes fear. The adrenalin had left our systems and in its wake was a kind of carelessness — as if life and death no longer mattered. This feeling, and the fatalism it produced, were not new to either of us. Perhaps for Sadegh it was rooted in religion; Islam, after all, means submission. He certainly had a Middle Eastern way of expressing disdain for destiny, a characteristic soft click of the tongue. In fact, I was never sure if he appreciated the seriousness of any situation beneath his insouciance. More often than not, he presented himself to the world as happily nonchalant. No matter what the mess, he would clean it up. No matter what was wrong, he would fix it. He exuded a damnable self-confidence. "Who knows?" "Who cares?" "It will be all right" were phrases he used often.

In my case, it was my profession that fostered fatalism. Journalists become accustomed to being swept up by the tide of events. For better or worse they go with the flow. There are calculations and rules for survival, but on the whole we worry later about whatever ghastly mess we have floated into and how we are going to get out.

Paris was already receding from my mind as the car drifted past the soft lights. Iran lay in the future at the end of a runway. The flight would be the beginning and end of a journey, a way of life, a dream, for the man sitting beside me.

"And if we do survive, if the revolution succeeds, what then? What is your part in the future government?" I asked.

"Nothing, I hope. I'm tired."

After a lifetime of struggle and sacrifice dedicated to this revolution, nothing? After years in the wilderness of exile, was Sadegh going home only to leave again? Now Sadegh was sitting at Khomeini's right hand. He was Khomeini's representative, his spiritual son. Did he intend to step down, to leave?

"Actually I see you as foreign minister," I suggested.

"No, no," Sadegh replied emphatically. "I want no part of all that. I've spent my whole life working to bring down the Shah, to make all this possible. I don't want to govern. That's for the others now. I want a normal life. I want to just sell whatever I have left in Iran and leave. We'll go live in Quebec, in the country." He grinned.

"Why Quebec?" I asked.

"I don't know. I like the idea. Wherever you are, when my part is done, I'll come and find you and we'll go live in Quebec."

The snows of Trois-Rivières and Sept-Iles seemed even more remote than the deserts of Iran. Sadegh's attitude made no sense to me even though he had told Christian once, "I don't want power. I have seen what it does to other people. I am afraid of power."

I did not know if Sadegh's desire to live with me in Quebec was the fantasy of an overtired man, or if it was really what he wanted. Certainly what he said he wanted was far from what I believed would happen. I had met him in exile. Once he returned to Iran, I believed I would lose him completely, just as an only partly tamed animal is lost to human friends when returned to the wild. I was both fearful of, and resigned to, my coming loss.

The car moved on. Suddenly Sadegh brightened. "Did you see my article in *Le Monde* today?"

I had. It was an explanation of the religious foundations of the revolution. In it he had written:

> Religion has never been separated from the political life of
> the Moslem man without misery and unhappiness replacing
> it. The spiritual dimension is the basis of thought, in order
> that the individual, in taking the part of the universal cause,
> may sacrifice himself for society. An Islamic government
> does not mean a theocracy in the strict sense of the term.
> Divine law and Islamic principles govern the application of
> equality, justice, liberty and fraternity.

"It's a bit Utopian, isn't it?" I asked. "Can it work that way? Have you worked out how? Don't you have to be there to implement it?"

"We'll see," he replied with a shrug. There it was again, the insouciant answer that in the future would drive to distraction those who interviewed him. But underneath the studied indifference there was a man who was running both toward and away from a terrible destiny, a man who would remain a puzzle even when I thought I'd put the last piece in place.

Sadegh brought the car to a halt in front of Place St. Michel. I had an appointment at a café there. He dropped me and went on to his own meeting.

* * *

At two in the morning I opened the door to Sadegh. His jaunty astrakhan hat and gray worsted coat were wet from the winter rain.

As he shed them he seemed to shed their stylish strength. He collapsed on my sofa in exhaustion, his eyes darker and his words dimmer than ever.

"We are leaving tomorrow night, but it's too soon."

Sadegh knew the dangers. Shahpour Bakhtiar, the Shah's compromise prime minister, might still pull the military together or the military might stage its own coup. Iran had modern weapons and trained fighting men. Our plane might well be shot down. Sadegh also knew there was anarchy in the streets.

"Khomeini wants to go," was all he said.

Sadegh was awake again at five-thirty to face the first day of the realization of his dream. He was calm, but clearly had a lot on his mind. I watched as he dressed, and thought that although we would be on the same plane, I might never be alone with him again.

"See you on the plane." He leaned over and tenderly kissed me good-bye.

* * *

Not until later did I learn that Sadegh had spent his last days in Paris frantically collecting and depositing money, and assuring the safety of the plane.

The original plan was to send an Iran Air jet from Teheran to Paris to fly Ayatollah Khomeini home. But at the last moment, the Shah's followers crippled all Iran Air's jets on the ground, on Bakhtiar's orders.

In Teheran, representatives of the LMI (Liberation Movement of Iran) met with the managers of Air France in their offices on Shahreza Avenue and a deal was made. They paid the airline from the ample funds that had poured into the mosque and their own headquarters. The rest they left to Sadegh in Paris.

But Shahpour Bakhtiar threatened to blow out of the sky any plane that carried his archenemy, Ayatollah Khomeini, as soon as it entered Iran's air space.

Many of the Ayatollah's followers at Neauphle were inclined to call Bakhtiar's bluff, but Sadegh had played for time to make his own arrangements. If they wanted safe entry, he reasoned, only the Americans could hold Bakhtiar back. Sadegh contacted a friend who, in turn, sounded out his old acquaintance, the American ambassador to UNESCO. In this way, he avoided contacting the American administration directly. Sadegh was then put in touch with Irving Brown, officially the representative of the AFL-CIO

(American Federation of Labor–Congress of Industrial Organizations), but less officially the representative of the Central Intelligence Agency, according to the friend.

Brown acted as broker for the plane's safe-conduct. The Americans had finally decided to join what they could not beat. To attack the plane was out of the question. It would be full of people.

Negotiations with Air France went ahead, but the Paris managers, having decided that the situation in Iran was unpredictable, demanded that 500,000 francs (about 100,000 dollars) of the charter fee be paid in francs rather than in Iranian rials.

Early in the morning, shortly before Sadegh arrived at the offices of the French lawyers, Bertrand Vallette called Claude Chayet, at the French Foreign Ministry. By now the French, too, were willing to assist in the inevitable. Chayet assured Vallette that the French government would pay Air France if necessary, and that the Iranians could later repay the French republic.

When Sadegh arrived, Vallette told him the good news, and together they went to Air France to sign the contract. But Monsieur Pauli, of Air France, was unenthusiastic. He made it clear that Air France did not regard the French government as a reliable creditor. Air France wanted payment now.

As they left the office, Sadegh rushed off with a hurried assurance to Vallette that he would get the money. Hours later, the three lawyers were still wondering *how*, when Sadegh reappeared with the air of a sleek house cat, and plunked down a heavy plastic shopping bag. "There!" he announced. Inside were the 500,000 francs demanded by the airline.

Sadegh had put in motion the wheels of the Iranian opposition's financial network. Calls to cohorts in Germany were the beginning. They contacted the banks in Hamburg and Zurich that held the bank accounts of the revolutionaries, and arranged for cash payments to Sadegh from bank branches in Paris.

Over the years the mosque, and later the *bazaaris*, had contributed large sums of money to the overseas work of the Liberation Movement of Iran, the group Sadegh worked with. There were accounts in several countries, including France and Germany.

Money in hand, Vallette and Sadegh tore off to Air France, where they handed Monsieur Pauli a check for the full amount. As soon as the contract with Air France was signed, they rushed across the city to put the money in the bank on which their check was drawn.

Later in the day a colleague from NBC news, Steve Mallory, offered me a lift to the Khomeini compound, where we were to pick up our tickets for the flight to Iran. We went in the limousine NBC had hired for the day's frantic commuting between its Paris office and Khomeini's headquarters. A slim, refined-looking blond, Steve had the indefinable raw edge peculiar to journalists who spend too much time in war zones. Belonging to neither side, war correspondents wear a psychological cloak on which seems to be stenciled "I'm not here, I'm only watching." But bullets and shrapnel penetrate the cloak by accident as well as by design, and the Middle East has claimed more than its share of journalists.

"I'd rather be in Beirut than where we're going," Steve muttered. He had spent a lot of time in that city, one of the most nerve-racking combat zones, where violence is displayed on a daily basis. Then he added, "Everybody's cat will have a gun. Hysteria will be general. How will the mobs react to us? We've got no way of identifying the factions."

I was hardly reassured by his words. The black knot in my gut drew tighter as we drove.

It was drizzling rain when we approached Khomeini's compound late that afternoon. Over the past weeks the yard around the small house had been trampled to mud by the impatient feet of journalists, disciples of the Ayatollah and security forces. Now the three groups mingled in an uneasy state of mutual distrust and puzzlement.

We waited in the cold and talked. After three hours a young mullah appeared on the porch to tell us that names had to be cut from the flight list because Air France complained there were too many.

After another three hours he appeared again. "You will find the tree with your country's name on it," he announced. "At that tree, a brother has your ticket if you are on the list. You will need twenty-four hundred francs, cash. May Allah be with you."

Three hundred disgruntled journalists stampeded into the trees like a pack of fevered hounds. It looked more like a carnival race than a once-in-a-lifetime opportunity either to be blasted into eternity by the Shah's Phantom jets, or, with luck, to be hurled into the murderous anarchy of the Islamic revolution.

"I can't find the British tree! Good God! Is there a British tree?"

"I think it's over by the Swedish tree."

"Is this the American tree?"

"No, it's in the back! I think it's that shrub over there."

The trees were identified by a penciled piece of paper stuck to the bark with scotch tape. Each one bore the name of a nation.

I found the Canadian/Swedish/Danish tree. Underneath it was a "brother" dispensing Air France tickets. My name, as Sadegh had promised, was on the list. I handed the brother my money and he handed me my ticket.

I drove back to Paris with Jean Reitberger, a cameraman from the French network of the CBC, and one of the lucky ticket-holders. Like Steve Mallory, Jean was a reluctant traveler because he'd had extensive experience in wars and revolutions. His nervousness intensified my own disquiet.

Back at the office, I called our crew who were already in Teheran. Don Dixon, our field producer, said without preamble, "It's insane here. The CBC is crazy to send you. Oh my God, don't come to Teheran!"

At midnight we all assembled at Charles de Gaulle Airport. There had been so many delays no one believed we were actually leaving. Journalists who were not on the list stood outside the rope barrier with hangdog expressions, envying those of us about to take our lives in our hands. A group of Iranians bent to the ground and prayed on the tiles in the harsh glare of the departure hall lights.

At last we boarded.

Khomeini, Bani Sadr, Sadegh and the rest of the entourage arrived together in the final departure area. Bourguet and his wife, Christine, were there, as were Bertrand and Geneviève Vallette. François Cheron came, too, but his wife Véronique did not. "I am a Greek," she had said, "and my people didn't fight the Turks for five hundred years so that I could put on a Persian veil instead of a Turkish one."

The lawyers came to say goodbye to Sadegh and his revered leader, but Khomeini swept past them and all his well-wishers like a Byzantine emperor.

In the first-class cabin, Sadegh sat beside Khomeini, each staring ahead. Seen together they could easily have been father and son. But in the end a vast distance separated their minds: it was the distance between two stars, between the cheek of Jesus and the kiss of Judas, between Hussain, the Shi'a martyr, and the curved knives of Yazid's warriors.

PART TWO

THE MAN IN THE MIRROR

※ 6 ※

I don't know when during the fall of 1978 I realized that I was in love with Sadegh, that he had a hold over me no one else had. Did he love me too? I was never certain that we both defined the word the same way. I knew there was a cultural chasm between us, which Sadegh's Western appearance only partially disguised. That chasm always held me back and caused me to spend the next four years fighting my feelings for him, running away, then returning.

I felt like a moth drawn to flame. And at the heart of the flame was Khomeini, dark and implacable. Why did Sadegh follow him? Who was he? What was he?

Throughout the time I struggled to know Sadegh, I kept wondering how he could be drawn to Khomeini. Sadegh was gregarious, articulate and full of humor. He could be politically intense and passionate as well, and his ideals were always in evidence. Khomeini, by contrast, was dour and severe. He appeared to be unconcerned with people. Side by side, they seemed to represent life and death.

After Sadegh was gone, I had to know everything about him: what had influenced him, his history, his conflicts. I traveled the places he had traveled and talked to his friends and his enemies. Eventually I pieced his story together.

Sadegh Ghotbzadeh was born in Teheran. Some of his papers give the year of his birth as 1937 and others as 1938. Sadegh was vague about it.

The Teheran of Sadegh's youth was not the Teheran of today. It was a large, typical Middle Eastern city of winding, dusty streets and dark, narrow pathways leading into the bazaar or marketplace. Merchants hawked Western goods such as brightly colored linoleum floor tiles, electric lamps, treadle sewing machines and radios. They also sold magnificent Persian rugs, baskets, copper goods, hand-tooled leather goods and jewelry — some of it gold studded with diamonds, some worthless metal set with cut glass. In the artificial

light of the bazaar the worthless and the priceless took on a similar
sparkle to beguile the shopper. Outside on the dusty streets, food
was sold from carts. The smell of cumin was everywhere, and one
did not have to venture far to find hot flatbread stuffed with spiced
meat.

Today, the mosques of Teheran vie with office buildings for the
attention of the tourist. When Sadegh was young, the spires of the
mosques dominated the skyline, their elegant turquoise and gold
turrets rising toward heaven like a protective army. In those days
only the palace of the Shah, with its gardens and reflecting pools,
competed with the mosques' beauty and grace.

But Teheran contained more than enticing bazaars and stately
mosques. In the teeming desert city, there were also slums filled
with aching poverty, there was child labor and there was death in
the streets from disease. Old men, their backs permanently bent
from years of work as human beasts of burden, were a common
sight, as were sightless children suffering from trachoma.

On the winding avenues were the houses of the middle class,
and on the sloping hills above the city were the homes where most
of the foreigners lived.

Sadegh's father, Hossein, was a prosperous lumber merchant
and an austere parent. His mother, an extremely religious woman,
doted on her four sons and three daughters. They led a comfortable
life. Hossein Ghotbzadeh was a leader of the bazaar. The word *bazaar*
refers to more than just the marketplace; it also refers to Teheran's
network of commerce and businesses. The bazaar is a Middle
Eastern institution, and it wields enormous power. Indeed, Teheran's bazaar became the financial backbone of the revolution.

The Ghotbzadeh family lived in a large house on Qasvin Street.
The family set a generous table, which often groaned with food for
dozens of guests. In the beautiful garden, there was a pool. But
beyond the walls of the garden the slums crept close. There was a
brothel across the dirt road, and garbage in the street.

The sons of Hossein Ghotbzadeh were not allowed to swim in
the pool in their father's presence. His daughters were allotted
certain hours in the water, but were scrupulously segregated from
their brothers. The seven children called their father *Agha*, meaning ''sir'' or ''master.''

Hossein felt a special affection for his second son, Sadegh, and
that affection was returned, although neither father nor son was

demonstrative. Hossein was deeply religious and imbued his family with his faith, but with the faith came strictness, and Sadegh, always adventurous and curious, often crossed the patriarch. More than once he found himself strung upside down by the ankles as his father beat his fettered feet with a heavy stick. Throughout the punishment, the son never uttered a sound.

Exerting an ancient matriarchal power over all of them was Ashraf, their overwhelming mother. Their father was *Agha*, "sir," but their mother was *Madar*, "mother," not "madam." Her big figure and broad features swathed in the black or gray folds of her *chador* were possessed of a vitality that anchored her children. Only in the privacy of their home did she remove the veil that was the habit of her profound religious faith. At home, and only at home, mothers, sisters, daughters and wives appeared in the dresses they wore under their veils. Thus they became rare treasures, known only to their husbands and fathers in their paneled sanctuaries. Anonymous in the streets, they possessed a strangely sharpened and concentrated identity and power within the home. Sadegh's mother was a strong woman, conservative and devout, from a plain background. She wanted her children to be successful, married and pious.

Sadegh seemed unlikely to fulfill his mother's desires. He was unruly and headstrong, forever getting his clothes dirty, wandering where he should not and falling out of trees.

In his early teens Sadegh took to roaming the streets with his friends, rabble-rousing in general and shouting imprecations against the Shah in particular. His mother believed the Shah was Allah's punishment on Iran for sins past and present. She was certain Allah would take care of the Shah, but she worried about her son. He wanted to give the divine machinery a kick.

Unlike his wife, Hossein Ghotbzadeh did not believe the Shah was a punishment. More sophisticated in his political views, Hossein was among those *bazaaris* who saw their businesses eaten up by royal hangers-on. Everywhere they looked they saw corruption and greed. Foreigners stripped the country of most of its wealth while the Shah, his family and friends took most of the rest. There was great poverty and great wealth; the Ghotbzadehs were one of a few families who fell in between the two extremes. They lived on the edge. They knew a comfortable life, but saw the result of exploitation all around. Sadegh ate heartily, but he knew that beyond the wall in the garden some of his friends went hungry. This knowledge made him politically aware, as did the conversations he overheard his father having with other leaders of the bazaar.

Hossein, Sadegh's father, became a supporter of the opposition party, the National Front, and a friend of its leader, Mohammed Mossadegh.   مصدق

Mossadegh had been elected to parliament under Reza Khan, the Shah's father, who at the time had been only prime minister not shah. When Reza Khan seized the country and took full powers, crowning himself king of kings, Mossadegh resigned. He returned to parliament only during the Second World War, when Reza Shah was forced by the British to abdicate.

After he became prime minister in 1951, Mossadegh, with the Shah's blessing, nationalized the oil industry. But the two men clashed as Mossadegh pushed for more and the Shah saw with alarm his dealings with Moscow, his radical economics. The people took to the streets.

So violent were the demonstrations that the Shah was forced to reappoint Mossadegh prime minister. The two clashed often in the following months. In July 1953 the Shah left Teheran, ostensibly for a vacation at his summer palace on the Caspian Sea. It was in reality for his safety during the now famous coup instigated by Britain and the United States. The Shah was returned to power before the end of the year. He banned the National Front, and Mossadegh was sent to prison. Ironically, though Western leaders claimed he was pro-communist, the Tudeh party helped overthrow him. Moscow thought he was allied to the CIA.

When he was released from prison in 1956, Mossadegh retired to his home in the village of Ahmad Abbad, near Teheran. Though he owned a large estate, Mossadegh was short of hard cash and to raise money he tried to sell the beautiful little tabrizi trees he had cultivated on his property. The trees were in great demand as decorative plants. When he called his old friend Hossein Ghotbzadeh to help estimate their value, Hossein sent his teenaged son, Sadegh, who remained with the old man for two weeks. In those two weeks Sadegh absorbed Mossadegh's words and beliefs and developed a deep affection for the birdlike old man with the bald head. What he saw as Mossadegh's brand of nationalism—Iran for Iranians and Iranian resources for the good of the country—became a part of Sadegh's political belief. But how did this fit with Islam?

Although the National Front was banned by the government and its members pursued by SAVAK, people kept its torch burning. Many even worked from jail, some from SAVAK's torture cells. Sadegh and other young members of the National Front were attracted to two leaders in particular: Mehdi Bazargan and Ayatollah Mahmoud Taleghani, both of whom had been in prison. Bazargan, a small, dapper, gray-haired man, was an engineer, a professor of thermodynamics and an Islamic scholar. His kindly eyes belied a fierce temperament.

Bazargan's was the first layman's voice to be heard espousing a revitalized, modern Islam. The mosque in Iran in the 1950s was not unlike the Church prior to the Council of Trent. In those days many priests, monks and friars demanded money to perform religious duties, many were involved in matters of state, corruption ruled supreme and any change was fought against. At first attempts to reform the Church were met by the Inquisition. Later, the Reformation forced change on the church.

The Shah had attempted to force a reformation as part of what he called his White Revolution, a series of sweeping social reforms that included land redistribution. The mosque fought the Shah as he expropriated its land and diminished its prerogatives. Some clerics remained loyal to the Shah, either with an eye to the main chance or sincerely wary of their brethren. Those who led the opposition to the Shah were arrested by SAVAK.

Bazargan agreed with the Shah on only one point: the mosque had become a force for intolerance and dogma, whereas it had once, under Arab domination, been a force of enlightenment, tolerance and learning. The Prophet Mohammad had once written that the ink of the scholar was to be as revered as the blood of the martyr. But on the whole, the mosque feared the ink of the scholar as much as the Shah did.

The mullahs, Bazargan believed, jealously protected their right to interpret the faith and thus closed the mosque to any new ideas. What Bazargan saw was the antithesis of the living, breathing faith he believed the Prophet had given the world. In this view, Bazargan was joined by Ayatollah Mahmoud Taleghani, one of Iran's most beloved holy men.

Taleghani was a longtime veteran of the battle with the Shah. He was first arrested in 1935 (by the Shah's father) and re-arrested many times after that. But however determinedly Taleghani fought the

Shah, he expended an equal amount of energy in resisting his reactionary brethren in the mosque who were opposed to the spread of knowledge.

Bazargan and Taleghani maintained a religiously oriented group within the National Front. They named it Nehzat e Azadi e Iran. This was the Liberation Movement of Iran, or the LMI.

To the outside world, the Shah presented Iran as a constitutional monarchy. It had a parliament with two houses and a cabinet (as it has today). There were elections. But the parliament was a rubber stamp for the Shah's decisions, and he appointed the cabinet. Elections were rigged; those who voted for other parties were persecuted. Now and again, a few opposition members were allowed to be elected to parliament, and there were those who refused to keep silent and escaped real harm. Bazargan and Taleghani were among those who, though often in and out of jail, were allowed relative freedom. Bazargan's power rested in his being an Islamic scholar well known outside Iran. His persecution would have attracted international attention. And Taleghani had followers who could be counted on to cause trouble in Iran. By allowing both to continue with only minimum restrictions, the Shah demonstrated his ''democratic bent'' to his Western friends.

But what the Shah really wanted was a return to the glories of the days of the Persian Empire, once the largest in the world. The days of Cyrus, Darius, and Xerxes, ruling from Susa and Persepolis. Ruling before Islam, as Sadegh reminded me. The Shah ensconsed himself on the Peacock Throne of Persian antiquity. He was, he said, sent by God and guarded by angels. The American government was the backbone of the Peacock Throne. A growing American political and military presence made this fact obvious. From a cramped office building, the American embassy grew until it was an eleven-acre compound. American personnel proliferated in the country's industrial and military life. Their overwhelming and overweening presence fueled the resentment of Sadegh and his friends.

In 1957, Sadegh was one of 90,000 applicants vying for the 10,000 places available at Teheran University. He was rejected. But he hung around the campus, consorting with his friends in the Front and attending lectures given by Bazargan and Taleghani. Listening to Bazargan lecture, Sadegh and his friends were inspired by his idea of Islam reborn. Bazargan's theological ideas and scientific scholarship made it seem possible for old values to live side by side with modern science. He and Taleghani called for a democratic republic based on progressive Islam, an idea entirely compatible with Mossadegh's nationalism.

Sadegh delivered revolutionary tracts and then began to help write them. He met with leaders of the Front, and together they discussed strategies to elude the iron hand of the Shah. But Sadegh was being watched. SAVAK was keeping tabs on him. Many of Sadegh's friends at the university were regular guests in SAVAK's cells, and as Sadegh's political activities increased, his parents became increasingly concerned.

Alongside the Front and its internal religious organization, the Liberation Movement of Iran, other organizations were spawned in the prisons. The Mudjahedeen e Khalq — The Warriors of the Faith — was made up of students who believed mainly in a disciplined mix of socialism and Islamic law. This group became an extremely important faction in and after the revolution and hostage crisis. Taleghani, in and out of prison with them, was their chosen spiritual leader, even though he did not belong to their organization. The Mudjahedeen went beyond Taleghani's teachings; they soon turned to guerrilla tactics, attacking SAVAK posts and assassinating key government and police figures. They went to prison by the dozens, and, as is usual in police states, many others went to prison with them. Priests, students, teachers and bewildered citizens went into the SAVAK cells. Many were whipped and boiled in oil to make them confess what they had not done. Many died in agony.

In those early days all those who opposed the Shah were allied by their common enemy. But beneath the alliance of opposition, there were secret factions and clandestine struggles. Different groups had different political beliefs and fundamentally different ideologies. And perhaps most important, each group mistrusted the others. This suspicion was a sine qua non of Persian politics, and later it resulted in betrayals, assassinations and anarchy.

But the tragic flaw within the Front and the LMI was their faith. Those in the LMI believed so intensely in the good of Islam that they did not see the need to change and reform the evil in the mosque before placing the nation at the mercy of Allah and the mullahs.

It was in this atmosphere that a friend warned Hossein Ghotbzadeh, in May 1958, of his son's impending arrest.

A few days later, the family and friends saw Sadegh off at Mehrabad airport.

In spite of himself, Sadegh was excited and even eager. He was going to America, to Georgetown University in Washington, D.C., the belly of the beast. But when he arrived in the capital, he was nonplussed to find the beast at home bore a close resemblance to the mouse that roared. To his more sophisticated mind, Americans were astonishingly open and guileless, naive to the point of innocence. They were like large children with dangerous toys. The citizenry in the capital of the free world seemed more preoccupied with their football team, the Redskins, than with politics. "Half their heads are hamburgers," Sadegh reported, "and half football."

The moment Sadegh landed in America, he plunged back into the politics of Iranian resistance to the Shah, becoming, with other students from New York to San Francisco to Paris, the core of the opposition movement abroad. They had been active in Iran, now they became the overseas arm of the LMI and were in constant contact with Bazargan and Taleghani.

Among those who formed the core of the student movement in America were three men in particular—Moustafa Chamran, Ibrahim Yazdi, and Ali Fatemi.

Chamran, a solid tree of a man, was a brilliant student of physics with a clear and rigorous mind whom Sadegh had known in Teheran, where they had both worked for the LMI. Stable and sensible, he became Sadegh's rock. Ibrahim Yazdi was an angular young chemistry student with frizzing hair who looked intently out at the world through thick glasses. Yazdi was earnest, intense and difficult to know. Ali Fatemi was a tall and impressive economics student who still burned over the torture and execution of his uncle by SAVAK. His uncle had been Mossadegh's foreign minister.

Sadegh was welcomed into the group. He was already known as a good organizer, a passionate speaker and a tireless worker. Gradually they drew more apathetic Iranian students into the fold and fired them with political fervor. The movement grew, and, mainly on Sadegh's initiative, formed itself into the Iranian Islamic Students' Association. The name was chosen for strategic reasons. "It will be harder for the Shah to attack us," Sadegh told his fellow students, "if we have a religious character and if we avoid political labels."

The association decided to attack the Shah on humanitarian rather than political grounds. Human rights was the association's best weapon precisely because it was the Shah's weakest flank.

In the summer of 1960 the Shah gave his soldiers orders to shoot to kill after an attack on the car of Prime Minister Eghbal at the University of Teheran. As a result several students were killed.

In America the Iranian Islamic Students' Association responded quickly. They held protest marches and demonstrations in front of the Iranian embassy, the United Nations and American government offices in Washington. They sought maximum media coverage and often wore paper bags over their heads to conceal their identity and thus protect their families at home from reprisals. Sadegh took a special delight in these events because he felt the association was actually "doing something."

But the American public did not respond. Sadegh found their ignorance of Iran appalling and their celebrity worship of the Shah sickening. He turned his attention next to the person of Ardeshir Zahedi, the Shah's ambassador to America and a man for whom Sadegh harbored particular loathing. Zahedi, who had learned his English while studying dry-land farming and poultry husbandry at Utah State University, was married to the Shah's daughter, Shahnaz. He was the son of the general who had led the 1953 coup against Mossadegh. Zahedi, barely thirty, represented Iran to the American nation and was rapidly becoming known as Washington's most lavish diplomatic entertainer. To Sadegh, Zahedi was a "jumped-up chicken farmer" who squandered his nation's wealth on evenings of imported pomegranates and stuffed peacocks and on hundreds of flowers and expensive "gifts" for influential Americans. Sadegh saw the ambassador as the epitome of rot in Iran, a man who personified the corruption and nepotism of the Imperial Court. He devised a plan to make a point, and have a little fun at Zahedi's expense.

Sadegh and a fellow student named Bejan Savadkovi sat drinking tea in Sadegh's cluttered basement flat on Q Street. Sadegh leaned back.

"Noh Rooz has always been my favorite holiday," he intoned, a half-smile on his lips and a mischievous glint in his eye. Noh Rooz was the Persian New Year.

"The embassy is having a party for Iranian New Year," Bejan added. "I'm going to speak at it on behalf of the students loyal to the Shah."

Sadegh knew this. "Help us," he said, leaning toward him. "Get sick, let me speak for you."

Bejan shook his head. "I'll get in trouble."

Sadegh smiled, his charm fully engaged, his arm around Bejan's shoulders. "No. No. It will be all right. Look, we'll fix it so you really can't speak, okay? You'll be sick. And if there's trouble, you'll just say you didn't have any idea what I'd say."

"But I'm not sick. I'm in perfect health."

"Come early in the morning the night of the dinner. Come early and I'll prepare you."

Bejan hesitated, but soon gave in.

The morning of the dinner, he arrived just after breakfast.

"Go! Go! Where! We wanna touchdown over there!"

"Louder!" Sadegh coached.

"Yay, team! Yay team! Get that ball and kick!"

Bejan Savadkovi leaped and shouted, as hour after hour Sadegh egged him on in the dingy basement flat. Outside, citizens of Washington were enjoying the first whiffs of spring, smelling the damp earth and rejoicing with the birds. It was a perfect day to stroll through the leafy paths of nearby Rock Creek Park.

"Friends, Romans, countrymen, lend me your ears!" Bejan was now reciting Shakespeare at the top of his voice.

Sadegh pressed him on. "Louder, louder!"

Bejan whooped and squawked until by dusk he was barely able to whisper. Sadegh smiled broadly, patted him on the shoulder and told him to go home and get dressed. He himself dressed in borrowed evening clothes and set off for the Statler Hilton.

Limousines and Cadillacs swung up to the hotel entrance in busy downtown Washington, disgorging the elegant haut monde invited by Ambassador Ardeshir Zahedi to celebrate the Iranian New Year. It was March 20, 1961.

Inside, the rustle of Dior originals mixed with the low din of animated voices and ice tinkling in glasses as American dignitaries and notables of other nationalities mingled with the smaller contingent of Iranian guests.

As the guests sat down at tables for dinner and speeches, Sadegh watched Ardeshir Zahedi.

His face flushed, Zahedi introduced Bejan Savadkovi, son of an honored military officer. Clearly the ambassador was thrilled to have a student speak. There had been a lot of trouble with students demonstrating and protesting lately, and this student's loyalty would impress his American guests.

Bejan rose and in a hoarse whisper apologized for being unable to speak. He then introduced his fellow student, Sadegh Ghotbzadeh, who would speak in his place.

Before the appalled Zahedi could act, Sadegh took the microphone and in loud, clear, Persian announced to the surprised assembly that in Iran this was not March twentieth, but the twenty-ninth of Isfand, by the Persian calendar. It was the day before Noh Rooz, the New Year, and it was also the anniversary of the nationalization of the oil industry by the great and courageous Dr. Mossadegh. On cue, Bejan and the other students cheered and applauded. Not understanding a word, the Americans, French, British and others politely joined in the ovation as the Iranians sat in nonplussed silence.

SAVAK guards immediately cut the microphone, but Sadegh continued without it, insulting Zahedi, hurling out imprecations against the Shah and demanding freedom for Iran. While he shouted his speech, the room exploded in disorder. SAVAK agents moved in on him, overturning chairs and tables, while enthusiastic students and irate guests hurled buns and tomatoes. Furious and wild-eyed, Zahedi shrieked Persian obscenities, and his terrified wife cowered behind an upturned table, while Sadegh harangued them from the tabletops.

As Sadegh was finally hauled off by the Washington police, he thought of Zahedi's anger and was satisfied: against such people the revolution could succeed. He was held for a few hours, then released when the embassy, preferring to avoid publicity, refused to press charges.

For Zahedi and his friends in the American administration, the incident was the last straw. Ghotbzadeh and his gang were obviously communists, working for Moscow. It was known that they had contacts with the Algerians and other Soviet puppets. Both the Iranian embassy and the FBI began to build a fat file on Sadegh Ghotbzadeh.

But Sadegh was not a communist. In fact, he had developed elaborate stratagems to ferret out the communists who infiltrated the student organization. When he sent their newsletters to suspects, he misspelled his and his friends' names, keeping a list of who received which spelling. Then, when he and his friends received the literature of the Iranian Communist party, the Tudeh, in the mail, the spelling of their names on the address labels told them all they needed to know.

"See?" Sadegh chuckled to Ahmad, another of the students. "It worked. Goddamn communists. They're worse than the Americans. Or would be if they had the chance."

"Worse?" Ahmad questioned.

"By a long shot," Sadegh replied.

The son of Hossein Ghotbzadeh had no love for the Soviet Union. His father had made sure of that. Imperial Russia had always been the enemy of Iran, and the Soviet Union was simply imperial Russia in another form and as expansionist as ever. Communism, moreover, was clearly the enemy of Islam. Sadegh was as viscerally opposed to Moscow as he was to Washington and the Shah.

Now Sadegh turned once again toward Zahedi, the Iranian ambassador. He decided to engineer a takeover of the embassy-funded student group.

When it came time for the group's annual convention, Sadegh and Fatemi loaded their friends into cars with promises of a good time and drove to the convention at Eastern Michigan University.

The assembly hall was full when Zahedi rose to speak to the students. When he referred to the "glorious uprising of 1953," Fatemi interrupted to correct him, pointing out that it had been a coup, not an uprising. Others rose to speak of nationalism and justice, and, on cue, one of their group rose to say that the Islamic group wished "no dissent with its brothers and sisters, and hereby joins itself with the others." In effect, they now "packed" the meeting. There was great applause as Sadegh was introduced to speak for the "Islamic" students.

"Iran," Sadegh declared, "needs educated people to develop, people who could learn about democracy here and take it home." As Zahedi began to redden with embarrassment, Sadegh launched into a tribute to Mossadegh. Growing ever more impassioned, he turned on Zahedi. "In Iran," Sadegh declared, "there's no way Iranians can speak out. Here we can for the first time, and we're here to tell you what we think of your government and your Shah!"

As Sadegh grew more heated, Zahedi spluttered furiously. Sadegh then suggested that the students of Iran could possibly do better than study chickens, though such study might result in their being appointed to ambassadorships.

As the meeting recessed for lunch, the ambassador turned to the embassy treasurer and, unaware his microphone was still on, hissed in Persian, "Don't give a penny to these motherfuckers."

When the students voted to choose a new executive in the afternoon, four of the five executives of the Iranian Students' Association were from the ranks of the newly joined revolutionaries. Ali

Above: Sadegh at his studies during student days in Iran.

Left: Sadegh at about age twelve.

Paris 1967, from right to left: Hassan Habibi, another friend, Abolhassan Bani Sadr, and Sadegh, holding Bani Sadr's daughter, Firoozeh.

Above Left: The Ayatollah in exile.
A photo of Khomeini in his home in
Najaf, Iraq, believed taken by Sadegh.

Above Right: Sadegh in Damascus on
one of the dozens of trips he took
from Kuala Lumpur to London
speaking publicly and meeting allies
privately for the Nehzat e Azadi.

Left: Some members of the Libera-
tion Movement of Iran (Nehzat e
Azadi e Iran). Front row left to right:
Ezatollah Sahabi of the National
Front, Ayatollah Mahmoud
Taleghani, and Mehdi Bazargan.

Right: Mohammed Mossadegh, the
controversial prime minister and
grand old man of the National Front,
hero to some, anathema to others.

Nuri Albala and Sadegh together in Paris in the 1970s.

Moustafa Chamran and Ahmad Khomeini posing for a booklet
on the training of the new Amal militia in South Lebanon.

Sadegh Tabatabai during a trip to Beirut with Ghotbzadeh in the 1970s.

Sadegh in Paris in the early 70s wearing his trademark astrakhan hat.

Top Left: Neauphle le Château: Sadegh on the left and Yazdi on the right translate while Joe Schlesinger of the CBC, bottom left corner, interviews the Ayatollah. (Photo courtesy of Joe Schlesinger)

Bottom Left: The momentous flight home: Sadegh sitting at Khomeini's right hand. (Canapress photo)

Above: Sadegh at Friday prayers in Teheran immediately after return to Iran. Bazargan in dark robe on left. Taleghani in black turban leading prayer.

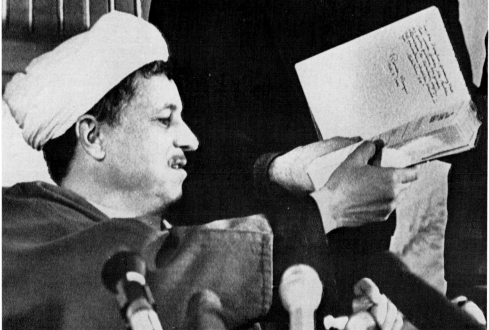

Above: The classic portrait of a revolution. Demonstrators burn the Star Spangled Banner on the wall of the American embassy, Teheran, November 9, 1979. (Photo: Canapress)

Above Left: The formidable Ayatollah Beheshti on the left with Bani Sadr on the right at the opening of the new Iranian parliament, May 28, 1980. (Photo: Canapress)

Left: The Shark, Rafsanjani, seen here at the height of power years later as he displays the Bible sent to him by President Ronald Reagan during the arms affair of 1986-1987. (Photo: Canapress)

The camera crew: Dennis and Bill with Canadian Press photographer Peter Bregg in the corridor barred off between the embassy wall on the right and the demonstrators bussed in on the left, February 1980. (Photo: Carole Jerome)

The main embassy gate in December 1980, after the hostages were moved elsewhere. (Photo: Carole Jerome)

The foreign minister.

At the war front; visiting reporters can be seen behind the Iranian soldiers at the advance gun emplacements moments before an Iraqi mortar barrage. (Photo: Carole Jerome)

Soldiers of the Imam at the Allah-o-Akbar Heights. (Photo: Carole Jerome)

Above: The golden holy mausoleum and the sacred shrine of Ali, son-in-law of the Prophet, Najaf, Iraq.

Right: The author shopping in Isfahan in her black bag. (Photo: Dennis Packer)

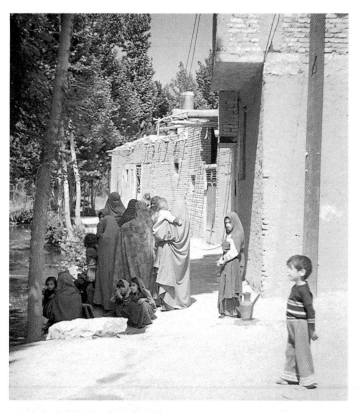

The other Iran: scenes in the village outside Isfahan. (Photos: Carole Jerome)

Left: The author interviewing at random at a pro-Shah rally, February 1979, moments before strangers told her that they had ''got that bastard Ghotbzadeh''. (Photo: Olivier Rebbot)

Below: Behzad Nabawi, the man Sadegh called the worst of the lot at a press conference after the hostages release, January 28, 1981, claiming that rumors that the hostages were tortured were mere lies. (Photo: Canapress)

The last known photograph of Sadegh at his trial in Evin prison, August 28, 1982. (Photo: Canapress)

Fatemi was elected chairman. Sadegh was elected recording secretary. Zahedi had lost.

Gleefully the students moved into the Iranian Students' Association offices furnished by the embassy on the top floor of a hotel on Forty-seventh Street in New York.

Not that life was one long political meeting. Sadegh and his cronies had their university classes, and they enjoyed outings for dinner, to movies and group picnics, sometimes with American friends, sometimes with the Iranian cabal. On these outings, Sadegh was often the despair of his friends, who tried in vain to get him to loosen up with a drink and chat up the girls they brought along for him. He usually preferred to sit scowling into a glass of orange juice. Most of the girls gave up, though a few got to know him well enough for the privilege of helping with his essays. For a while he dated a dark-haired nurse named Barbara.

When a close friend suggested he should find a girl and settle down, he shrugged. "And ask her to share SAVAK tales and death threats? No."

It was partly sacrifice, partly the instinct of the lone wolf. For all his gregariousness, Sadegh was essentially a maverick, a single-minded loner who liked to do things his own way. The Statler Hilton episode had been his own show. This attitude gradually alienated Ali Fatemi. As much as he loved Sadegh for his intelligence and commitment, Fatemi grew wary of Sadegh and his politics of Islam. There did not seem to be any room for anyone else's ideas of either Islam or democracy. The two young men began to drift apart. This was to become a pattern in Sadegh's life.

It was during these early years in America that Sadegh received two shattering personal blows: first, news of the death of his father, from illness. Then, as the result of a doctor's negligence, the sudden death of his favorite sister, the beautiful Aghdas. Sadegh crumpled, alone in a way he had never before known.

In 1960, a new wave had swept over America with the election of John Fitzgerald Kennedy. America's new president was young and vigorous, a man of vision and integrity. Among his first moves was an attempt to redirect American foreign policy. He encouraged America's allies to institute greater political freedom on the premise that progressive societies were more stable and durable, and thus less vulnerable to communist agitation.

For the Iranian opposition, the new policy was a godsend.

Kennedy exerted considerable pressure on the Shah, exacting a one-third cut in the army and pushing for the elimination of government corruption. The Shah balked, afraid of his relatives, afraid of a loss of power.

When the Shah came to America on a state visit in April 1962, he was feted and feasted by the Lord of Camelot, who wanted to preserve Iran's support for three main reasons: Iran provided a buffer against the Soviets; it was an oil-rich country; and being non-Arab it was Israel's only friend in the Middle East. The Iranian students felt betrayed by Kennedy, who, they had believed, shared their ideals. They marched and chanted bitterly as pro-Shah Iranians heckled and Americans looked on with distaste. SAVAK agents, always allowed to operate in the United States, unobtrusively snapped photographs of Sadegh, Fatemi and the other students.

When the students heard that Bobby Kennedy was going to Iran as part of a world tour, sixty of them demonstrated outside the attorney general's office, protesting the proposed visit.

"What's this about?" the attorney general asked on his way into the building.

"We're Iranian students. We're protesting your trip to Iran," Sadegh told him bluntly.

"If you want to make your point, why don't you come up and see me?" Bobby Kennedy proposed.

The surprised students filled all the available chairs in the large paneled office. Some sat cross-legged on the floor; others leaned against the wall. It was a heady moment. They were in the heart of the American capital, in the center of its powerful government.

"I've heard it all before," Kennedy said bluntly, perching on the edge of his desk as if he were presiding over a student seminar. "If you give me more rhetoric and bullshit you can get out. If you've really got something to say, I'm here to listen."

Fatemi carefully presented their case. He talked about the economic situation—the great wealth and the great poverty. He talked about censorship, about the fact that all opposition was harassed by SAVAK, and he talked about SAVAK and its methods. The others described political repression, censorship and the fate of their colleagues in prison. They gave hard facts and they argued that repression in Iran was not, in the long run, in the interest of the United States. It created unnecessary enmity. If Iran had a true democracy, they argued, it would be a far better and more reliable ally.

Their message was clear: Don't go to Iran. Don't give your stamp of approval to the regime anymore.

Kennedy thought for a few minutes, seeking a solution that would satisfy the students and the needs of state. He said he would still go, but only if he was allowed to meet with the opposition. He invited the students to supply him with a list of those he should meet. They were overjoyed. The attorney general of the United States had actually listened to their case.

Sadegh came away with an immense respect for Robert Kennedy that bordered on hero-worship. Sadegh had profound objections to some of JFK's policies, but Robert Kennedy seemed to him a man of intelligence and integrity, tough and even ruthless if need be, but compassionate, a true American patriot and a friend of mankind. For Sadegh, a true American patriot was necessarily a friend of mankind. He felt strongly that those Americans responsible for the regimes that oppressed millions around the world betrayed America and all she stood for. To Sadegh, America meant, above all, liberty. Robert Kennedy, tough and just, was to Sadegh what an American should be.

The list of opposition leaders the students supplied was passed on to the president. Impressed, JKF informed the State Department that he wanted Bobby to meet Iran's opposition groups. Appalled, the mandarins of State insisted that such visits would be diplomatic dynamite, a supreme insult to a monarch who was already touchy. It could, they feared, be the end of the Shah if Robert Kennedy consorted openly with the Shah's foes.

Kennedy insisted.

State argued.

Kennedy was adamant.

They compromised. Bobby Kennedy did not go to Iran at all.

*　*　*

Zahedi struck back at the students in July. It was almost a year since Sadegh and his friends had taken over the Iranian Students' Association. The embassy announced it would review the passports of the forty-five hundred Iranians in America on student visas. Those with less than a B average would be called back, even those with permanent resident status.

Sadegh's grades were unsatisfactory. His first priority had always been to organize the Iranian students and lobby the American students. He had struggled to learn English. His professors had despaired. When they talked to Sadegh, they received a lecture on Iran. Under the embassy's new dictum, he would have to return. Moreover, it was rumored that Ali Fatemi was also to be forcibly repatriated.

The Islamic student movement's considerable resources were instantly and awesomely mobilized in Teheran. Thousands of angry Iranian students poured through the great iron gates of the university to protest on behalf of their two leaders overseas. The Committee of Students of the National Front had asked a young economics scholar to address the throng. It was the first time Abolhassan Bani Sadr had heard the name Sadegh Ghotbzadeh.

Abolhassan Bani Sadr, one day to be the first president of Iran, had unimpeachable status. He was both a student and a lecturer, and a member of the National Front. He was the son of an ayatollah, and as such he brought to the gathering the weight of Islam. He spoke fervently in defense of Ali Fatemi and Sadegh Ghotbzadeh.

In London, Munich, Geneva, Vienna and even Sydney, Iranian embassies were picketed. The *Washington Post* featured a photograph labeled, ''Irate Student.'' It was of Sadegh. With his black hair and smouldering eyes he looked part matinee idol and part juvenile delinquent.

Next, Ghotbzadeh and Fatemi took their protest into the ambassador's living room. They led a delegation of fifteen into the magnificent residence at 3003 Massachusetts Avenue.

Zahedi remained out of sight and sent his legal counselor and a consular official to meet his adversaries. After hours of discussion, the exhausted diplomats told Sadegh and Ali they could spend the night and resume discussion in the morning, but that the others would have to leave. The students refused, and at 3:45 A.M. the police were summoned. The students were marched peacefully to paddy wagons and whisked off to a cellblock at the municipal court, where they were fed and soon released.

''I only wish the jails in Iran were as nice as this one,'' Fatemi cracked to reporters when they were released.

When asked for his comment Sadegh told them, ''Sooner or later, the future of Iran will be in our hands.''

It was Bobby Kennedy who made it possible for Sadegh to remain in the U.S. when the embassy withdrew his student status. The attorney general had taken a liking to Sadegh and the students from Georgetown University in Washington, and they, in turn, kept him

informed on events in Iran. When told Sadegh's student status was
to be withdrawn, the attorney general helped arrange for Sadegh
to have a special discretionary visa.

In the fall, the embassy announced that Sadegh and Ali were to
be summoned back to Iran by a civil court. The charges against
them included treason. If they did not return, they would be tried
in absentia.

*   *   *

On November 22, 1963, America's dream imploded. John F.
Kennedy was assassinated while driving through downtown Dallas
in a motorcade. Sadegh was stunned and horrified, just as millions of Americans were. America's humanity and its peculiar
fragility were crystallized before him. He shut himself in his room
and wept.

When the wheel turned again, Sadegh's position was less secure.
Bobby Kennedy warned the students at Georgetown to adopt a
very low profile. Even though he was to remain attorney general
under President Johnson, he would no longer have a special voice
at the White House. Not surprisingly, when Bobby Kennedy left
office to run for president, Sadegh's discretionary visa was withdrawn. Sadegh was stubborn to the core. Rather than try to obtain
a passport from Algeria, as Fatemi did, he forged an extension on
his Iranian passport and left for Europe.

As he left, his feeling toward America remained, characteristically,
both affectionate and idealistic. With some help from an American
girlfriend he wrote an essay, which included the following para-
graphs:

A few selfish men have dragged the name of America in the
dust, have extinguished the everburning lamp of liberty as
symbolized by the Statue of Liberty at her shores, have
denied her flag the claim to glory and respect. The legitimate
aspirations of a hundred million people over the decades have
been thwarted, and history shows us that they cannot be
thwarted forever. When this is realized, the contents of this
paper shall serve to vindicate a century of crushed hope. . . .

Finally, let it be said that I, during four years of my studies
in the United States of America, have found the American
people to be freedom-loving, liberty-conscious, and helpful.

My friends, in particular, have been stimulating, and the
true American showcase of global brotherhood.

*   *   *

The Hotel Asia is typical of the small, cramped establishments that
cater to the denizens of Paris's Latin Quarter. The cubbyhole rooms
are home to students, drifters, penniless political refugees, Algerian
immigrant workers — legal and illegal — and disillusioned blacks
and Arabs from the former French colonies who are lost in the
capital. There they have a bed, a sink and a bidet. Next door there
are fine buildings with spacious apartments for those who can afford
a much sought-after address on the Left Bank. But the neighborhood derives its flavor and its modish appeal from the students
and their seedier cohorts, from smoky, dirty cafés and hole-in-the-
wall stores dispensing Arab sweets and pungent kebabs.

Two men hunched over papers spread on a lumpy bed under a
bare lightbulb in one small room of the Asia. Abolhassan Bani Sadr
and Sadegh Ghotbzadeh were building a revolution that their own
stubborn rivalry would later help destroy.

Bani Sadr, the student-lecturer at the University of Teheran who
had spoken out for Sadegh when the Iranian government canceled
his passport, had come to Paris with his wife, Ozra, in November
1963. He came to study and to agitate. Sadegh, in turn, had come
from the United States to seek out the leaders of the movement in
Paris.

From the beginning Sadegh and Bani Sadr were two mismatched
donkeys in harness together — Sadegh, bigger and brasher, snort-
ing and yanking; Bani Sadr, smaller and scholarly, checking all the
buckles first — but both intent on getting the cart moving. Sadegh
was a doer, Bani Sadr a maker of lists with points and objectives.

And there were others. Shin, no longer a student, but an engineer
with a job in Switzerland; Hassan Habibi, a mild-mannered, auburn-
haired friend from their student days in Iran; Ibrahim Yazdi, whom
Sadegh had known in the United States; Karim Khodapanahi, a
tall dour hanger-on; and a brilliant young student of economics
named Ali Reza Nobari. Some of these men would later betray
Sadegh, forming part of the web that encircled him after the revolution.

Then, however, they were allies, their aim to rid Iran of the Shah.
They wrote and they published. They met with student groups all

over Europe and the Middle East. And there was intrigue, the intrigue born of the left's proliferation of organizations. In addition to the monarchists and liberals of the National Front, there was the Communist party — the Tudeh — which was still loyal to Moscow. No one in the mid-sixties considered the Tudeh significant save Sadegh and SAVAK, perhaps their only point of agreement. The Fedayeen were another lot, a mixed bag of Marxists, Maoists and Islamic leftists whose organization was so loose they scarcely knew one another. Some Fedayeen cells allied with the Tudeh. The main cell, Cherik, was more independent. And there was, of course, the huge Mudjahedeen e Khalq, which was still growing. The Mudjahedeen were acceptable to Sadegh, who regarded them as genuine Islamic guerrillas, but he disliked the other organizations intensely.

Shin returned to Iran and took a position with a construction firm. As the revolutionaries in Paris plotted, things got worse in Iran. Shin, who kept his views to himself, sent word of every arrest and each new measure of repression.

Every day SAVAK scooped up more and more of the Shah's detractors. Flung in prison cells in Evin, Qasr or Ghezelghaleh, the state's accused enemies were beaten, scorched and boiled in oil. Their feet were whipped into swollen stumps, their legs broken with steel bars. They were suspended on the Horseman or hung upside down on the Parrot's Perch; they were electrocuted and violated with bottles and cattle prods; their spines were seared raw and their genitals mutilated with electrodes and weights. Women were raped and men sodomized. And when their tormentors were finished, the broken bodies where shut into dark cells to lie in agony and to wait for death from bleeding, infection or sheer pain. Sometimes the bodies healed and were taken to the firing squad or noose. Food came mixed with filth and broken glass. In Bandar Abbas, a city in the south, the victims expired in suffocating heat. The ones who escaped from SAVAK's prisons were not always glad they survived. They had to live with the knowledge of human savagery, hearing the screams of their fellow prisoners forever. Sadegh's hatred for the Shah grew with every arrest and every outrage.

8

In 1967, after three years in France, Sadegh returned to the United States, hoping to continue his studies there. He went with a new identity. The Iranian government had revoked his passport on a trip to Switzerland when he brazenly went to the embassy to renew it. Marooned, Sadegh had called on other friends in Syria. The Syrians came through, but they transliterated Sadegh's name into the Arab style (as opposed to the Persian style) and used only part of his full name, Sadegh Ghotbi-Asfahani. Thus, on his new Syrian passport, his name read, Sadegh Asfahani.

To lend credibility to his Syrian nationality, Sadegh rented a room in Damascus on Avenue Jole Jamal, and called it his permanent address. But in truth, he used it only on trips to Syria. Two of his closest Syrian friends were Hafez al Assad and his brother Rifaat. Hafez Assad was to become president of Syria while Rifaat would become his powerful lieutenant and rival.

On Sadegh's return to the United States in February 1967, the Syrian passport was responsible for his almost immediate expulsion. He had hardly settled in when the Immigration and Naturalization Service rejected his application for student status. The following day a letter from the department informed him that the visitor's visa, issued by the American embassy in Paris, was canceled by the Department of State. He had till August 14 to leave the country.

Geoff Keating was one of the lawyers, hired by friends, who accompanied Sadegh to the State Department, in the hope that a personal encounter might have the desired effect.

A scowling State Department official brusquely bade them enter his office.

"Good of you to see us," Keating began. "We . . ."

"It's not good at all," snapped the man. "Carry on, I've seen the file."

Taken aback, Keating picked up his presentation. "We simply want to make it possible for my client to finish his degree here at Georgetown. The department has made a lot of technical objections over his place of residence, but I assure you, we can satisfy all requirements.''

"And he wants to be a student?''

"Yes. Full-time. At Georgetown.''

"A student.''

"Yes,'' Keating repeated. "He's already invested a good deal of time in . . .''

Springing angrily out of his chair, the official cut him short. "Student!'' He seized a bound stack of thick files from his desk and flung it down in front of them. "You have a nerve to come here, to tell me this guy is a student! We know exactly who he is and who he works for. It's all in here. And let me tell you something else,'' he hissed, leaning on his knuckles and fixing Sadegh with a malevolent glare, "if we had known who you were, pal, when you showed up with your so-called Syrian passport, you would never have gotten in at all.''

Geoff Keating and I later spent years trying to find out what was in the file. We petitioned under the Freedom of Information Act and received back stacks of paper. Only Sadegh's name and description were visible. All other information was blacked out, remaining classified even five years after Sadegh's death.

At that moment, in 1967, Keating was transfixed by the five-inch-thick file. He wondered what information it contained and who had furnished it. Bobby Kennedy once had Sadegh investigated by the FBI, but at that time Sadegh had been told he was clean.

Keating was also profoundly taken aback by the official's brutality. He told me later that in all his years of dealing with government, he had never encountered such naked hostility. The official refused to enlighten him further. As they left the State Department, Keating asked Sadegh what might be in the file.

Sadegh clicked his tongue. "The usual,'' he said.

The State Department's objections hung on a technicality: they did not, upon examination of Sadegh's papers, "find him a bona fide nonimmigrant having a residence in a foreign country to which he intended to return.'' The implication was that he intended to stay in the U.S. forever, and that he used a questionable name in a dubious passport.

Sadegh was given a chance to defend himself at a hearing in a Virginia courtroom. But in the end, the case was lost on the grounds that when Sadegh was in the United States previously, he had "too often engaged in activities clearly inconsistent with the normal pursuit of a college degree. His arrests and demonstrations while a guest of the United States Government were not in the public interest.'' Ghotbzadeh was to leave the country.

Again Sadegh approached Robert Kennedy, but Kennedy's efforts on his behalf did not change the government's decision.

The most obvious place to go was Canada. To Sadegh, Canada was the place where the second sons of families in English novels went to live and were heard from no more. And he knew there were wheat, snow, mounted policemen, a French problem and some rather good universities buried in snowdrifts.

Sadegh was granted a short extension on his American visa while he made arrangements to leave. He applied to several Canadian universities, then set off northward to present himself in person.

At the Vancouver airport, the Canadians turned him back. He needed a valid American visa in his passport before he could enter Canada, they informed.him. The Canadian embassy had assumed he had one when they had issued him his visitor's visa. Sadegh put his suitcases down in disbelief. He couldn't enter Canada and they had now revoked his U.S. entry visa so he couldn't go back, either. He was marooned by a catch-22 in the no-man's-land of airport passport control.

''Wait here,'' he was told. And what choice was there? He watched as the Canadian official went off to talk to his American colleague.

Finally Sadegh was summoned by the American, who stamped him back into the United States. Disappointed and frustrated, Sadegh found himself on a flight to San Francisco. For two weeks he lived with friends and waited to hear from a Canadian university. He needed a student visa. Yazdi, now a Ph.D. teaching chemistry in Texas, wrote him a recommendation.

Simon Fraser University turned him down, but Notre Dame University in Nelson, British Columbia, accepted his Georgetown credits and pronounced him acceptable.

On January 7, 1968, Sadegh was admitted to Canada as a student. He moved into a small flat on Baker Street in Nelson, and within a few weeks he was knee-deep in student politics, forming a small Iranian group in the student union. Once again his driving will and ruthless manner in political matters made him enemies. Some professors and students regarded him as brutal and opportunistic. But others liked him and in the end he was actually voted student of the year.

Sadegh loved Canada. The mountains rising up from the sea over the stands of Douglas firs and pines, and the deep snow. It was a magnificent country. But Canada had another quality that appealed to him: its people, he felt, were closer to the ground — salt of the earth.

When he got his degree in 1969, a bachelor of arts in history, Sadegh called Bani Sadr and Habibi to tell them he was coming back to Paris.

It was in Paris in the seventies that Sadegh met the French lawyers who later played an important role in his life and in the Iranian hostage crisis that followed the revolution. It was Sadegh's idea to recruit some reputable Western lawyers to go to Iran on a fact-finding mission so they might publish a report of the sort published by Amnesty International.

Sadegh soon learned that Bourguet was familiar with the Middle East. The son of one of his clients had once hijacked a TWA passenger jet to Beirut for the benefit of a Palestinian group. Bourguet had found himself in Beirut defending the boy. In the process, he had rubbed shoulders with Palestinian commanders, Lebanese officials and the Druze chieftain Kamal Jumblatt.

Just two days after he met Sadegh, Bourguet was on a night flight to Iran with two colleagues. Their subsequent report on repression in Iran was the beginning of a long partnership between Sadegh and the lawyers and their wives.

It took Sadegh a little longer to get to know François Cheron and Bertrand Vallette, the other two partners in the law firm. They formed a human rights organization called the Association Française de l'Amitié et Support Pour l' Iran (AFASPI).

Bertrand and Geneviève Vallette and Sadegh lived in the same building on rue Moulin de la Pointe. They spent many evenings playing backgammon in Vallette's flat above Sadegh's. Bertrand's sons grew very fond of their big friend, calling him "papa".

For Christian and Christine Bourguet, Sadegh became a member of the family. He alternately energized and exhausted them. Sadegh was a son, a friend, a client, a phenomenon. Bourguet, unlike many who met Sadegh in those days, was fully aware of just how Eastern his friend was. He knew Sadegh was only superficially Westernized, and that the clothes, the language and the evenings in Paris restaurants were only a façade. Bourguet knew from long hours of conversation with Sadegh that Sadegh's character was Persian and that he was deeply committed to Islam.

Bani Sadr, Nobari, Habibi, Khodapanahi and the others Sadegh conspired with became equally familiar faces around the legal offices, dropping in to ask advice or to get help translating their latest press release.

They published now under their new name, the Organization of Moslem Students. The old group, the Student Confederation, had become a chaotic conglomeration of ideologies and rivalries, badly infiltrated by the Tudeh communists.

Though Bani Sadr and Ghotbzadeh still chafed one another, they were united in opposition to communists and the like. They made a decidedly odd couple, though: Ghotbzadeh railed at Bani Sadr's interminable theorizing, while Bani Sadr fumed at Sadegh's tendency to hold sit-ins or other demonstrations without consultation. Each grew suspicious of the other's closest confidants and Sadegh acted independently rather than trust a secret to Bani Sadr's loose tongue. The seeds of their future fall were sown.

But there was one in whom they all trusted. Ali Shariati. When he arrived from Teheran to meet the group in Paris, there was harmony. In 1970, Ali Shariati was a young sociologist who had emerged as the poet-scholar of the new Islam. Though he was only twenty-seven, his books on the sociology of Islam became a cornerstone of the revolution's ideology. Sadegh, Bani Sadr and Habibi spent many hours in Paris cafés listening to Shariati, who became a sort of Lenin to the Iranian revolution.

Sadegh's devotion to Shariati bordered on worship. Both young men believed in God not as a bearded crank in the sky but as a benevolent presence in all living things. Since God was in man, and man in God, man was both predestined and responsible. The old fatalism that characterized traditional Islam had no part in their view. They believed man must use his intelligence to nourish the gift of the universe.

Shariati warned them to beware of the mullahs, just as Taleghani warned them of the depth of political ambition in the mosque. But Shariati saw Khomeini as something different. Khomeini's life in exile in Iraq was symbolic. Living in a simple home, eating onions and bean curd, this Spartan man represented Islam cleaned of power and elitism. And Khomeini had consistently stood against the Shah with great courage and considerable political acumen. Some of his writings dealt with old-fashioned notions of religious hygiene and dogma, but far more of it contained lucid analyses of imperialism, economics and Islamic government.

Khomeini was now working on a new "lesson" called the *Velayat e Faghih, Rule of the Sovereign Religious Guide*, and this caused the leaders of the LMI more concern. Parts of it read rather like an Islamic *Mein Kampf*. But they were sure Khomeini was at heart the man they needed. They could not have an Islamic revolution without a religious leader. And Taleghani could not deliver the mosque. Khomeini could.

With the blessing of Bazargan and the LMI in Iran, Bani Sadr and Habibi agreed with Shariati that Sadegh should be the one to go to Iraq for them, to make contact with Khomeini.

*   *   *

Baghdad was caught in suffocating summer heat when Sadegh arrived. Two men from the Ministry of Information met Sadegh's plane and took him to a hotel, where he was told to await a third, his "guide." Sadegh knew that, in reality, the guide was an agent of the Ministry of Information, which made it its business to "see to the needs" of visitors, like Sadegh Ghotbzadeh, who were known to represent "the opposition in exile" of a neighboring and none too friendly country. The Iraqi government also kept close tabs on their "guest," Ayatollah Khomeini and his entourage of family and followers.

On that first day, Karim, the guide, took Sadegh on a short pilgrimage. They joined the dense traffic on Al Rashid Street and moved among the shoppers who crowded the small, cheap shops that lined the pavements: stationers, photo stores with heaps of frames and posters, cluttered pharmacies, clothing stores full of old-fashioned Western styles in cheap fabrics. To their left, shoppers plunged into the darker alleys that led into the *souk* — that uniquely Arab marketplace. On its narrow winding paths were stalls where brass- and coppersmiths sold their great flame-hammered plates and samovars, rug merchants offered tasseled fakes, yellow gold glittered brittle in jewelers' windows and among authentic Kurdish tapestries, hundreds of shopkeepers offered a dazzling array of other wares on their shelves. Beneath it all in the darkest and most remote corners of this shopper's paradise, countless drug dealers and perpetrators of nameless crimes lived a clandestine existence. Sadegh and Karim left the shops behind and turned up Imam al Adham Street, past the graceful beauty of the Imam al Adham Mosque, to the Aimma Bridge, and there they crossed the Tigris.

Sightseeing! Sadegh realized he was being taken sightseeing. And so it was the next day and the next. Impatient to leave for Najaf and his meeting with Khomeini, Sadegh had to resign himself to killing time in the stifling heat. In the afternoons he slept, but in the evenings when it was cooler he wandered out into the streets. In a sidewalk café, he watched the city go by. "What a mess," he thought. "The traffic is even worse than Teheran—Teheran twelve years ago, anyway." And he noted that all the cars were American and German. The people appalled him. Scraggly shoeshine boys stared at posters of pop stars; hawkers roamed up and down the sidewalks; men lingered over pictures of luscious red-lipped Arab beauties or red-haired Western dreamgirls. None of these sexual fantasies actually walked the streets. Sometimes a woman in a black veil passed, or demurely dressed young girls in twos or threes, but they did not linger.

Over everything loomed the image of the president: his face stared down from posters, photographs, billboards and giant cut-outs festooning the city squares, lampposts, and trees. The populace was constantly reminded that President Hassan Al Bakr was the leader of the revolution of 1958 that brought the Socialist Arab Ba'athist party to power. Sadegh hated this iconolatry, and he began obscurely to hate Iraq.

All the more surprising was the scene at the hotel discotheque. There, Iraqis and foreigners danced to a band that played exclusively English songs.

Sadegh was thirty-two and filled with righteous indignation. Back in his room he wrote:

The only thing revolution brought to this country is the change of leadership. . . . In the streets one can see a lot of women and men working very hard under the burning sun for a bit of bread. But one also sees very up-to-date American and European cars. One can find people in cabarets dancing every night until dawn. The revolution has benefited only one group, and it was only a materialistic benefit that has destroyed the culture."

And his most telling comment:

I cannot understand how they can forget about believing in God and worship a president instead. They have his photo everywhere, they call his name. One cannot find a Mullah to call God with the same tone. . . . Although the Iraqi nation is not as corrupt as Iran, in a few years' time they will reach the same level of corruption. There is not a ray of hope for this country.

What Sadegh saw in Iraq was definitely not what he wanted for Iran. Ba'athism, developed by Michel Aflak, a French Arab scholar, was supposed to combine the best of Islam and socialism (with bits of a few other ideologies thrown in). As far as Sadegh could see, in Iraq it manifested itself as a repressive, totalitarian regime that rather resembled the Shah's. It was a travesty of social justice and of Islam.

In Iran, Sadegh wanted no extremes. He wanted balance, integrity, true responsible liberation for men and women, real suffrage for all, and he wanted it all guided by the finest principles of Islam. Sadegh wanted something new in this world. He did not want a country lost between Islamic moral codes and Western permissiveness. With these matters on his mind, Sadegh traveled on his fourth day in Iraq to Najaf.

After an hour's travel Sadegh reached Kerbala, where, at the end of a dusty street, the shrine of Hussain, the Shi'a Islamic martyr gleamed in the sun. Hacked to pieces by the swordsmen of the Arab Caliph Yazid, the remains of Hussain are entombed in gold and crystal at the heart of this shrine.

Sadegh knelt at the tomb as if it were that of a friend, one who might have died yesterday rather than thirteen hundred years ago. Sunni Moslems came and went from the shrine, but Hussain belonged to the Prophet, and thus to the Shi'a Moslems, to Sadegh's heritage and to him.

After prayers he traveled for another hour out into the desert. Najaf announced itself with the banal appearance of oil storage tanks, a crowded bus depot and cars honking down the boulevard. Palms and quina trees lined the road, while mimosa and wisteria flowed over walls to mingle with the harsher realities of a desert town. The twin aromas of the Middle East, jasmine and urine, floated in the air.

An introduction had to be arranged first, so Sadegh went to the home of a sheik he knew. Hassan, an old friend from Paris and now the personal secretary to the sheik, took Sadegh to an old man who knew Khomeini. Hassan explained that Sadegh represented the Moslem students abroad and the Nehzat e Azadi e Iran (the Liberation Movement of Iran). A long conversation followed, and in the end the old man agreed to arrange an appointment.

The next day, Sunday, Sadegh went to meet the Master.

The house was small and plain, but Sadegh felt as if he were entering a shrine. He tried to minimize his size as he walked down a narrow hallway that led to the courtyard.

Khomeini sat cross-legged on a small Persian carpet, his back braced by a pillow against the bricks of the courtyard's far wall. He wore a black turban and robe. He had a high wide forehead, barely lined, heavy arched eyebrows over dark-lidded eyes, and a straight nose sloping to a sculpted mouth.

Sadegh knelt and kissed the Master's hand. Khomeini nodded once, but otherwise sat in silence. Sadegh had no idea how long he would be allowed to remain, so he first expressed his joy and gratitude at being given an audience, then he plunged into the exposition the students had agreed on in Paris. For over an hour Sadegh talked. As he did so, he watched Khomeini and tried to assess him. Khomeini had a stern expression. "His face radiates dignity," Sadegh wrote later. "He is distinguished by his extreme simplicity. And he knows it. This man knows his power. He is analyzing me, too. I've been introduced by three different sources and he knows my work and my name, but that isn't enough for him. He has been looking at me the whole time, making up his mind about me."

Sadegh felt he had stirred Khomeini's interest, but, noticing signs of fatigue in the old man, he offered to leave and asked to return again the next day. Khomeini agreed readily.

That afternoon Sadegh called on other religious leaders and learned something of the intrigue and rivalry that seethed around the Ayatollah's little establishment. He was disturbed to learn that the Tudeh had already begun to work on Mustafa, Khomeini's oldest son. They had turned him away from the Liberation Movement and were agitating for immediate armed revolution. Isolated as he was, Mustafa had no idea they were communists. He thought they were the Second Front, a group claiming to be the successors to Mossadegh.

Prepared to dislike Mustafa, Sadegh went to visit him. He was won over immediately by Mustafa's warm, outgoing personality, but he did not succeed in changing his views. Mustafa thought armed revolt was the way now, and Sadegh worried about his influence on his father.

The next morning Sadegh returned to Khomeini, determined to clarify certain matters that now troubled him. Khomeini greeted him with faint familiarity.

"With all respects, Agha," Sadegh said, "these are our thoughts: people do not really know anything about the reality of Islam. If we introduce it to them properly, they will accept our ideas. I have told you what we have been doing in our organization. Now we need to go further and we hope to do that with you, Master."

"People do not know the real Islam, that is true. We expect great improvements, but we stay home and do not do enough. I have written a lesson called *Velayat e Faghih, Rule of the Sovereign Religious Guide*. Do you know it?" Khomeini asked.

"Yes. It is what is needed, but there are certain problems," Sadegh answered.

"Yes, I am aware of the problems in the lesson. Here in Najaf it has caused a great disturbance among some of the religious men who say these ideas will destroy Islam."

"These people who claim to be pro-Islam have covered up Islamic truth with a lot of nonsense. The only thing they have done is build mosques with paintings and mosaics and called that Islam," Sadegh commented.

"The Islamic movement is political, economic and social. But no one talks of these things. These concepts should be brought out of the dust and we should let our people know them," Khomeini agreed.

Sadegh picked up the question of a larger following and, as forcefully as possible, outlined his movement's reservations about the vagueness of Khomeini's lesson. "There is much that can be taken as too rigid, too orthodox and old-fashioned unless it is clarified, such as the question of dress for women. It could mean you insist on the chador. If you say that, we will have many women against us instead of with us."

Khomeini gestured mildly with his hand. "No, no. The chador

is not necessary. It is only necessary that they cover their hair.''

"And the part about the Jews," Sadegh pressed. "It would be better if you specify Zionists, rather than all Jews."

Khomeini glowered. "Jews have rewritten the Koran and left out the parts they don't like."

Sadegh was taken aback. Recovering, he skirted the issue. "Well, perhaps that is another problem, but in the lesson it is really the Zionists you are talking about, so it should say so clearly."

Khomeini considered and finally agreed.

"If you allow us," Sadegh went on, "we will translate the lesson into Persian and publish it." Khomeini wrote in Arabic, the language of the Koran. Sadegh felt the lesson could be controlled that way. He didn't want it misinterpreted by factions who would use it against the movement.

They went on to discuss the death of Ayatollah Hakim, a revolutionary cleric, and the murder of Saeidi, a young cleric who had died in the Shah's prison, as well as other clergy who had been arrested at the same time. Khomeini became emotional, close to tears.

Sadegh could offer no information. But he knew that the day before, some of the scholars in Najaf had sent a delegation to Khomeini questioning his principles and pestering him to take a position for armed revolution using Saeidi's death as a battle cry. Khomeini had lost his temper. "I am not going to give up my common sense for a bunch of children like you! I have not got enough information! I hear different stories of his martyrdom. Until I have facts, I can do nothing!"

Sadegh agreed with Khomeini. "You must be careful," Sadegh warned. "Religious questions can be answered because you find the answers in scripture. But when the questions are political, you must find out the truth first. As Master, you should just answer the very important questions."

"My action should be through faith and religion, not through politics," Khomeini agreed.

Sadegh listened to him with satisfaction. He broached the subject of Mustafa, but Khomeini assured him that Mustafa did not interfere with his decisions.

Sadegh left Khomeini impressed with the man's dignity, faith and firmness. They had forged the beginnings of an alliance.

"He is a real politician," Sadegh wrote in his diary. "Sometimes, he confirms subjects without mentioning them directly. Sometimes, when he hears something indirectly, he doesn't say anything until the action has been taken on that matter and he knows that it cannot be changed; then he rejects the action. Because by doing that he covers himself as a leader, but the matter which had to be said or done is already done. So, nobody can blame him for it.

"If he is surrounded by a group of intelligent and faithful people, he could be a great leader and run everything perfectly. Unfortunately, that is not the case. A few people who are close to him are faithful but have no intelligence."

Shadows grew over Najaf as the earth turned it away from the sun; and as the soft evening gray stole over the harsh glare of the day, the muezzin's high cry called believers to prayer. They readied rugs and prayer stones in their homes or made their way through the streets to the mosques.

In the Mosque of Imam Ali, the lilac and green and gold seemed even finer in the darker light, quieter and deeper. In the vast courtyard, those who had spent their day in the shelter of its walls and arches, reading or visiting friends, gathered themselves up to face Mecca: black-veiled women, some old with running eyes and missing teeth, some young and exquisite, scruffy young boys, old men with looks of pain or peace in the corners of their eyes.

"*Allah-o-Akbar*. . . ." the muezzin cried. "*La Illah'a Il Allah*! There is only one God and He is Allah."

Sadegh looked contentedly around him. Political complexities receded as he looked on the great shrine of Ali. Here was their source and their guide, their radiant center. Ali, the Prophet and Allah.

When I went there myself years later, I pondered Khomeini in the shadows of the shrine of Ali. Even a cursory reading of his work revealed the intensely atavistic and bigoted nature of the man. The *Velayat* did resemble *Mein Kampf*. And Khomeini rejected everything from music to modern science. Even the Shi'a clerics in Najaf had been chilled by him.

"God has seventy thousand veils of light and darkness," he wrote in another essay. "Veils of light are no less veils for being composed of light, but we have not even emerged from the veils of darkness; we are thoroughly entangled in veils. What is to become of us? Learning has entirely negative effects on our souls."

I felt a veil of darkness brush by me in the sunlight in the gold and turquoise mosque.

But Sadegh had seen only the light, felt only the presence of Ali.

When he looked at Khomeini, he saw only the reflection he wanted to see of his own ideals. In his notes, he had written the truth, that Khomeini was a politician, an acute manipulator. But in the fatal illusion in the mirror he forgot that. He ignored the shadows, even when Mustafa later warned them all, "My father will kill to realize his vision, will kill more than the Shah could imagine."

Sadegh returned to Paris to work with renewed vigor for an Islamic revolution, giving a glowing report of Khomeini to Bani Sadr and the others. The revolutionaries continued their campaign against the Shah in the name of God. The Shah responded with SAVAK and a certain amount of guile.

On one occasion in 1975, one of Sadegh's allies in Teheran, Alef, was picked up on the street by three burly agents of the secret police. To his surprise he was taken not to Evin, but to the prime minister's palace, where one of the senior officials, without preamble, told him to take a message for Ghotbzadeh: the Shah would offer Sadegh amnesty and a job in the government if he would break with the "communist agitators" and come home.

Alef smiled. He knew what the answer would be.

"Those bastards!" Sadegh exclaimed. "You tell them I'll fight to the last!"

In the fall of 1976, the Shah's men tried another tack: SAVAK sent an assassin to kill Ghotbzadeh.

But the man they sent, Jules Khan Pira, lost all heart for the job. He phoned Sadegh to warn him. Pira was a petty thief with a limp, a prison record and a trail of failures in business. With Sadegh's help he arranged to see someone in the DST, French intelligence, to reveal how SAVAK recruited him and furnished him with a Walther .22 and a silencer. But the meeting never happened. The DST kept his written deposition and closed the door to him. Two years later, upon learning that Pira had died in lonely misery in a local hospital, Sadegh went to the funeral of his pathetic would-be assassin.

Over the years, Sadegh and his companions were spurred on by the deaths of their friends. One dropped dead as he stood on a New York City subway platform next to Sadegh. SAVAK specialized in heart attacks.

In 1977, Mustafa Khomeini, the Ayatollah's eldest son, died. Publicly the LMI accused SAVAK, privately they thought it might have been a real heart attack caused by overeating. But they mourned the amiable Mustafa.

A few months later there was the most devastating loss of all. Ali Shariati died. After the meetings in Paris, he had returned to Iran to teach his classes on politics and Moslem sociology. He inspired huge crowds and popular posters of him soon appeared. He was imprisoned and tortured. Then, due to international pressure, he was released and allowed to go to London, ravaged by illness, where he died in March 1975. He had asked Sadegh to be the one to arrange for his burial in a holy center in Syria. Sadegh flew to Damascus with the body of his friend cold in a coffin in the hold. Whether Shariati had been assassinated in London, or died of his illness, SAVAK and the Shah were the enemy who had killed him. For both sides, politics was war.

During the 1970s Sadegh was also involved with the PLO, and was on friendly terms with Yasser Arafat. But when Palestinian commandos of Black September murdered eleven Israeli athletes at the Munich Olympics in 1972, Sadegh was appalled. Christian Bourguet recounted some of his memories of those years to me and I listened, piecing together more of Sadegh's life before I met him.

Leaning back in the heavy chair behind his desk, Christian packed the tobacco in his pipe and lit it, filling the room with billows of pungent smoke. "Yes, Sadegh was close to Arafat and the PLO at one point, and he was friends with the PLO man in Paris, too."

"Who was that?" I asked.

"Mahmoud Hamshari. Actually, his wife, Marie-Claude was a client of mine."

"Everything is interconnected, isn't it? Did Sadegh actually work for the PLO?" I asked.

Christian shook his head. "Not as an agent. As a friend with a parallel cause, if you like. Sadegh was determined to make all the Moslem organizations work together. It was hopeless. And he was very upset about what happened in Munich. He didn't believe murdering innocent athletes served anyone's purpose. Sadegh told me, 'It's a strategic error. Murdering innocent Israelis is no way to gain public support for the Palestinians or for the Moslems of the world. It just makes them look like barbarians.' And it *was* barbaric," Christian added.

"Hamshari is dead now," I said, remembering the news story. In December 1972, a bomb had gone off in Hamshari's apartment. It was widely rumored, and subsequently mentioned in several books, that the assassination had been carried out by MOSSAD, the Israeli intelligence agency, as a reprisal for the murders in Munich. Rumors and conspiracy theories abound in Middle Eastern politics and one must always be wary of them, but in this case the rumor seems too logical to ignore.

"Sadegh's relations with Hamshari were strained after Munich," Christian confided. "But when Hamshari was killed, Sadegh temporarily ran the PLO office in Paris—just until a replacement could be sent. I think it was then that French intelligence started monitoring our phones." Christian smiled. "And I'm sure the Israelis also took a certain interest."

*   *   *

The Israelis had powerful reasons for taking an interest: during the 1970s Sadegh traveled extensively forging revolutionary alliances in the Arab world. He went most often to Beirut. For there, in the beautiful, beleaguered Lebanese capital lived the "other" Imam, Mousa Sadr.

Mousa Sadr was a giant in his world and in Sadegh's life. In Lebanon, Mousa Sadr was a Shi'a religious leader of incomparable power and prestige. For the Lebanese Shi'a he far outranked Khomeini.

Sadegh's devotion to Mousa Sadr, and his involvement in the Lebanese imbroglio, were ultimately crucial factors in his destruction. The enemies Sadegh made in Lebanon decided his destiny.

It was one of the revolutionary coterie of friends in Europe who introduced Sadegh to Mousa Sadr. Sadegh Tabatabai was a sharp-witted, well-heeled young man about town, a bright bon vivant with a ruthless streak. He and Sadegh were well-matched, close friends and he was the nephew of the Mousa Sadr. When Mousa Sadr came to France to attend the Shi'a World Conference in Strasbourg in 1968, Tabatabai arranged a meeting between his uncle and his friend Sadegh.

Mousa Sadr was an imposing figure: even taller than Sadegh, he stood over six feet, four inches. But it was his eyes people always noticed. They were a startling green that seemed to mesmerize the beholder.

Sadegh at first seemed immune. He chafed at the regal mullah's pacifism. Mousa Sadr's rhetoric was not fiery like Khomeini's. But gradually, Sadegh fell under the Imam's spell, growing to respect, admire and finally revere this remarkable man some ten years his senior.

Mousa Sadr was born and raised in Qom, where he studied at the great Madrasseh. His family was partly Lebanese in origin, and partly Iranian. There was also a branch that lived in Iraq. He became a famed teacher in Iran, but he was drawn to Lebanon, the country of his not-too-distant forefathers. In 1960, he succeeded in finding a place teaching in the Mosque of Tyre, where, after a time, he was acclaimed as the religious leader of the Shi'a of the region.

Though only in his twenties at the time, he was the choice of Lebanon's Shi'a leader, Sheik Abdel Hussein Sharafeqdin, to succeed him. Sadr worked ceaselessly for his people.

"The Palestinians are refugees," he would say. "The Shi'a of Lebanon are refugees in their own home."

When Lebanon negotiated its independence from France in 1943, 53 percent of the population was Christian. The many groups that inhabited Lebanon signed a national pact that became part of the independence agreement. It guaranteed that for every six Christians in parliament, there would be five Moslems. In a complex distribution of power, the pact also called for a Maronite Christian president, a Sunni prime minister, a Shi'a speaker of the parliament, a Druze defense minister, and so on.

But by the 1970s birthrates and Palestinian immigration had changed the ratio. Moslems, including Druze, were now about 58 percent and Christians barely 40 percent, but the old power-sharing formula still held. To complicate matters, the majority of Moslems were now Shi'a. As a result, of three million Lebanese, almost one million were Arab Shi'a, yet unlike the other groups, they had no separate representation.

Mousa Sadr set about changing that.

He had maintained good relations with the Christian rulers. The hallmark of his ideology was mutual respect and tolerance. But he decided mere goodwill needed a bit of muscle. In 1968 he created the Shi'ite Superior Council, and the Lebanese parliament recognized it as legally representing the Shi'a interest. Its members were twelve mullahs, including Moussa Sadr, twelve shi'as who were not mullahs, and nineteen Shi'a deputies.

Mousa Sadr was a religious leader with political teeth. He forged an alliance between the Shi'a rich and poor, handing out religion with one hand and revolution with the other. He nourished a new movement: the Movement of the Disinherited, or Mostazafin, which would one day become Amal, the cutting edge of the battle for Lebanon.

Mousa Sadr had a great vision of a worldwide brotherhood of Moslems. For him, the Shi'a of Lebanon were a starting point. They were Arabs, as were most of the Sunni, but they were Shi'a, as were most of the Iranians. Perhaps the Lebanese Arab Shi'a could reconcile Arab and Persian Shi'a and Sunni. And there was an economic element. Mousa Sadr's movement was to be a movement of the deprived. Like Ali Shariati, he taught a potent blend of Islam and socialism: he embraced all creeds, and he wanted to shatter the barriers of Arab Moslem nationalism.

Khomeini and Mousa Sadr knew each other. Mousa Sadr had proper reverence for Khomeini's status as one of the religious scholars and leaders of his time. The two men conferred on political theory and even went over some of their speeches together, usually by correspondence. Over the years Mousa Sadr helped to smuggle cassettes of Khomeini's speeches into Iran through Lebanon. Both men saw religion and politics as indivisible, but some of Khomeini's teachings were out of harmony with Mousa Sadr's nonviolence.

Across the Mediterranean, another Moslem leader took note of Mousa Sadr. He was Colonel Muammar Qaddafi of Libya. Having overthrown the Libyan monarch, King Idris, in 1969, Qaddafi swept into power on a wave of anti-Western, anti-Zionist, Islamic revivalism. At this stage in his career, Qaddafi was an avid exponent of pan-Arabism and Moslem unity. Hoping they would serve his visions, Qaddafi began sending money to groups that also preached unity, among them Mousa Sadr's Lebanese Shi'a.

But Sadegh did not trust Qaddafi, and Mousa Sadr was wary. Each day Qaddafi's Islamic revival looked less and less like Islam. Qaddafi did not uphold Shari'a law, the collective common law of Islam, or any form of progressive Islam. He professed to be anti-Marxist, but his Green Book of ideology, which came to be known as the "Watermelon," green on the outside and red on the inside, was full of Marxist theory.

By the mid-seventies, tension between the Lebanese Shi'a and Qaddafi had increased, largely over the question of the Palestinians. When they had first begun to arrive in Lebanon after being expelled from Jordan in 1961, the PLO guerrillas and their families had been welcomed by their Moslem brethren in Lebanon. But that fraternity had soured as the PLO increasingly abused Shi'a hospitality, demanding rights and seizing property from the Shi'a themselves. And the PLO, at that time, was the particular favorite of Qaddafi.

Sadegh traveled often to Beirut, sometimes with Sadegh Taba-tabai, to see Mousa Sadr and the men of Amal. On occasion, the two Sadeghs would stay together with friends. Other times, Sadegh would lodge with one of the up-and-coming Amal militants, Nabbih Berri, in his home on Barbour Street.

The meetings with Mousa Sadr usually took place in the big châteaulike headquarters of the Shi'a Superior Council in Hazmieh on the east side of Beirut.

There, as often as not, they were joined by Moustafa Chamran, Sadegh's old friend and mentor from Teheran school days and exile in America. Chamran, more thickset now, with thinning hair and horn-rimmed glasses, had come to Lebanon, met the Imam and stayed. He worshipped Mousa Sadr, who in turn deferred to Chamran. Everyone recognized in Chamran the unusual spiritual powers of a Sufi. Chamran was working in the south of Lebanon, where most of the Shi'a lived, setting up a polytechnical school near Tyre.

When they all got together in the mansion in Hazmieh, they wrangled over present problems and future policies. It was generally agreed that Qaddafi had to be lived with, but not trusted.

But they disagreed violently over the PLO.

Chamran reported to Mousa Sadr about the growing resentment over the Palestinian presence in the south, as the PLO confiscated houses and refused to pay rent, acting, as Mousa Sadr had said, "like an occupying army."

"We'll have to arm," said Chamran. "If we don't fight the PLO, we'll certainly have to fight the Israelis. It's inevitable."

"You know I don't want it to come to that. It's not the way," Mousa Sadr intoned.

The discussion went on in dismal circles. To arm or not to arm?

Sadegh grew impatient. How could they talk of fighting the PLO? It was madness. It was suicide, pitting Moslem against Moslem, while Israel sat crouched over the border. Give the PLO part of Lebanon, let them have a few houses, let them level the place and start over on this benighted country.

The following day they again gathered at the home of one of the senior Shi'a men in South Beirut. A jeep rolled up outside and several armed men clambered out. A few minutes later, Yasser Arafat entered the room.

Yasser Arafat was a contradiction. His casual military dress and three-day growth of beard were worn as a trademark. His face was clownish, with its bulbous nose and hanging lower lip. Sometimes he seemed self-effacing and not quite serious. He didn't appear to be a leader of men, but the Shi'a leaders knew he was not only a leader, but a tough customer. And however many of them disliked the PLO, they respected Arafat.

Sadegh stood by him, in spite of the fact that Arafat disparaged any idea of revolution led by the Liberation Movement of Iran. "You'll never overthrow the Shah," he used to tell Sadegh. "Not that way. Not with an impotent political movement, students and newsletters."

They settled in to discuss the matter immediately at hand: the relations between the PLO and the Shi'a of Lebanon. Chamran and others were implacable, Mousa Sadr as diplomatic as possible. Arafat held that the PLO needed to maintain a certain control, and the discussion, as always, got nowhere.

Sadegh brooded in considerable distress. They had to keep the link with the PLO. A split would lead to God knew what, and would certainly do harm to their own efforts against the Shah. A rift with the PLO would split their own already cracked ranks, Qaddafi would manifest his displeasure and who knew what the Syrians might do.

Sadegh did not want to be forced to choose sides. He had carefully built alliances with all. He met privately with Arafat, then with Mousa Sadr to repair the damage but to no avail. The strife between the men of the PLO and the Shi'a on a day-to-day, neighbor-to-neighbor basis was too great to overcome.

Walking along the Corniche, Beirut's colorful waterfront promenade, Sadegh reflected on the disintegrating situation in Lebanon. In spite of the fighting that had gone on, the Corniche was still filled with office buildings, bustling restaurants and nightclubs. On the other side of the street, bathers romped in the warm surf. Sadegh shook his head sadly.

What should they do? Who could be trusted? Arafat? Though he deplored the useless violence often used by the PLO, Sadegh liked the Palestinian leader who had fought so bravely for so long. They mustn't break with him. As he walked along he considered the problem and recalled bits of conversation from the meetings he had attended.

Sadegh knew there was another PLO faction, a pro-Qaddafi group that operated here and had ties to Iran. Their leader Djalalo-din Farsi had the looks of Sherlock Holmes and the soul of Professor Moriarty.

Sadegh knew Farsi, a smooth-talking manipulator with limitless ambition. He wasn't sure of him, even though he and Farsi exchanged friendly letters and had amicable visits in Beirut. But more and more, Farsi openly supported Qaddafi and attacked Mousa Sadr. Working from the office of the PLO in Lebanon, he accused Mousa Sadr of being a pacifist who was selling out the Palestinians.

"Farsi's an agent," shrugged some in the Shi'a group. "He's an agent for Qaddafi or Moscow — whoever. You'd better keep your eye on him, you know he's got his own connections with your group in Iran."

But Sadegh persisted in trying to work with Farsi and his men, believing in his dream of Moslem unity. Farsi would not only help shatter that dream: he would become a mortal enemy.

Veterans of Lebanon's factionalism looked at Sadegh with pity. Undaunted, Sadegh made pilgrimages to Moukhtara. There in the Chouf Mountains east of Beirut, the Druze warlord Kamal Jumblatt ruled his fiefdom. Sadegh wanted the Druze in his vision, too.

Back in Paris, Christian Bourguet found his life hopelessly entangled with sundry Lebanese factions, as Sadegh's apartment became a hotel for everyone from Kamal Jumblatt to Mousa Sadr and his family. Whenever they traveled to France, these powerful warlords and warrior priests of Islam sought Sadegh out and stayed with him.

The French lawyers were chilled by Mousa Sadr. Sadegh had spoken warmly of him, but the Imam refused to meet with their wives and they found him cold and aloof. When they accosted Sadegh, he made excuses for the Lebanese Imam. Kamal Jumblatt, too, was a dubious quantity. In Paris, he was genteel enough, but in Lebanon the situation was worsening, and there he was merciless. Jumblatt was waging war on the Maronite Christians in the Druze heartland, the Chouf Mountains, east of Beirut, saying he wanted to drink blood from Maronite skulls.

By the time the Syrians sent in their troops in 1976 to rein in the PLO and put a lid on things, Mousa Sadr had thrown in his lot with the Syrians. This made Qaddafi angry. And Sadegh sided with Mousa Sadr and his own Syrian friends, the Assad brothers who ruled now in Damascus. But Sadegh harbored no illusions about Hafez al Assad. When the news came that Kamal Jumblatt had been assassinated in 1977, Sadegh was one of those who found it plausible that the Syrians had been behind the deed.

Unable to prudently attack the Syrian machine, Jumblatt's Druze wreaked vengeance on Christian civilians as Kamal's son, Walid Jumblatt, pleaded impotently with his father's men to desist.

When Sadegh returned to Lebanon, he, Chamran and Sadegh Tabatabai met for a few moments privately with Mousa Sadr. For all their commitment to the Shi'a of Lebanon, these four were Iranians first and foremost, and it was Iran they wanted to discuss with Mousa Sadr. His Iranian roots made him one of them.

Even though a revolution in Iran seemed years away, Sadegh saw Mousa Sadr as one of the most important figures in the future of both Iran and the Moslem world.

"When the time comes, we will need you," he told the Imam.

Mousa Sadr retreated. "No, my place is here . . ."

"And Iran," Sadegh insisted. "Khomeini will need you. *We* will need you."

"Ah, yes, Khomeini — one does what one can," Mousa Sadr replied. His green eyes were filled with disquiet and the ambiguity of his words was lost on his listeners.

When the Israelis did invade Lebanon in 1978, Chamran emerged as a hero in the fight against them. While the PLO withdrew to safer ground, the Amal militia began to emerge as a force to be reckoned with.

* * *

My opinion of some of Sadegh's friends — Khomeini among them — was never high. But I contemplated the Lebanese and Syrian assortment with new horror. The blood-drinking Jumblatt, and the savagely ruthless Assads — how could I love a man who called these people friends? Sadegh had a ruthless streak, but he was not savage. Were these people only necessary allies in a larger battle? Or did Sadegh have some spiritual kinship with their darkness? I could not believe he did. Bertrand, too, had been troubled by this, and of course all three of the lawyers had been taken aback by Khomeini.

"Sadegh took the situation in Lebanon with a kind of melancholy cynicism," Christian told me. "He felt Lebanon was doomed, but he believed that if anyone could rescue anything from the debris, it would be Mousa Sadr."

Then, despite his years of fighting agents of Moscow, in the last weeks Sadegh spent in Paris before leaving for Iran, the French government had tried to expel him as a dangerous Soviet Libyan agent. Their agents in the DST, one of France's numerous security police departments, had been keeping a close watch on Sadegh for some time. Sadegh's close relations with the PLO convinced them that he was in all probability a Soviet agent and an important one at that.

First there was Sadegh's connection to the PLO and Hamshari, the PLO representative who had been killed in retaliation for the Munich massacres. Sadegh had stepped in and run the PLO office till Hamshari's replacement could be sent. They saw Sadegh deal with French Communist Party members and with the infamous Muammar Qaddafi, and drew the wrong conclusions, not knowing he worked against these powers. Agents of the SDECE, yet another French counterespionage service, had followed Sadegh to Tripoli, where, they noted, he had visited Libyan agents and then Qaddafi himself. The French station chief in Libya sent back word: Ghotbzadeh was an agent for Qaddafi. The Israelis confirmed it. MOSSAD confided to the French that after Tripoli, Sadegh had gone to Geneva where he opened a bank account into which five million dollars was deposited. The source of the five million, they said, was Hafez al Assad, Moscow's staunchest ally in the Middle East.

The SDECE and the DST had already pushed their government to expel Khomeini, but the Shah had vetoed that idea. Now they could at least remove Sadegh from the center of things. The Ministry of the Interior informed Sadegh he was to leave France.

Vallette phoned Claude Chayet at the Quai, and he met with Sadegh. Chayet believed Khomeini would come to power and he did not want to risk bad relations with the future government. He called the Ministry of the Interior and reluctantly they backed off.

Furious, the DST and MOSSAD went further. They passed their information to senior American journalist Arnaud de Borchgrave, who duly reported it in *Newsweek*. Two Israeli officials also gave their confidences to a French journalist, Yves Cuau. Cuau was not convinced Sadegh had actually sold his soul to Moscow, but the evidence from the Israelis was intriguing. A five-million-dollar bank account?

Sadegh never had such funds, Cheron assured me. The Israelis must have known he was no friend of Moscow. But he was pro Arab. It had to be pure disinformation.

Ultimately, this web of deceit would mislead Washington into losing its last chance to defeat the Libyan-Soviet faction of clerical extremists in Iran. That chance was Sadegh.

* * *

During the 1970s Sadegh traveled widely on behalf of the revolutionary movement from Kuala Lumpur to the United States, always under the watchful eyes of SAVAK, the DST, the CIA and the FBI. Oddly, he was now able to visit the United States on tourist visas, but on occasion he went with false identification from his collection of passports. When his luggage mysteriously vanished for long periods at American airports, he was unconcerned, knowing full well who was inspecting it.

He treated SAVAK with elaborate contempt, making sure the agents following him didn't lose his trail. "Then they send someone new," he told a friend, "and I have to figure out all over again who it is."

In November 1977, the Shah and his shahbaŋou, Farah, came to Washington and a lavish reception given by President Jimmy Carter. It seemed as though Sadegh and all the rest had worked for the past twenty years for nothing. In the corridors of power nothing had changed. The Shah needed AWACs from the president and Carter needed the Shah's backing for Anwar Sadat's proposed trip to Jerusalem and a scheme for peace in the Middle East.

Howling mobs of Iranian students protested outside the White House during the welcoming ceremony. Police in riot gear fired tear gas that then floated over the White House lawn. Shah and shahbanou, president and first lady, stood stoically with streaming eyes.

When the Shah came to France, Sadegh went underground, as French police rounded up all members of the Iranian opposition and sent them temporarily to a "hostel" on a coastal island. He and his friends then organized a sit-in hunger strike at the church of a sympathetic priest in the old Marais district. Their heads covered in paper bags, the students settled in a side chapel, drawing attention to the continued imprisonment of one Ayatollah Taleghani in Teheran. Small demonstrations occurred in Iran; the first strikes began.

But still the Americans were unimpressed. Jimmy Carter went to Teheran in December 1977 to spend New Year's Eve with his staunch friend and ally the Shah. As they toasted in the year 1978 with champagne, Carter raised his glass.

"Iran," he said, "is an island of stability . . . a great tribute to the respect, admiration and love of your people for you."

And immediately the storm broke. The strikes and demonstrations escalated. It was Muharram.

The Shah published a letter claiming Khomeini was a foreigner, a homosexual and the son of a dancer. The next day, January 8, 1978, the faithful rose in predictable fury in Qom. When the police shot and killed a number of demonstrators they began the fatal forty-day cycle of new demonstrations in mourning for the dead of the one before. The revolution had reached its boiling point. For the first time, the cry *"Marg Bar Shah!"* was heard. "Death to the Shah!"

The momentum eventually brought Khomeini to Paris.

It had been Khomeini's decision to leave Iraq when president Saddam Hussein muzzled him. Millions would die later in war as Khomeini avenged himself on Saddam.

Sadegh approached the Syrians. Hafez al Assad and his brother were willing to allow Khomeini to visit, but they realized the Ayatollah's revolutionary waves might well rock their own boat.

Next, Sadegh considered Lebanon. But Beirut, he concluded, was out of the question. That left two possibilities where the movement had an infrastructure: Kuwait and Paris. If Khomeini moved to Kuwait, Sadegh was prepared to settle there with him.

Sadegh flew to Iraq to see the Ayatollah.

"The French would never permit me in the country," Khomeini grumbled.

Sadegh argued that they would and suggested he come as an ordinary tourist.

"A tourist?" Khomeini arched a dark brow.

"The Americans and the Shah will be thrilled. They think if you're forced to go to Europe, you'll be isolated from Iran. You'll be just another ranting exile. The Americans don't understand."

"They might be right," Khomeini replied.

Sadegh disagreed. "Paris is not as good a choice as Kuwait, but we could still send the cassettes to Iran from there and we would have access to the Western press. And we can phone Iran direct from Paris . . ." Sadegh himself pondered the advantages. He then added, "The French can be dealt with. Besides, they're sentimental about revolutions."

When Sadegh left, Khomeini hadn't made up his mind. Sadegh knew that many of Khomeini's supporters in Najaf wanted him to stay in the Middle East, and out of the clutches of the coterie in Paris. Of course, the separate members of the coterie in Paris were equally anxious to keep Khomeini away from each other's influence.

Khomeini pondered and finally announced his decision to go to Kuwait. The Iranian embassy issued Khomeini a new passport. They were happy to have the Ayatollah away from Iraq. They were also smug in their knowledge that the doors to other countries of the Middle East would also soon be closed to their nemesis.

Khomeini, however, was refused entry at the Kuwait border. He would, after all, come to Paris via Damascus. Sadegh flew to Damascus to escort the Ayatollah to Paris. On a stopover in Zurich, he learned Khomeini had changed his plans and was now planning to fly direct to Paris. Sadegh phoned Cheron and Bourguet to warn them to be ready to meet the Ayatollah. He then flew directly back to Paris.

On October 4, 1978, Sadegh, Cheron and Bourguet drove out to Orly airport. With them was Nuri Albala, a Jewish-Turkish-Moroccan lawyer well known in left-wing activist circles. It was he who had introduced Sadegh to Christian Bourguet. To their dismay, Bani Sadr and his cohorts were also waiting at the airport. Sadegh was puzzled. He had been certain only he knew of Khomeini's arrival.

Bani Sadr had been equally sure he alone had been told of the arrival. It turned out that Ahmad Khomeini, the Ayatollah's youngest son, had notified both Sadegh and Bani Sadr. Bani Sadr's religious credentials, Ahmad explained, would assure the masses at home that Khomeini was indeed in Islamic surroundings and not indulging in wicked Western ways. Bani Sadr feared the old man would make rash remarks to the Western press, and ultimately ruin everything.

Was Ahmad sowing discord, or had the enclave in Najaf assumed that to talk to one of the Paris group was to talk to all of them? The question lingered in Sadegh's mind.

When Khomeini stepped from the plane, he seemed out of his element. The Shah would have rejoiced to see this clerical fish so patently out of the water. Just another ranting exile among the hundreds in the French metropolis.

Sadegh saw it differently. The idealist in him burned brightly. He firmly believed Khomeini was the glue that could hold them all together. He saw Khomeini then as an indomitable holy man, strong on any soil. In his heart he knew this was the turning of the tide.

Sadegh's face glowed with joy and excitement as he went forward to greet his spiritual father who, like his natural father, showed neither joy nor warmth. Rigidly, Khomeini extended his hand and allowed it to be dutifully kissed.

Cheron and Bourguet were greeted with regal indifference by Khomeini, for whom they had done so much for so long. There was no greeting and no thanks offered for their years of work. Khomeini gazed frigidly at the floor. Cheron looked into the implacable black eyes of the Ayatollah and for an instant saw the abyss.

Outside the terminal, Bani Sadr ushered Khomeini into a gleaming Mercedes that slid up to the curb. Cheron urged Sadegh to jump in with them, but Sadegh waved Cheron away with a gesture.

"Remember the story of the son of the Prophet," Sadegh said to Cheron as he left.

Sadegh was referring to Mohammed, who remembered that it was his adopted son, Ali, who was, in the end, the most loyal.

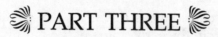

PART THREE

THE OTHER SIDE OF THE MIRROR

9

The sky was dark outside the aircraft as we flew over Europe towards Iran in the early hours of the morning of February 1, 1979. While apprehensive journalists drank orange juice or tea — not their usual fare — dark-haired men crouched in the aisles, praying. A young Iranian named Mahmoud told me he wasn't afraid: he wanted to join his dead comrades in Iran.

"Welcome aboard Air Khomeini," sang out the Air France steward. I looked at another reporter in disbelief.

After an hour in the air, it was announced that Mr. Ghotbzadeh would hold a casual press meeting in the forward economy section. Khomeini remained out of sight in the first-class cabin.

Elaine Sciolino of *Newsweek* spoke first: "Sadegh, if there is enough security for this plane to land in Teheran, why was the decision made not to take any Iranian women or children?"

"It's not the safe plane you may think it is. I should say at this time that when the Ayatollah decided to return, he told us very clearly that he saw a great danger. He told us he didn't want anyone to take a risk for him, so if anyone decided not to come, he wouldn't mind. He told us to tell that to everyone — even the journalists — so everyone would take their own risk."

There was cynical laughter from the reporters. We had assumed as much. Indeed, if this flight had any insurance, we were it.

"What *is* the risk?" inquired a cool British voice.

"They may shoot down the plane," came the lighthearted reply.

"What's the likelihood of that?" an American asked.

"Let me say this: the Ayatollah has said that this trip holds four possibilities for him: either he gets killed, he is arrested, he is placed under house arrest or he will be free with his people."

Sadegh answered some questions in French. Then another reporter asked if the strikes now in progress in Iran would be called off.

"When the monarchy is ended and the new Islamic government is in power, the strikes will end. We're not kidding, you know. We're serious."

I asked about rumors that the army would surround the plane when we landed. Was this for protection? Or was it a threat?

"We'll see when we get there," Sadegh answered, then disappeared to join Khomeini.

The American beside me muttered, "Some goddamn' press conference."

But it was typical of dozens of press conferences Sadegh would give in the future. Seemingly candid and friendly, but refusing to engage in a serious discussion in the open, he never revealed his deepest concerns. The obfuscation was necessary in his peculiar position, but it was also partly a result of his playfulness. Most of all, it was a Persian tour de force. He both engaged and enraged journalists.

Then the sands of Iran were under the wings, receding to the soft rise of the snowcapped Alborz mountain range. A small imperfection at the foot of the beautiful mountains grew and resolved itself into the sprawling buildings of Teheran, dirty white blocks in the beige of the sun and sand. Teheran looked oddly like an archeological ruin. The Shahyad, the Shah's monument to his dynasty, rose above it like a ghost.

The huge aircraft passed low over the city, as if making a regal salute, then slowly turned to approach the runway. We were so close to the ground we could see individual figures on the tarmac when suddenly the engines screamed and we streaked upward into the sky.

My stomach turned over as we made a frightening vertical climb. All conversation in the plane ceased as fear and curiosity manifested themselves in total silence.

The *Time* reporter next to me remarked, "He flies this thing like a Piper Cub." His crack belied the tension we all felt as the plane climbed up and away from Teheran.

What had gone wrong? Was the army waiting on the runway? Were the Shah's Phantom jets pursuing us? We climbed still higher, than banked and circled.

We circled again, then again headed in for a landing. At last the wheels of the plane touched the tarmac.

In an eerie calm we filed out of the plane while Khomeini and his men waited in the forward cabin. At the bottom of the steps, we jostled for good positions from which to take pictures and ask questions while an elite corps of air force men kept us under tight rein.

The plane looked like a giant buzzing insect bearing a seed from another time to take root in the soil. Then the black seed appeared: Khomeini. He was immediately enfolded by his two brothers – Ayatollah Pasandedeh, Khomeini's brother by birth, and Ayatollah Hossein Ali Montazeri, his religious brother.

Near me I saw a cameraman I knew. He had often photographed the black turbaned enigma in exile. Through his lens, Khomeini was focused and distilled, every line picked out, every extraneous person or thing blocked out.

"He's changed," the cameraman said, looking through his camera.

I asked him to explain.

"In Neauphle he seemed to have a human soul—but here, now, it's gone."

One mask had been replaced with another.

"How do you feel?" my colleague shouted to Khomeini. "It must be good to be home! Tell us, what do you feel?"

Hard eyes, hard mouth, dark, menacing eyebrows. "Nothing," was Khomeini's only answer.

An air force officer muscled the cameraman aside, pushing an automatic rifle across his collarbone.

Then I saw Sadegh. He emerged behind Khomeini and stood on the steps of the plane. I looked at him for a long minute, then allowed myself to be carried along with the others into the airport building.

"*Allah-o-Akbar!* God is great! *Khomeini e Imam!*" The words rose like one enormous voice from the throng of people who had come to proclaim the Imam, the savior. It was lilting, like a children's song. "*Khomeini e Imam, Khomeini e Imam . . .*"

My attention was caught by a young child with wide eyes who sang a mournful verse from the Koran. Then suddenly Sadegh was at my side.

"What next?" I shouted over the din.

Sadegh was flushed, excited like a schoolchild. He shrugged and smiled. "I don't know, I really don't."

"Did you know this would happen? Did you know so many people would come?"

"No. Well, it was supposed to happen. But the fever! It's more than I expected."

"Are you frightened for him?" I asked, referring to Khomeini. "A little bit."

Even though I'd asked the question, I couldn't imagine anyone being frightened for Khomeini. I was frightened *of* him — and of the fact that things were already moving too quickly. Deep inside, I knew Sadegh and the others had already lost control, or, worse, they had never had it.

"Are you in control now?" I asked.

"I really don't know what the organizers here have planned," he answered.

I hadn't meant in control of this demonstration, but Sadegh was too taken aback, too excited to understand.

"Who's in charge now, the government or the troops?" I pressed.

"Our friends over there." He waved his arm toward some armed men. Then he laughed again in disbelief at the crowds.

"Is there a motorcade?"

"I don't know." He was next to me and he was a million miles away.

"You don't know? Wasn't that planned before we left?" I began to wonder about Sadegh's liaison with Teheran from exile.

"How do you feel about being home?" I asked, playing journalist. His look of euphoria combined with bewilderment had in effect answered the question.

"I don't know. I really don't know. But I'll let you know tomorrow."

In seconds the crowds swallowed him up again, and I once again joined my colleagues.

I had the sudden feeling I wouldn't see Sadegh again for a long time, and that when I did, the situation would be very different. I was right, because for Sadegh and me tomorrow was delayed for almost a year.

As we all crowded through the airport doors into the street, journalists, clerics, revolutionaries, the reality of the city struck in waves. Waves of sound first — cars honking, people yelling and chanting. The air, which had looked misty from the plane, was filled with dust. There was no moisture. It was hot and dry and smelled of spices and sewage, of perfume and sweat. Normally at this time of year it would be cold and snowy. "It's an omen," one marshal said to me deliriously. "Khomeini brings the sun."

Revolutionary marshals, identified by their armbands, gesticulated and shouted orders at the crowd, and at us. Mostly young men in drab pants, jackets and shirts, they were fired with their triumph, though I thought I sensed panic in their eyes, too. But perhaps it was only my own panic as I looked at the forces they had to control.

The press were herded toward a collection of vans and buses parked by the curb. I clambered aboard one, and we headed off to follow the Imam. Frenzied devotees clung to the van's fenders and open windows. Others marched alongside as we inched our way along Eisenhower Boulevard through a sea of people. Most of the men wore work clothes or jeans. Some wore old suits. The women were engulfed in the long black or blue folds of the *chador*, looking like blackbirds. Occasionally a fold would lift in the breeze and reveal jeans and men's black running shoes, or leather boots and a bright skirt.

For hours the motorcade crept slowly through the city past mobs of Khomeini's people. We saw no skyscrapers, but the buildings we passed were modern — modest, plain, concrete blocks with no frills. Their white and buff color was what gave the city its romantic archeological look from above. On the ground the buildings looked drab, shoddy and insubstantial.

By contrast, the Shahyad was monumental and imposing, its fluted columns spread like the legs of a huge wrestler settling his weight. It towered over everything else, but the man who had built it was gone, and Teheran now belonged to Khomeini.

I was mesmerized by the spectacle, and fascination soon overcame my fear. We were in the middle of one of the great historic events of the twentieth century, and we knew it. It was exhilarating beyond all measure, even for jaded journalists. We scribbled and recorded every detail as we drank it all in.

As we moved slowly through the mobs, more people crawled onto the fenders and clung to the sides of our van.

"I hope they don't roll the van," a veteran British correspondent muttered. "Sometimes they do."

I stared out the window and watched with horror as a policeman handed his gun to a grim-faced, nine-year-old revolutionary. Children with guns. I shook my head and wondered what would make a policeman give a child a real gun.

At the entrance to Behesht Zahra cemetery — the name means "paradise" — a group of earnest young boys waited for us. They were a scruffy but cheerful lot, dressed in a mix of worn shirts, pants, rough jackets and jeans.

On the hoods of their rickety trucks they had laid out cheese and big flat rounds of bread for us. The food looked as grubby as the boys and some of the press held back. But the rest of us fell on it ravenously, suddenly aware of how long it had been since we had eaten. The boys grinned and nodded, offering us their bread and cheese with happy openheartedness and humble hospitality. We were guests of their revolution.

The graveyard, which lay beyond an enormous arched gateway, was already filled with a living mass of humanity. Hundreds of thousands of feet shuffled over the dead below the ground, as the masses moved slowly toward the podium on which Khomeini now sat. At the end of the motorcade, a helicopter had ferried him over the cemetery. The people filled the avenues and spaces between the trees and bushes, and they sat wedged together on gravesites. It reminded me of a medieval tapestry; the figures flowed together without the differentiation of perspective. The near and far, the quick and the dead, all on the same plane, crystallized in one moment.

And as we approached, led by the boys from the trucks, who acted as marshals, the masses parted to allow our passage. Wave upon wave of black veils drew back while they murmured a chant of ''Allah-o-Akbar . . .''

Paris seemed far more than a quarter of a world away. We had not just been transported to the realm of a different and exotic culture, we had been brought to a monumental moment in a nation's history. And we had been transported through the looking glass. ''It is a great huge game of chess that's being played, all over the world, ''Alice exclaimed when she entered the realm. Only being a mirror world, the chess game was played backward. It started with the king already dead. Checkmate — Shah mat. And now the bishop ruled the board.

We reached the small platform set among the tombs and sat down on the gravestones and the sun-baked earth to listen as Khomeini announced the death of the regime of the ''criminal Shah'' and the birth of the Islamic Republic.

It did not occur to me to wonder why the great homecoming was staged in a graveyard. It seemed most appropriate for this revolution to flower in the tombs. Although the revolution had been brought about largely by passive resistance — by strikes and demonstrations — death and martyrdom were at its heart. That brutal truth was reflected by Khomeini himself. Seated on a small platform with other mullahs, he was immobile and expressionless. His cold voice issued forth as if from one of the cadavers below his feet. He was there to bear witness for those who died under the Shah, but I heard the voices of those yet to die. As the tremendous crowd listened with rapt attention to the words from the loudspeakers, sometimes they shouted, ''*Allah-o-Akbar*,'' a chant that grew into a roar as Khomeini finished and prepared to leave.

The helicopter that had spirited Khomeini from the crush of the procession to the cemetery appeared to once again whisk him away. Heedless of whirring rotors, people flocked after him, chanting and crying. But the chopper clattered upward, out of reach. Then it hovered just over our heads, seeming to struggle to stay aloft. Suddenly it veered and began to fall. Our young marshal screamed and beat his way through the crowd, pulling and dragging us out of range. But, just as disaster seemed inevitable, the chopper slowed its descent and rattled up and away.

I had no time to indulge in nervous aftershock. The marshal rounded us up and led us back through the crowds. It took hours to reach our vans. The crowd had not dispersed, and on the drive to our hotel, we stopped here and there to check out a celebration, or to talk to a guard, a policeman or a marshal.

It was late by the time we reached the Intercontinental Hotel and I connected at last with the CBC team, which included Joe Schlesinger, Don Dixon and for radio news, Hal Jones.

We sagged into chairs or sat on the edge of the beds in Dixon's room and compared notes.

''I told you not to come,'' Dixon said. ''Fun, isn't it?''

I had assumed Don was being chauvinistic when he warned me off, but now I saw he meant it for himself, too, and Don Dixon was a cool veteran newsman.

''It's a nightmare out there,'' he continued. ''We're getting out ASAP — as soon as possible.''

Schlesinger was, as always, the old pro on top of the situation, but he was no less anxious than Dixon to leave.

''It's a great story,'' he said. ''And you can have it.'' He smiled like a fond uncle offering a booby trap.

I decided to bow out before I passed out. I tottered off to get some sleep. It had been fifty-six hours since I had last closed my eyes, and the next day I was going to school with Khomeini.

The Teheran organizers of Khomeini's triumphant return had prepared a temporary headquarters for him at the Refahi School, an old religious girls' school. The squat building was just behind the parliament buildings.

For the first time in twenty-six years, Khomeini and his partners in exile would all meet face to face with the other clerical leaders and their accomplices in Teheran. Khomeini had been flown to the school by the clattering helicopter. This morning the press corps rushed for taxis once again to fight the heavy traffic and mobs of humanity of Teheran's streets. The posher networks hired cars.

Outside the Refahi School, a long line of women in fluttering black stretched three deep for a hundred yards. As they waited patiently to move forward to glimpse the Imam, they sang a song whose cheery tune belied the meaning of the words — "Death to Bakhtiar."

Again they reminded me of warbling blackbirds, and suddenly I thought of the hapless Protestants who were dressed up in black feather disguises for the amusement of King Louis XIII, who chortled as he took careful aim and shot them as they hopped about his garden. A hundred years later the incident had become a nursery rhyme: "Four and twenty blackbirds, baked into a pie . . ."

I shook my head in sorrow at these women who voluntarily donned the robes of degradation. "Long live Khomeini!" they called to me. We would never speak the same language.

I walked over to the women to record their singing and to ask a few questions. They sang obligingly and I asked why they supported Khomeini.

"Khomeini is good, the Shah was bad," one who spoke some English replied.

Perhaps, I thought, it was as simple as that for most of them.

"Do you like our revolution?" they asked me.

I couldn't honestly say. So far I had seen little save mayhem. During the next ten days, however, I would see more. I would work long days and then return to my hotel to edit tapes and write scripts late into the night.

The Intercontinental was the hotel of choice for the press corps. There is one such hotel in every hotspot. In Teheran, the Hilton was more elegant, but the Intercon, an ugly edifice that looked like an upended typewriter, was more central. It had telexes and phones that worked, as these things astonishingly do in the midst of chaos.

The Intercon also had fair to excellent food. The coffee shop offered edible buffets; room service served; and upstairs we had our choice of the Polynesian Room or the French Restaurant, where we consoled ourselves with mountains of cheap caviar and excellent wines from the city's finest cellars — cellars that were doomed. Every supper was a kind of sacramental last supper before St. Emilion was martyred and Pepsi reigned supreme in what was soon to be the teetotaling Islamic Republic.

The lobby was huge and undistinguished, with green carpet and nooks with armchairs where journalists mingled. Revolution was good for the Intercon, which overflowed with some five hundred of us from around the world, guests who cared little about decor. The rooms were modern, functional replicas of hotel rooms anywhere. All we wanted was hot water and a phone that worked.

I fell back on my bed each night and wondered where Sadegh was and what he was doing. I had tried in vain to reach the friends he told me I could trust. I asked about him and so did other members of the press, but the mullahs denied knowledge of his whereabouts, or they said he was on a secret mission.

It was frustrating to be cut off from him, but it was to be expected. In any case, he had his job and I had mine. Later, perhaps, I would find him, or he would call.

10

In the midst of the uproar it was extremely difficult for foreign journalists to distinguish events and participants. We worked twenty-hour days, and felt like swimmers moving against a swift current in a river full of debris.

On the streets, the general message of the mobs was joyous, but there was an undertone of dark violence. Friends and enemies wore the same uniform and showed the same face to the press and to each other.

"You American?" they would ask accusingly, nose to my nose.

I soon learned to reply, "*Man Faransavi hastam*—I am French." In those days, it was best to be French, and preferably from Neauphle le Château. The population of Teheran harbored the fond illusion that France had embraced their beloved leader when all others rejected him.

One day, the foreign journalists went to a pro-Shah rally at a small arena near the parliament buildings. Since the pro-Shah demonstrators expected an attack from Khomeini's hoards, armed soldiers surrounded the building. Inside, a shaft of sunshine from a skylight pierced the gloom, lending an air of apotheosis to the assembly. The atmosphere was electric with defiant fear as desperate supporters of the monarchy poured in and filled the tiers of seats.

I pushed through to an empty space at the center of the arena, and began asking questions of those in the first rows.

"Hi!" a cheerful voice behind me said. As I turned, he snapped a picture of me in the beam of light from the ceiling.

"Great shot. Having a good time?" he asked.

My photographer was my old friend Olivier Rebbot, a good-looking Frenchman with a manic American manner. He was one of the most popular of the press photographers. We all called him the Happy Rabbit, since his face had brightened up many of the world's combat zones. He was in Iran for *Newsweek* with Elaine Sciolino.

He leaned over and asked the first row of Shah supporters, "Having a good time?"

"Javid Shah!" clamored hundreds of drowning souls. "Long live the Shah!"

Nearby, a plump bleached-blond woman was in near-hysterics. Her heavy makeup had been smeared and her hair was wild, as if set on end by an electric current. Tears flowed shamelessly down her face as she desperately shouted long life to a king who was already gone.

In the midst of the tumult two men came up to me and pointed angrily at my microphone. I held it up to the elder of the two, a stout, balding man.

"We've got that bastard Ghotbzadeh!" he spat. "He's finished."

"Who does? Who are you?" I asked frantically. Why had they picked me out of this mob? Did they know?

"We've got him," the man said, and they both turned and disappeared into the turmoil. I stood frozen to the spot. Who had him? Where was he? Was he dead or alive?

"Javid Shah!" wailed the fat blond woman.

I told myself it was a coincidence the men had picked me. They were just looking for a reporter. And Sadegh's all right, I said over and over. But I was shaken and I wished again I could get in touch with him or his friends.

*   *   *

On the day of Khomeini's return, the populace had appeared as one giant organism. Now cells broke away and formed whole new organisms which throbbed with life and spread over the city like amoebas.

Out on the streets were the Mudjahedeen — the Warriors of the Faith — led by Massoud Radjavi. Their religious mentor, though not actually a member of their group, was Ayatollah Mahmoud Taleghani. He was lying low. The Mudjahedeen believed in a mixture of Marx and Islam. They had opposed Khomeini from the beginning.

The Hezb'ollahi — or Hezbies, as the cynical comics in the press came to call them — were rabid followers of Khomeini. Hezbe Allah means "Party of God." They, too, roamed the streets, killing members or suspected members of the Mudjahedeen. They also killed anyone who thought well of the Shah.

The Fedayeen were out-and-out leftists whose ideology combined Maoism and radical socialism. They were enemies of the clergy and hence of Khomeini.

The Tudeh, the Communist party of Iran, outwardly supported Khomeini while it tested the temperature of the population.

The remnants of the National Front, the nationalist party founded by Mohammad Mossadegh, believed in nationalism and social democracy. They, too, initially supported Khomeini. Most of their leaders were working on a constitution, deluded into believing they would be allowed to implement it.

The Islamic Students' Organization was split into various factions. One group, the Sepah Pasdaran, or Army of the Revolutionary Guards, patrolled the streets. They were allegedly former volunteer marshals who had patrolled the streets in the final days before the total collapse of the Shah's government. With its usual wit, the press dubbed them the Rev Guards.

All the groups were infiltrated by other groups and by agents of various Middle Eastern governments and factions. The Iraqis, the Syrians, the Jordanians, the Libyans, the PLO, the factions in Lebanon and the Israelis all had interests in Iran. Iran became the living example of the old, ironic joke: "Invite four (here you simply fill in the name of any Middle Eastern nationality) to dinner, and listen to the views of six political parties."

Almost any of the groups who wandered the streets or plotted for power could have targeted Sadegh for assassination. I fretted helplessly, terrified. But after a couple of days, some colleagues heard he was either in Mashad or Isfahan, in the north or south, on a mission for Khomeini and would be back soon.

Sadegh, when he returned from his mission, went to stay at the home of his old friend, Alef. Eventually, I met Alef, one of the few whom Sadegh trusted, and, as it turned out, could trust. It was Alef who told me of those turbulent days after Khomeini's return to Iran, days during which I wondered where Sadegh was, and worried about the rumors I heard.

Sadegh was back in Iran at last, in Alef's comfortable little house with its adjoining courtyard and garden. He felt dazed. The unmistakable dry, spicy atmosphere of Teheran flooded over him, and he felt a thousand sensations as he once again breathed Persian air.

Alef, a tall, thin man with angular features and dark, kind eyes, brought tea prepared the Iranian way in small clear glasses on a silver tray. The two men savored their reunion and Sadegh's homecoming. Then they discussed the situation in Iran.

Alef was certain they did not need to worry about the military. It had already disintegrated. Every day more soldiers and airmen came over to their side.

"The moment for a military coup has passed," Alef assured Sadegh.

Sadegh smiled and leaned back in the comfortable chair.

"Yes, it's all over now," Sadegh said. "Everything is under control. Now I can go and live my life in the West."

"What?" Alef was astonished. He stared at Sadegh. "Where?" he added, then, "Are you all right?"

Sadegh made a motion with his hand. "Of course I'm all right. Don't you see? I've done my part. I'll go live in Canada. I want a place in the country. Maybe a small farm. With chickens and things."

"Canada! Chickens!" Alef was on his feet now. "Sadegh, you'd last about ten minutes. What's this all about? You're home."

Sadegh sank into another moody silence.

Alef was worried. Sadegh had been away nineteen years. Alef, by contrast, had spent a great deal of that time in Iran. His view of the mullahs in general and of Khomeini in particular was far more cynical than Sadegh's.

"Don't leave Khomeini alone with the mullahs," Alef warned. "If you want him to stick to the plans you made for this revolution, you'll have to stay with him day and night."

"Don't worry about Khomeini. They won't be able to twist him."

"They won't have to! In his heart and soul, Khomeini's a führer!"

Sadegh was enraged. "Khomeini is a man of God! He has devoted his life to Islam! He's gone to prison for Islam and spent years in exile. He never stopped working toward a revolution. Never! Now you sit here and call him names! I won't have it! Who the hell do you think you are?"

Alef had not expected Sadegh's anger. He waited. Then, sensing the outburst of temper had subsided, tried reason.

"Calm down, Sadegh. All right, let's say Khomeini is all you think he is. The problem is, you don't know the mullahs. I've tried over and over to tell you, to make you understand. They're dangerous. This is not the Iran you left. They've come out of the mosque, all of them. Not just men like Taleghani who want reform, but all of them. The mullahs smell power."

Alef knew he had to be diplomatic. He continued with conviction. "Whatever Khomeini's beliefs are, and regardless of his loyalties to you, the mullahs are his natural brothers, and the mosque, for all its rivalries, is a closely knit family. Khomeini is home after a long exile. While he was gone, the clerics here fought and suffered, too. Khomeini owes them a huge political debt — and a spiritual debt, too. He won't want to offend them and cause a rift. Sadegh, you have to stay here. Your work in Paris was only part of it. The mullahs have their own organization here, and it's powerful. You can't just sit back and let matters follow their own course.''

''I don't want political power.'' Sadegh sank back in his chair. ''That's up to Bazargan and the rest.''

''Fine,'' Alef replied. ''But you have to help make sure those who do get political power are the right people.''

Alef wasn't the only one beating this drum. Sadegh's old friend Karim Lahidji tried to make him listen to the same warnings about the mullahs. Karim Lahidji, head of the Association for Human Rights, was a courageous man who had been severely beaten and left for dead on the street by seven SAVAK agents in 1978. Lahidji, too, had lived in Iran while Sadegh was in exile. He knew the mullahs were the flip side of SAVAK.

But Sadegh was not worried. He had talked to the mullahs who had come to Neauphle. Rafsanjani and Montazeri seemed all right, he said. In any case, Lahidji and Habibi were working on a constitution. The Islamic Republic would start life on a solid foundation. ''Maybe some mullahs will argue, but they won't defy Khomeini,'' he concluded.

Alef groaned. ''They won't have to,'' he said. Then he repeated his old advice. ''At least get together with Beheshti. I'm not sure you're right about Rafsanjani and Montazeri. They're ambitious and Rafsanjani is clever. But Beheshti is vital. If you can get him to cooperate with you, it would be much better. He's ruthless, but he's sincere and he's very sharp. If he thinks he can be powerful within the government you have in mind, he'll work for it. If not, he'll be the most dangerous of the lot.''

Ayatollah Mohammad Beheshti was a highly controversial figure. It was rumored he had been in the pay of the Shah even though he had harbored revolutionaries in his Islamic center at the mosque in Hamburg. Beheshti had emerged as one of the key clerics in the movement, an alert politician and an able leader and organizer. But now it seemed that Beheshti had ideas of his own. Alef knew that Beheshti and some of the strongest mullahs were forming a political organization of their own. He regarded them uneasily.

Lahidji had warned Sadegh and his allies for years about the mosque. Still, Alef found Beheshti to be intelligent and warmhearted and quite a family man in spite of his cool manner. He reasoned that if Sadegh and Beheshti could work something out, the danger of the mullahs taking over everything would be reduced.

But Sadegh only shook his head and dismissed Beheshti. "Nah, he's only small-fry."

Sadegh's astonishing assessment of the formidable Ayatollah Beheshti was partly disingenuous, partly wishful thinking.

Frustrated by this wall of obtuse self-assurance, Alef began to bang his head against it. "For the love of God will you listen to me! You haven't been here for nineteen years! We've been dealing with the mullahs and we know a damn sight more than you do! If you don't get going and organize against them, they're going to make the Shah look like Prince Charming! And Khomeini will lead them all the way. They'll rip your constitution to shreds!"

Like Macbeth encountering the three witches, Sadegh encountered his soothsayers. But unlike Macbeth he ignored their opinions. Already he and Bani Sadr had separated, each with his own coterie. Had those warning him circled and urged, had they joined together and pressed their point, the future might not have turned out as it did. But there, in the familiarity of a Persian setting, with tea in clear glasses, Sadegh didn't listen. Perhaps he was still too much in the world of student revolutionaries, for whom argument is a kind of aphrodisiac unrelated to reality. Perhaps to him it was just another argument—and hadn't he had enough such arguments with Bani Sadr?

Not listening to Alef and the others in those early days was a tragic mistake. Beheshti marshaled the mullahs' strategy sessions into an agreement to rule by "consensus of clergy." Agreement by consensus was his only hope of keeping a rein on the fanatic elements among his brothers, while at the same time tapping the enormous power of the mosque itself. Beheshti needed the liberals on his side to counterbalance the clerical fascists, but he also needed to maintain his own primacy over them and co-opt Khomeini.

Beheshti also encouraged the idea that as meritorious as some of Mehdi Bazargan's and Ali Shariati's proposals to modernize Islam were, ultimately only the mosque had the right to pronounce on Islam. Ancient words and timeless gestures issued from the ring of turbaned brothers, a circle unbroken for a thousand years. Alliances and strategies of today were carefully tucked into the folds of the robes of yesterday, for tomorrow's battles.

The mullahs nodded. But if they had looked, they would have seen Khomeini nodding above them.

*   *   *

In spite of himself, Sadegh began to have some misgivings. He visited the Refahi School and was appalled by the collection of mullahs. Half of them, he realized, were sanctimonious hypocrites and medieval morons, but they gathered round Khomeini and left Sadegh and the other secular leaders out.

Bani Sadr had also been swept aside. He stayed off in a corner scribbling lists of theoretical problems with solutions A to Z. He seemed blissfully unaware that his task was useless. While the mullahs were marshalling their troops, he was attempting to reason with Khomeini.

A few days later, Sadegh returned to the Refahi School with Alef. There, sitting with Khomeini, was Ayatollah Falsafi, who had long been an intimate of the Shah's. An ardent enemy of Mossadegh, Falsafi was famous for his public statements, especially his pronouncement that if bees had queens, it was natural for Iran to have a king. Now Falsafi sat with the heir apparent.

Sadegh exploded with anger and horror, pointing at Falsafi. "That is the end of the revolution! Him, there! It's all over!"

Dragging Alef with him, Sadegh left, vowing to wash his hands of the whole bloody lot and go back to Paris.

"Khomeini," he muttered, "will come to his senses."

Khomeini summoned Sadegh later. They met alone.

"Sadegh, what's wrong with you?" Khomeini asked.

"I'm leaving until you've finished with these parasites and want to work with me again. How could you sit with Falsafi?"

"It is necessary to bring all the brothers together, even those whose ways must be mended. Have you lost faith in me?"

"No. But I have none in them," Sadegh replied, not bothering to hide his disgust.

"You need only have faith in me," Khomeini replied.

"I do."

"I need you here. I don't want you to leave. There is a great deal to be done. I want you to take over the direction of the radio and television."

Sadegh was stunned. "Me? I don't know how to run a television network. I'd be lost. Whose idea was this?"

"I want you to do it."

Sadegh considered. No doubt the mullahs thought he would flounder and drown in the impossible task, and that they would be able to control him. But as director of broadcasting he would have a powerful weapon against them and his other ideological enemies who were trying to co-opt the revolution. And he would regain the status he had held in Paris as a leader alongside Khomeini.

Khomeini was equally certain that, in Sadegh, he had a son who would do his bidding.

*   *   *

I obtained the home phone number of Ayatollah Mohammad Beheshti, the mullah Sadegh had dismissed as a "small-fry." The number was given to me by an Iranian reporter who was standing about the lobby of the Intercon. I phoned, and Beheshti told me he had agreed to an earlier request for an interview from ABC News, but that I could come too. I found the ABC radio reporter, Bill Dowell, an old friend from Paris, and we tore off in the ABC car.

Some twenty minutes later we found Beheshti's small, white house in a neighborhood that, with its rows of closely packed ticky-tacky dwellings, looked like a suburb of Cincinnati. Inside, the resemblance faded.

A young acolyte dressed in mullah's robes ushered us into a bright room. It was empty save for an enormous carpet and a few cushions. Beyond it, in an alcove, a sofa and armchairs were grouped around a low coffee table. Minutes after we arrived, we were joined by Peter Jennings of ABC television news.

We were taken to the alcove and seated. In moments Ayatollah Beheshti glided in, a confident, wordly figure in a brown cloth cloak and white robe. Beheshti showed a cool face to the press. He had a falcon's features and manicured hands, which he rigidly controlled. When he did succumb to an irresistible private joke, the effect was bizarre, as though a statue suddenly laughed. When he was speaking English, German or Farsi, his droning monotone rolled slowly over words chosen with great deliberation.

Smiling in a distressingly feral way, he indicated a small room crammed with electronic equipment — tape machines, a patch console, recording gear and a telephone.

"You remember the phone at Neauphle?" he asked. Then, not waiting for the answer, he went on :"Well, this is the other end."

After two hours of conversation it was apparent that this was a man to be reckoned with. He assured us that "consensus of the clergy" was an operative concept, and we realized it was a consensus he guided.

When we talked of human rights in the new republic, I naturally brought up the subject of the role of women. Women, he assured me, were to be fully equal with men in the Islamic Republic.

"Then why," I asked, "have you not looked me in the face for two hours?" During our entire conversation, Beheshti had answered all questions, including mine, by addressing Peter Jennings and Bill Dowell, who sat directly in front of him, while I had been seated at right angles next to him.

"Oh, I was only talking straight ahead," he replied with geniality. "But I have answered all your questions, more even than theirs," he added, while still looking at them. "A woman will be respected for her own qualities," he went on. "But her beauty must not be used as a motive, as a cause to do so or so as it is in America or Europe or in Iran before today. I have seen women act this way in France, in Germany and so on. Please, please try to be a woman, an active woman, in every field, but only have sexual relations with your husband."

"I'm not feeling beautiful this morning," I answered, then persisted, "but surely if the problem is that men can't control their bestial instincts, the solution is to teach the men, not cover the women."

"We shall do this, too. But things must not be done for sexual reasons in offices and in the streets."

"Then I ask you again, why haven't you looked at me in these two hours. How can I be the social equal of someone who won't look at me?"

At this point Peter Jennings made a smart-aleck crack. I didn't catch his elegant phrasing, but the gist was clear, and this bit of man-talk was roundly enjoyed by all the boys, including the ayatollah, who broke into restrained laughter.

Regaining control, Beheshti said to me, looking at them, "A man is better not to gaze at a woman and a woman is better not to gaze at a man. So I answer all your questions and I value you as much as the men, but I do not gaze at you. Is that clear?"

Is it ever, I thought to myself as we all left. Beheshti was the epitome of the political mosque, a cool and self-righteous Machiavellian. His ideas were anathema to me, though ironically I found him appealing, not as a man but as a human being. Perhaps more exactly, I found his intellect appealing. And he had a style, a certain élan. Beheshti was, I concluded, an enthusiastic manipulator, a man of many faces. He was capable of infinite bamboozling, and was to be approached with great caution by either friend or foe. For those reasons, I dubbed him Ayatollah Kissinger.

*   *   *

One day I went to the university to a rally called by the Mudjahedeen leader, Massoud Radjavi. Thousands of excited people filled the vast field in front of the podium.

I backed away from the surging crowd and climbed the steps of one of the graceful white university buildings for a better view. Before me, on a small bench under an ornamental tree, a young woman draped in the black folds of the *chador* sat with a young man. Together we watched as a gang of Hezbies wielding clubs and guns swung around the building and headed for the crowd. They fired their guns in the air and chanted, "*Khomeini e Imam!*"

Suddenly the rally exploded in violence, as Mudjahedeen and Hezbies clashed. Outnumbered, the Hezbies beat a retreat, running breathlessly past me. I looked around. The young couple were still talking, unperturbed by the mobs around them. This sort of violent eruption was now an everyday occurrence.

The other factions held rallies too, but since none wore uniforms it was difficult for foreign journalists to distinguish one group from another.

The next day I found myself at the university again. Roughly shaven young toughs pressed against my microphone and yelled threats against the Shah and the West.

"You just tell them we're armed," said a dark, heavy fellow, "and we're ready to fight if they try anything!"

He stabbed his finger at me. "And we've got the guns to do it."

"Are you a guerrilla?" I asked, feeling I had to say something. I had no idea if these boys were Mudjahedeen, Fedayeen, students, Pasdars or Hezbies.

"Never mind," he growled, and melted away into the crowd that had pressed around our cameras.

"He's a Mudjahedeen man, and he means it," another man told me.

Spying Bill Dowell off in the distance, I moved slowly away to join him.

"You've heard about anarchy," he remarked. "You've read about anarchy. You've heard theorists theorize about anarchy. This is anarchy," he concluded.

Mass revolution, that rarest of all animals in man's political jungle, had indeed brought its twin, anarchy. Rough beasts both, fabulous and deadly. These self-appointed bands — guardians of revolutionary truths — prowled the streets, arresting people at whim and releasing them according to their own arcane creeds. Remnants of SAVAK also stalked the night, killing anyone they could, while they in turn were savaged and murdered.

At the university grounds a group of professors invited me to join them for a special event. I hesitated, looking around at the crowd, but the professors pleaded, so I followed them to a bus. The bus headed out of the city along the now familiar streets toward the cemetery where Khomeini had made his first speech.

At the cemetery they explained that after a death Moslems commemorate the seventh day, the fortieth day and the day one year after a death. This was the fortieth day after the death of their beloved colleague, Kamran Nedjatolahi. He had been shot on his balcony by a SAVAK sniper during a demonstration.

It was a dry day. As we walked across the vast grounds of the cemetery, a strong wind swirled the dust up in clouds around us. A curious wailing sound grew in the distance as they urged me forward. The scene before me wavered and floated in the haze of dust and my own exhaustion.

"Be careful," cautioned one of my guides.

And looking down, I saw what I had dreamed about in Paris. Then it had been a horrible nightmare. The reality was even worse. Hundreds of newly excavated, empty graves honeycombed the ground. They had been dug in expectation of the future dead of the ongoing revolution. It was not won yet. The bones and screaming faces of my dream were yet to come, but I froze as if they were there before me, moaning and shrieking.

My guides propelled me forward along the narrow paths afforded by the walls between the empty graves. Women, draped in black, sat on the edges, as their feet dangled in the bodiless holes. We struggled through them toward our goal, a small mound not far away. Nedjatolahi's grave was surmounted by an enormous oval of fresh flowers, the Moslem funeral wreath.

When we reached the mound a woman with a tiny, agonized face embraced me. She begged me to tell the world of their suffering. "Long live Khomeini!" she said, weeping into the folds of her chador. She was Nedjatolahi's mother.

It was forty days after my dream in Paris.

*   *   *

Images of death and violence and small bizarre incidents occurred daily. In front of the parliament nervous young soldiers paraded with guns. Demonstrators gave them carnations and they in turn stuffed them into the barrels of the M16s. One young soldier gave me his flower and said he hoped the killing was over.

I phoned Bakhtiar for an interview. After briefly assuring me he would remain in office, he refused a meeting. When I went to the Prime Ministerial Palace anyway, a row of Scorpion tanks was pointed directly at the building.

Liz Thurgood of *The Guardian*, Tony Clifton of *Newsweek* and I set off to interview Mehdi Bazargan, the intellectual father of the revolution whose ideas had for years inspired Sadegh and the others. We drove across Teheran in a hideous old taxi full of gasoline fumes and cigarette smoke.

Mehdi Bazargan was a tiny gray-haired man with twinkling eyes and a neat gray goatee. He gently insisted that he could not make any premature statements, but we knew he would be named prime minister of a Provisional Revolutionary Government. He saw himself only as a kind of manager of the nation until a true government could be elected. It was difficult for us to connect the political storm with this frail-seeming little man, who smiled and spoke haltingly to us in French. Could he possibly be one of the forces behind it all? And could he now control what he had helped unleash? He was to be named prime minister on the next day, and then we would see.

I wanted desperately to see Sadegh. I needed him to guide me through the maze of groups, personalities and events. Finally I reached one of his friends, and he offered me some guidelines to find my way through the jungle, but he could not contact Sadegh, either. I decided it was best to keep a low profile where Sadegh was concerned. If he had enemies, then he did not need a Western ladyfriend making herself known.

*   *   *

We crowded into a tiny room at the Refahi School the next day for a makeshift press conference. Catherine Leroy, a renowned photo-journalist, Liz Thurgood of *The Guardian*, Elaine Sciolino of *Newsweek* and I were the only women. We rejected wearing the obligatory headscarf, and in spite of an officious mullah who was soon cowed by Catherine, we remained with heads uncovered.

Khomeini, Ibrahim Yazdi and Mehdi Bazargan entered with a few others and sat on a small platform a few feet from us. As Khomeini spoke, his calm, implacable voice spread a palpable coldness, each word a needle of ice. He announced that he had appointed Bazargan as prime minister, then he unveiled the face of the Islamic Republic: "Religiously, I am entitled to do this! So everyone should obey this provisional government! Opposition to this provisional government will be considered opposition to Islamic laws and regulations! Therefore, I am warning anyone who takes any action against this provisional government that the punishment for them will be very harsh under Islamic jurisprudence. Opposition to this government will be considered blasphemy!" Ibrahim Yazdi translated in strident tones, but Khomeini's dull drone froze the blood.

As the revolution rolled over the last resistance, I found myself trying to get a plane out of it. The Toronto desk wanted me back to put together a second documentary report on events so far. I was also expected back at my vacant post in Paris.

The central frustration, and the worst aspect, of radio and television reporting is that correspondents are parachuted in and whisked out on quick, commando-like raids. Just as you are mastering the situation in one hotspot, you are sent to another, or back home to attend to the more mundane aspects of reporting. But I had already been in Iran longer than the others. Don Dixon and the rest of our crew had left on a Hercules C-130 evacuation flight arranged by Canadian ambassador Ken Taylor. That left me to find my way home alone.

Dave Burnett, a top photographer with his own agency and a close friend of Olivier, the Happy Rabbit, arrived at my room with news that there was a slim chance of getting on a departing Air

France flight, which might be the last one for weeks. I wanted to stay, but I was ordered back. Many of those ordered to stay, on the other hand, wanted to leave the mayhem. One of these, Elaine Sciolino, modeled her new *chador*—safety prevailing over feminism.

Olivier wished us a cheerful farewell as Burnett and I scrambled off for the airport. Two years later, Olivier died in El Salvador, on the other side of the world, when a bullet found the armhole of his bulletproof vest.

In the madness, I had been unable to find Sadegh. Perhaps, I reflected, it was just as well. This was his home, not mine. There could be no place for me in his life in this strange and alien land and in the midst of this upheaval. In my heart and soul I wished him wisdom and love, and I said goodbye. But as the aircraft roared down the runway, I felt a terrible wrenching pain, as if I were leaving my only home.

Then we were airborne and Iran sank away beneath us in the growing distance. Far below, Shahpour Bakhtiar, who had been left holding the bag by the Shah, resigned. The army went back to its barracks. Revolutionaries swept through the streets in hijacked trucks. The Israeli embassy was looted and turned overnight into the embassy of the Palestine Liberation Organization. Bakhtiar's house was burned to the ground, and fledgling vigilantes of the komitehs — the so-called neighborhood committees organized by the mullahs and radicals — rounded up the Shah's military commanders, members of SAVAK, governors, mayors and anyone they could find who had held any kind of power under the Shah.

The mad chess game was engaged.

"Now *here*," said the Red Queen, "it takes all the running you can do, to keep in the same place. If you want to get somewhere else, you must run at least twice as fast as that."

The pandemonium receded as I left Iran behind and returned to the other side of the looking glass.

≈11≈

In early February, four men—SAVAK chief, Nematollah Nassiri; governor of Teheran, Mehdi Rahimi; governor of Isfahan, General Reza Naji; and paratroop commander Manuchar Khossroudad—were paraded on the roof of the Refahi School. Nassiri, once the strutting king of his own domain of dark cells, whips and pain, now cowered like a beaten rabbit as the mob below brandished knives and meat cleavers and screamed, ''We want to kill! We want to kill! Off with their heads!''

Khomeini's men stepped up behind the four and shot each in the back of the neck, then filled the bodies with bullets as they fell into the raging crowd.

By the end of February, the revolutionary tribunals had killed at least a thousand people. By midsummer, they would do away with over 70 percent of the Shah's senior officer corps. Then they went on to execute junior officers and enlisted men. The agreement Khomeini had signed, guaranteeing the safety of military men who went over to him, meant nothing in the new republic.

The tribunals operated under the gleeful guidance of Ayatollah Sadegh Khalkhali, a short, pudgy man with tiny eyes bulging behind thick glasses. He took enormous and obvious delight in ridding Iran of those he disliked, charging them with brutality, murder or ''war against God,'' and ''corruption on earth.'' The defendants were given two minutes to reply, then were sentenced and shot. Khalkhali sometimes administered the death penalty personally, and as he traveled throughout Iran delivering his summary justice, he became known as Judge Blood.

Each town, city and neighborhood had a committee, a komiteh, formed out of the ranks of the revolutionaries and guided always by the mullahs. The komitehs began to permeate every aspect of daily life, supervising the seizure and redistribution of property, arresting enemies of the revolution and policing the streets. They were especially vigilant about infractions against Islam or the revolution.

In Teheran the Central Komiteh soon grew to equal the Revolutionary Council in power. At NIRT, the National Iranian Radio and Televison network, Sadegh had to accept the komiteh's dictates, because the komiteh was fully backed by Khomeini. It was perched high on a hill at the north end of Teheran, and the director of NIRT was perched high in its headquarters. From his office on the thirteenth floor, Sadegh could see the city fanning out below, and from here he considered his dilemma. A nightmare he was not in control of was closing in around him. The Teheran Komiteh now pulled the strings, and at NIRT he danced to their tune.

They decided which revolutionary marches and tapes should fill the air time, and they chose the long speeches for the edification of the public. Then the komiteh sent Sadegh two "assistants," Moussavi Khoeini'a, a mullah, and Ahmad Khomeini, the Ayatollah's youngest son.

Before Ahmad's arrival at NIRT, Sadegh had paid little attention to Khomeini's son, a nondescript, colorless man with a sallow face and cowlike eyes. Ahmad had been a constant presence over the years, of course. Sadegh's path had crossed his in Lebanon, where both had cultivated allies. Ahmad also eventually had a role in Najaf, Iraq. He was one of the organizers of the move to Paris, and he had been in Neauphle. But Ahmad had never seemed important. To most observers, he was only an adjunct of his father, a little, bland, junior Khomeini. Indeed, the American journalists called him the Little K.

As he faced Ahmad in his office at NIRT, Sadegh remembered Khomeini's arrival in Paris. Had Ahmad manipulated him and Bani Sadr? He dismissed the thought; probably it was simply another of Bani Sadr's intrigues. But, he decided, Ahmad would bear watching.

The other assistant, Moussavi Khoeini'a, was a question mark. Prior to the revolution, this fat, bespectacled mullah had had a reputation as a speaker in the mosques, where he drew subtle parallels between Islam and Marxism. Khoeini'a had been at Neauphle, too. There, Sadegh recalled, he had tried to inject Khomeini's speeches with a clerical viewpoint while he and Bani Sadr had always tried to stress a broader emphasis.

Still, Khoeini'a's motives were not clear to Sadegh, though it was obvious the mullah had been given the nod by Khomeini and the Islamic Republic Party, the IRP, the political creation of Behesti and his brothers.

What Sadegh did not know was that Khoeini'a was closely involved with the Moslem Students' Organization, the same organization he and Bani Sadr had emerged from many years ago, and
that the Moslem Students' Organization was now being formalized
as a revolutionary structure to help carry out "Islamic" reforms in
the universities.

Sadegh watched with growing animosity as Khoeini'a set about
establishing a small clique of his own within the TV network. Ahmad
did his part as well. He began writing florid speeches in praise of
his father to be broadcast as if they were the words of liberal clerics
well known for their opposition to Khomeini. He knew these clerics
were now too frightened to protest the false use of their names.

Sadegh himself had dismissed a few of the old NIRT staff whom
he considered irrevocably corrupt. Ahmad and Khoeini'a dismissed
many more. In this they were aided by Karim Khodapanahi,
Sadegh's old friend from Paris whom he had brought in to serve as
his deputy at NIRT. Khodapanahi would emerge as one of Sadegh's
most treacherous enemies. His poisonous work began when he
helped devastate the television staff in Sadegh's name but without
his permission. People were left with the impression that Sadegh
himself had ordered all the dismissals. Sadegh knew, but could do
nothing.

One of Sadegh's braver employees journeyed to the thirteenth
floor in person to beard the detested lion in his den. Mohammed
Shahid, a young producer, had remained studiously neutral during
the months of upheaval. While the others were on strike, obeying
Khomeini's commands from exile, he doggedly went to work to
produce his little show on music in the cinema. Now Shahid wanted
his back pay so he could leave. He was prepared to face the new
boss whom so many of his colleagues hated.

Sadegh greeted him affably. "I'm told you want to leave."

"Yes. I want my rightful pay first. For the last six months I worked;
I was not on strike."

"Why didn't you go out on strike with the others?" Sadegh asked.

Shahid found himself answering the question easily. It had been
asked without menace. "I'm just not political, that's all. I didn't
support the Shah, and I don't support the revolution."

"Then why do you want to leave?"

"The Shah's is now the ancien régime. Maybe tomorrow you'll
be the ancien régime. So I just want to go."

Shahid immediately regretted his rash frankness and looked at

Khomeini's lieutenant in fear. But Sadegh leaned back and smiled.

"You're very honest," Sadegh said.

Assured by Sadegh's easy manner, Shahid made a joke. "You can be honest," he said, making a pun of Sadegh's name, which means honest or sincere in Persian. "But I am named Mohammed, like the Shah, so I can't be honest."

Sadegh laughed and asked Shahid to remain in his job, but the young man refused, though he agreed to broadcast the shows he had already prepared. Sadegh ordered Shahid's full six months' salary prepared, then asked if he would consider doing a program about Costa Gavras's films *Z* and *State of Siege*, Sadegh's two favorites.

"I already have," Shahid shrugged. "We broadcast those years ago."

"Under the Shah?" Sadegh asked, astonished.

"Of course."

Sadegh struggled to digest his surprise that Costa Gavras's left-wing attacks on fascism and American imperialism had seen the light of day in imperial Iran. Then he asked Shahid to show him his office. Downstairs, Sadegh examined the enormous film and tape archives with incredulity. "All this was allowed?"

Shahid nodded and asked if it would be allowed now. The Shah's censorship had been severe, but it was hodge-podge. The mosque might be more efficient. Sadegh assured him there was no reason to worry.

In the projection room they came across an enraptured mullah watching a film run backwards. Unaware of how to thread a projector or rewind it, he was marveling at how the cameraman could achieve such an effect. Sadegh closed the doors and rolled his eyes heavenward.

Soon another employee of the old regime complained that the staff was being harassed, that armed Revolutionary Guards came daily and stood at the doors.

"There is to be none of that sort of thing here!" Sadegh exploded. Then he sank back in his chair and reconsidered. Finally, he warned the man that those who were watched and harassed should not come to work anymore. They understood. Sadegh couldn't protect them, and he knew it. All he could do was give them a chance to save themselves. He felt he had to compete with the komiteh and the mullahs in militant rhetoric, or lose his own militancy and his power.

To try to counterbalance the stultifying effect of the relentless music, grainy graphics and the bombastic mullahs, Sadegh himself went on the air and worsened things considerably. He addressed the nation as "my people," and sanctimoniously informed them of the need for revolutionary vigilance in these early days of the new republic.

Sadegh was talking to a beloved and imaginary Iran he had idealized in exile. Real Iranians in their living rooms were taken aback. Who did this lout think he was? Never before had the director of television emerged from his office and invaded their homes. And they were certainly not his people. Worse yet, Sadegh had not gone to university in Iran. His Persian was rough, the street Persian he had learned as a boy. The Western press found Sadegh's words ever quotable, but in his own language his voice was not what Iranians expected to hear on television.

Sadegh maneuvered against the Front as much as he did against the extreme mullahs, closing the television to free debates in order to cut off both groups. Sadegh now saw the Front people as weak and was suspicious that some of them might be courting Washington. The only person he believed in was Khomeini—he still believed his Ayatollah was receiving bad advice. Like the White Knight he was moving dangerously close to putting himself out of the game, thinking he was checking his enemies.

*   *   *

"Where did you go? I couldn't find you." Sadegh's voice was warm and insistent over the crackling telephone line.

"I had to get back to Paris," I replied. "The network has its own logic."

"When are you coming back?"

"I don't know. Iran isn't exactly my normal territory."

"Tell them to send you back."

"It's not that easy. How are you?"

"Okay. Okay. It's a mess here."

"I know. Maybe I should apply for a job to help you run NIRT." Then, more seriously, I asked, "Sadegh, are you going to be able to get it all under control?"

He was evasive, worry underlying the familiar bravado, and I held back my anxiety and my anger, afraid to be brutal. That same fear strangled my mind in his presence. On the telephone, I was even more inept: journalist and lover locked in conflict. I sank paralytic into the ocean between us.

"Well, come as soon as you can."

Nothing can be said over the telephone, nothing meaningful, when other ears are probably listening.

"I will," I promised. "I must."

* * *

It went on. A Jewish friend of mine was called and told her brother was to be let out of prison. At the gate, her brother was brought out by a mullah who, before her eyes, unwound the turban from his head and wound it round her brother's neck, strangling him with a smile. "There," the mullah said, kicking the limp corpse toward her. "You can take him home now."

This horror and others occurred over and over as the revolutionaries wrought their divine justice. Often it was mixed with personal revenge or sheer bloodlust, and always it was tacitly encouraged by deliberate lack of control from above. (*"Khomeini doesn't say anything until the action has been taken, and he knows then it cannot be changed,"* Sadegh had written long ago when he first visited the Ayatollah in Iraq.)

Then Khomeini ordered the carnage stopped, and he put justice in the hands of the revolutionary courts. They soon outdid the disorganized vigilantes. As France had had its September massacres, its royalist prisoners butchered wholesale, so Iran, too, bathed their people in blood. Later, systematic terror would come.

And, as if it could all be stopped on decree, Karim Lahidji and Hassan Habibi worked on a constitution, while Bani Sadr criticized it, making lists of what had to be changed and citing objectives.

Next, the reactionary clergy moved against the liberal Ayatollah Taleghani. His sons and daughter-in-law were arrested. Only when he appeared with Khomeini and reaffirmed his faith in Khomeini were his children released. Close friends said that when he returned home, he wept and vowed to continue to fight. But Taleghani was a tired old man and his days were numbered. When he desperately tried to bring about a reconciliation of moderates, neither Bazargan nor Sadegh showed up for a meeting with him. The gap was widening.

Bazargan named a cabinet, but it did not have the power to govern. Only Khomeini had that power and he wielded it through the Council of the Revolution, which the Western press soon called the Revco. Khomeini named a volatile mix of clerical brothers and secular leaders to the council: Sadegh, Bani Sadr, Bazargan, Beheshti, Rafsanjani and Habibi, among others. Revco was to hold power until popular elections decided on a president and a parliament. The presidential elections where scheduled to be held first.

At the center of this complex web sat Khomeini, slowly spinning circles within circles. The people had baptized him Imam, a title of supreme reverence for the unique leader of the Shi'a. But for many others, he was literally the incarnation of the twelfth Imam, the inheritor of the mantle of the Prophet, their only legitimate ruler.

Khomeini returned to the holy city of Qom. This move was not, however, a disengagement from government; it was merely a relocation of the government. Khomeini held himself both above and outside politics, but no decisions were made without consulting him. The Revolutionary Council met every Sunday, Tuesday and Thursday at a different member's home. Once every two weeks they journeyed en masse to Qom to confer with Khomeini himself.

April brought new outrages. Amir Abbas Hoveyda, the former prime minister, had voluntarily stayed in custody when the mobs tore down the gates to release the Shah's prisoners. He was prepared to submit to due legal process, an act of unparalleled optimism and naiveté in the face of the approaching beast. Hoveyda had been left in prison as a scapegoat by his old friend the Shah.

In the middle of the night Hoveyda was brought before a kangaroo court, where he was tormented by a mullah and two "judges," one of whom was Ibrahim Yazdi, before he was sent back to his cell.

On hearing of the trial, Bazargan journeyed to see Khomeini and secured from the Ayatollah an edict that all trials and executions were to stop until the Revolutionary Council drew up regulations to govern courts and komitehs. But late one night, equipped with keys from the guards, two robed figures went to Hoveyda's cell and strangled him.

Bertrand Vallette and Christine Bourguet were chosen by AFASPI, their group in Paris, to go to Iran to report on the state of human rights since the revolution. Once in Teheran Bertrand faced his old friend, a revolutionary victor, in his spacious office at NIRT, confronting him over the murder of Hoveyda.

"Hoveyda was a bastard!" Sadegh insisted. "He would have died one way or another."

"What the hell's the matter with you?" Bertrand demanded.

"Even if he was a bastard — and you know perfectly well that he was probably the most decent of the lot — that's not the point! Where's your due process? Where are your human rights now?"

Sadegh shrugged. "You don't understand."

"Understand! I understand your revolutionary government is murdering people! Is it any different now than it was under the Shah?" Bertrand was in tears. He had arrived in Iran only hours before and had already seen the face of the revolution, and he didn't like what he had seen.

The bitter exchange continued until finally Sadegh acknowledged Bertrand's point. "But do you know how hard it is to save the life of someone like Hoveyda? If we spare the guilty like him, then even more of the innocent ones they have arrested will be killed. The komitehs will go mad."

As Bertrand pondered this tortuous logic, he suddenly realized that Sadegh simply wouldn't admit that he didn't have the power to control events. Sadegh had tried to save Hoveyda—or at least to try him legally. He had wanted the trial to be a showcase of imperial corruption and true revolutionary justice, but the mullahs pre-empted him.

Growing angrier by the day as I watched the debacle in Iran from my post in Paris, I wrote to Sadegh. It was not the executions of Nassiri, the former head of SAVAK, or his ilk that particularly concerned me. Those, I wrote, I could understand. It was the appearance of the apparatus of an authoritarian state that deeply distressed me. The censorship, the summary justice, the oppression of women — all these, I told him, I found unforgivable. I begged him to have the courage of his convictions.

Then, afraid the letter would fall into the wrong hands, I never sent it.

*   *   *

It was now spring and the waltz of the constitution began. Lahidji and Habibi completed their draft of the document. It resembled the constitution of the French Fifth Republic, with the notable exception that the powers of the president were far more limited. They had injected a system of checks and balances, not unlike those in the U.S. constitution. The result was a form of parliamentary republic.

Bani Sadr didn't like the constitution. Lahidji accused him of not liking it because he wanted to be president and, as it was written, the president would not have unlimited power. Bani Sadr did not deny his ambition, nor did he hesitate to admit he didn't want to be a toothless president. Lahidji argued that Iran must wean herself from her age-old tradition of authoritarianism.

Much to everyone's astonishment, Khomeini accepted the document as it was. Most astonishing was the fact that the proposed constitution had no *faghih*, that is, no power of church over state. And yet Khomeini suggested an immediate referendum to approve it. Beheshti and Sadegh agreed with him; Bani Sadr and Bazargan did not.

The Revolutionary Council met in Beheshti's bungalow. Bani Sadr argued that if a referendum was pushed through now it would look as if they were afraid of discussion. But Beheshti argued that if they waited the extremists in the mosque would destroy the constitution. This latter view was odd, coming from Beheshti, but Beheshti saw himself as a unique power, not one of the extremists.

Sadegh argued for the referendum, thinking any further delay would be fatal. Time would give their enemies the opportunity to completely co-opt the revolution. He had seen their legions: they would destroy anything in their path.

Finally, Bazargan persuaded Khomeini to submit the constitution to review by a government commission composed of Bani Sadr and others from the National Front. Lahidji watched in dismay and despair as they mutilated his handiwork. The presidency was invigorated and the legislature hog-tied. When the council approved the changes, it was sent to Khomeini for verification.

But now Khomeini wanted changes — nine in all.

The Ayatollah sat as always on the floor of the small, bare room in Qom. The first eight changes were no problem. The last was dramatic.

"Here," said the Ayatollah, "you must add the specific condition that a woman cannot become president."

Bani Sadr looked at Khomeini in surprise. "We can't do that," he protested. "You yourself said in Paris that any Iranian would be able to become president of the new Islamic Republic. A woman could become president, you said so."

Khomeini shrugged and, with a negligent wave of his hand, declared, "Oh, yes, yes, yes. I said a lot of things in Paris."

Bani Sadr was stunned. Had Khomeini just said that?

In the silence, Beheshti found himself taking up the cause of women's rights. "How can you go back on your word? It's impossible."

Khomeini airily ordered them away. "Find a way," he commanded with a shrug, "some kind of formula, then."

"Well, there we are," Beheshti said dryly as they left. Bani Sadr felt the cold creep deeper into his bones. Khomeini had lied. It was unthinkable. He was a man of God. Even if he hadn't believed everything he said in Paris, he had still spoken the words, and the word of a man of God was sacred. It was unthinkable. Who had brought him to this, who had persuaded him to break a sacred pledge?

When he heard what had transpired, Ayatollah Taleghani sank to his knees in protest on the floor of the parliament. "This constitution," he whispered, "is the greatest tragedy ever to happen to Iran," and he wept on the floor of the chamber.

Taleghani took his fight once more into the streets. On the anniversary of the Black Friday massacre at Jaleh Square, Taleghani spoke to a huge throng at Behesht Zahra cemetery. He warned his people, imploring them to beware of despotism masquerading as religion. It was against Islam, he said, to deny people the right to criticize, to protest and to express their grievances. Quoting the holy book, he made the Koranic sura of Al Imran echo through the graveyard: "Those who veil the verses of God, those who unjustly kill the prophets, and also unjustly kill those who have risen for equity, promise them painful agony!"

A few days later, Ayatollah Taleghani died. Hundreds of thousands followed his casket to Behesht Zahra in the largest demonstration in Iran's history.

Official reports said Taleghani died of a heart attack.

Friends said he died of a broken heart.

Foreigners said he was old anyway.

Others whispered it was assassination.

The referendum overwhelmingly ratified the constitution and the Islamic Republic. The faghih reigned.

This was the face of the revolution that greeted Christian Bourguet and François Cheron when they arrived in Teheran in September. It was with heavy hearts that they watched the life of the city outside the car window. At the same time, it felt good to know that now there was no Shah and no SAVAK. Surely Sadegh and his like would be able to prevail ultimately. In any revolution, there was a period of tremendous upheaval and even violence.

Bourguet said little to Cheron as they drove through the city. Both men were worried, but they wanted to be optimistic.

When they arrived at Sadegh's office they took the opportunity to protest again the fraudulent trials and executions, but he waved their words aside.

"I have hundreds of letters in the next room from ordinary people, applauding the executions," he said airily.

Bourguet looked at the friend he scarcely knew, one who, he feared, had now perhaps been caught by the narcotic of power he had once so accurately condemned. He and Cheron insisted on a long meeting with Sadegh later in the day.

And for two hours they attacked. When Sadegh continued to justify repressive measures in terms of temporary security and political necessity, Cheron finally hit home.

"Sadegh, I've just returned from a long session for political prisoners in Argentina. And your words are exactly the same as those of the Argentine generals. Exactly the same excuses, Sadegh, as a fascist junta."

Sadegh erupted in real anger. "Are you attacking the Islamic revolution?"

"Heaven forfend. I'm attacking fascism and tyranny."

"You don't understand! You don't understand anything!"

"Exactly. It's tyranny, pure and simple. There's nothing to understand. I imagine the Shah had good excuses too."

Finally, Sadegh grudgingly acknowledged the basic truth of their accusations, adding resignedly, "But there isn't time to go through all the proper legal wrangle with the komitehs to establish *all* the procedures. I just don't have enough time in a day for all that needs to be done."

Bourguet and Cheron received this hopelessly inadequate alibi with deepest dismay.

"Then you had better make time, mon vieux."

The lawyers watched in misery as the revolution they had worked for so long built the classic apparatus of oppression. On August 24, Khomeini closed down twenty-two more papers, and ordered all organizations opposing clerical rule to turn in their weapons. The Hezbies attacked the offices of all major political groups, concentrating on the liberals.

Once again, like a body stretched on a rack, the country felt the tension of repression. In Azerbejan, local revolts were ruthlessly crushed. Kurdish tribes of the northwest also rose in revolt, demanding autonomy within Iran. More than two thousand government troops died in battle, and the Kurds won a bloody standoff.

Reporters trying to cover events and the Western public trying to follow their reports reeled in confusion. Every day seemed to bring a new face, another unpronounceable name or a different group to the chaos. Even for those of us close to events and familiar with the participants, it was confusing. The clergy was split, the moderates were divided several ways, the leftists ranged from Islamic Marxists to Soviet Communists. Tribal groups rebelled. The fabric of the nation was stretched and torn.

The chaos was compounded by the rivalry that existed even between the players we thought were the closest in spirit: Bazargan, Bani Sadr and Sadegh. Even they could not work in trust and harmony. Like knights in the looking glass, their one rule of battle seemed to be that they always fell off their horses on their heads, fighting each other.

Was this pathological intrigue among friends inherent in their Persian roots? I decided not. Rather, I thought, it was the result of centuries of tyranny and secret police. Neighbors could not trust neighbors or even relatives. "I only trust my brother," the old Persian saying goes, "and I'm not even sure of him sometimes." Reared in North America, one does not always realize how much democracy and due process have done away with fears of plotters in the pantry. It is not that we have some superior hormone in our national bloodstream, it is simply that our system, however imperfect, has survived and has erased from our collective memory the court intrigues of old.

By fall, the situation in Iran was critical. Bani Sadr and Sadegh tried to overcome the burden of distrust. They met at Bani Sadr's home one night, alone, just as they had met during their years in Paris.

"It'll work if we operate the way we used to," Sadegh suggested. "You and Shariati write, and I'll carry out the ideas."

Bani Sadr smiled wryly. "You mean I should lock myself in a room and think, while you play the man of action?"

"Well, why not? I'm better suited to that role. They'll eat you alive."

"How come?" Sadegh asked.

"If I speak it is because I have something to say. You said so yourself, I'm the scholar. I've studied for years, I have hundreds of files; I prepare each speech. That's why Habibi and I told you to be serious about your studies when we sent you back to America. Then there was time for all that. Now there isn't. You're swamped with work. I'm not so busy so I have the time even now to prepare my speeches carefully. You can't just go around saying, 'Imam this' and 'Imam that,' the way you do."

"So what should I do?" Sadegh asked. Bani Sadr couldn't see the amused sarcasm behind the acquiescence.

"Let me send you some of my people to prepare your speeches." Sadegh agreed.

Bani Sadr was pleased. If he could harness Sadegh, there was a chance of saving the situation. They needed each other to outflank the mullahs. But as he blithely agreed to Bani Sadr's conditions, Sadegh was already balking, irritated at Bani Sadr's pompous superiority and patronizing attitudes.

And then they went over the wall at Fort Apache.

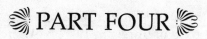

PART FOUR

THE HOSTAGE CRISIS

12

"We want the Shah!" the crowds had demanded ever since the first days of unrest in 1978. Now, in November 1979, nine months after Khomeini's return to Iran, the Iranians still did not have the Shah or access to the vast fortune he had accumulated. They wanted the Shah to be tried and sentenced. They wanted his wealth returned to the state. They wanted justice. But the Shah of Iran had powerful friends who protected him.

First the Shah lingered in Egypt, living in luxury. Then he moved on to Morocco and, still living in opulence, declared his desire to go back to Iran. He delayed going to the United States, apparently believing his image would be better if he stayed in Islamic countries.

Not that the United States had invited him. William Sullivan, the ambassador to Iran, and his chargé d'affaires, Bruce Laingen, both warned their government that to admit the Shah into the United States might be seen as a signal that the U.S. was planning to reinstall the king by force. Such a move, they warned, would endanger the embassy and the embassy staff, given the mood of the people in the streets.

The Shah went to Mexico, but he appeared to be seriously ill and his doctors said he needed to be treated in America.

In the Oval Office, Jimmy Carter pondered his dilemma. From the beginning, national security adviser Zbigniew Brzezinski had wanted the president to let the Shah in. He had wanted America to "stand by her allies." Two powerful Republicans joined Brzezinski in urging the president to allow the Shah to come to America; they were David Rockefeller and former secretary of state Henry Kissinger. Cyrus Vance, secretary of state, on the other hand, opposed the idea. Vance felt that if the Shah was admitted to the U.S., the Iranian government would be less than cooperative in guarding the embassy. Indeed, as a result of his fears, he had already reduced the embassy staff from eleven hundred to seventy-five.

When it was learned that the Shah was ill, Rockefeller sent his own doctors to Mexico. Their diagnosis was a malignant lymphoma compounded by possible internal blockage, resulting in severe

130

jaundice. Rockefeller wanted the Shah brought to New York for further diagnosis and treatment. The men in the White House met.

Hamilton Jordan, Carter's chief of staff, laid out the political ramifications: if the Shah died in Mexico, Kissinger would have a field day. ''He'll say that first you caused the Shah's downfall, and now you've killed him.''

Carter was furious. His concern was with American interests. He was not convinced the Shah needed to come to the United States. There were many other places that offered comparable medical facilities.

Cyrus Vance was willing to admit the Shah if it were made clear to Teheran that it was only for medical reasons. They asked Bruce Laingen to sound out Mehdi Bazargan and Ibrahim Yazdi on the idea.

Bazargan said the Iranian government would guarantee protection for the embassy as long as the Shah's visit was temporary and it could be proven that it was indeed for medical reasons. Laingen, the chargé d'affaires at the embassy, expressed profound doubts that Bazargan's people could enforce protection, and said the embassy would be in considerable danger.

Finally Jimmy Carter agreed. ''What are you guys going to advise me to do if they overrun our embassy and take our people hostage?'' he asked as the final meeting broke up.

The Shah arrived in New York on October 23, 1979.

At the same time, leaders from around the world gathered in Algiers to celebrate the twenty-fifth anniversary of the beginning of the Algerian revolution. Acting Iranian prime minister Bazargan, Acting Iranian foreign minister Ibrahim Yazdi, and Moustafa Chamran, now acting minister of defense in the provisional government, met with Brzezinski in Algiers. The Iranian agenda was simple: they wanted assurances that there would be no conspiracies against the new regime, recovery of the Shah's assets, continued military aid, and a discussion of the Shah's wealth. They also suggested that the Shah was not in the United States for purely medical reasons.

Brzezinski left the door to military aid open; he told them the courts of the United States were open to their suits regarding the Shah's assets; he assured them there were no plots against the new government; but he grew angry over the suggestion that the Shah was in the United States for other than medical reasons.

When the meeting ended, Brzezinski felt reassured. It had been cordial.

Both Secretary of State Vance and the press corps were taken aback when they learned of the meeting. Bazargan and Yazdi had left themselves open to attack by Iranian extremists. And didn't Brzezinski know that Bazargan was sitting on a powder keg? Didn't Bazargan himself realize the impact his meeting would have? It was hard to tell who had been the most naive, the Iranians or the Americans.

The meeting was the spark that lit the fuse.

* * *

The American embassy in the heart of downtown Teheran was no ordinary embassy. It covered eleven acres of ground, had several large structures and was totally walled in. It was a compound, where eleven hundred people had once worked. Its main entrance faced the street called Takht-e Djamshid. Because of the embassy's size, massive buildings and high walls, the Americans had nicknamed it Fort Apache.

The morning of November 4, 1979, was cloudy, and in the early morning gloom the massive stone buildings of the American embassy compound did indeed look like a fortress.

Protest marches in front of the huge compound had become something of a tradition. The previous February the Mudjahedeen and Fedayeen had actually broken into it, overwhelming the small number of marine guards. On that occasion they seized the ambassador, William Sullivan, and marched him out into the yard with a bayonet at his throat. Sullivan stood there, white-haired and dignified, while mobs roared at the gate.

When they learned of the attack, Prime Minister Bazargan and Foreign Minister Yazdi immediately ordered the guerrillas out. In this action they were backed by the Revolutionary Guards — the Pasdaran — who were only too willing to act against their rivals, the Mudjahedeen. After that attack, a contingent of Pasdaran was posted at the embassy to protect it, rather like setting the fox to guard the chickens. William Sullivan returned to Washington for consultations.

Since the first attack, the guerrillas had asked official permission to repeat the feat. The Organization of Moslem Students, specifically at Sanati and Teheran universities, had made noises about a preemptive strike — preempting the Mudjahedeen, that is. They asked Khomeini for permission to attack the embassy. Khomeini said neither yes nor no. The leader of the student organization at Sanati and Teheran universities was none other than Moussavi Khoeini'a, one of the two assistants previously assigned to Sadegh at NIRT.

Now the students had the perfect pretext: the U.S. had admitted the hated Shah, and to top it off, Bazargan had met with the Americans in Algiers! This was the key: the needed pretext not just to attack the United States, but to move against Bazargan and the moderates.

At first they marched past the embassy, then a few suddenly broke off to scale the walls of the compound. Initially the attackers numbered only a few dozen, then hundreds. The marines inside tried to repel them with tear gas, but there were too many and it was too late.

The Americans now discovered that some of their guards were in fact agents, who opened the gates to the attackers and helped cut the heavy chains with a bolt cutter and then stood aside as the mob stormed in. Once inside, the attackers drew guns and moved quickly to take over the chancellery. The embassy staff retreated, destroying what documents they could.

The marines held off the assault as best they could without resorting to the use of their weapons. This was Sullivan's policy: killing the invader might produce far worse results.

"Give up and you won't be harmed," a student leader shouted through a bullhorn. "If you don't give up, you'll be killed."

"If the marines shoot," said one student, "we'll have our martyr. If they don't, we'll have the embassy. Either way, we win." The marines did not shoot.

Finally, the marines at the chancellery could hold out no longer. The student attackers poured in. Their eyes streaming from tear gas, they ripped gas masks from the embassy personnel inside.

The Americans were rounded up and blindfolded. Then they were hauled outside and paraded in a humiliating show of victory. It had been a professional, well-coordinated strike, with a clear plan of attack. It was not a "spontaneous outburst," as the clergy later alleged.

But not all the Americans who worked at the embassy were there on the morning of November 4. It was soon learned that chargé d'affaires Bruce Laingen and two others were across town at the Iranian Foreign Ministry to see Yazdi. When officials at the Foreign Ministry heard of the attack on the embassy, Laingen and his compatriots were detained there — for their own protection. Others who had not come to work gradually made their way to other embassies, or to the homes of friends who sheltered them temporarily. Eventually, they would be taken in by Canadian diplomats.

Shortly after the seizure of Fort Apache, Sadegh answered the phone on his desk at NIRT. It was Moussavi Khoeini'a.

"The Moslem students have seized the American embassy! All the people inside have been taken hostage. I'm in direct contact with them. We want the support of the radio and TV."

"What do they want? Was anyone hurt?" Sadegh asked anxiously.

"No, no one," Khoeini'a assured him. "It's a gesture. It's the perfect insult to those bastards in Washington. We may even get them to throw out the Shah and send him back here. It shouldn't last long, two or three days."

Like the students, Sadegh had been genuinely outraged that the Americans had admitted the Shah. He had no doubt the Shah could be treated elsewhere. It was a calculated insult to Iran. And no doubt the Americans were hatching another coup with the help of Bazargan and Yazdi.

Sadegh smiled. The seizure of the embassy was not very practical, but it satisfied the Iranians' need for revenge. Sadegh promised the needed coverage. Soon the Iranian public saw and heard how the brave Students Followers of the Imam's Line, had struck a blow for the revolution.

A spokesman for the students soon appeared on Iranian TV screens denouncing Prime Minister Bazargan for deviating from the revolutionary line of Imam Khomeini. "As a result, our dependence on the United States has increased day by day," he stated. "The latest expression of this submissive government policy was demonstrated last week when Bazargan met with Carter's satanic agent Brzezinski in Algiers."

Sadegh knew immediately that Khomeini would see the act as a manifestation of God's will, a divine sign. When the Mudjahedeen had taken the embassy it was not seen as divine and had accordingly been squelched. But these students followed Khomeini and the mullahs; therefore, in his eyes they would be seen as instruments of divine will. Did Khomeini actually authorize the seizure, Sadegh asked himself. He wasn't certain, but whatever Khomeini's involvement, Sadegh decided, he was sure to approve the action.

Nor would the old man's humor be improved when he learned that pictures of him had been used as dart boards by the American diplomats, as Khoeini'a had told him. He would be angered and outraged.

"Death to Carter! Down with American imperialism! This CIA nest must be closed!" Thousands poured into the streets to converge on the besieged embassy. The Stars and Stripes was burned along with the blue and white Star of David, the flag of Israel. The crowds chanted more slogans for the PLO. The multitudes rose in a tumult of bitter elation, a mass of black joy.

It was as if the students had lanced an abscess on the body of Iran, releasing the poison. Anger and spleen ran in the streets as the terrible tension was broken and given an outlet. Moderate citizens who watched in horror as the pus poured forth were shocked by the depth of a hatred they had never suspected. But instead of healing, the release of the abscess spread its toxin.

When Ahmad Khomeini, the Ayatollah's son, appeared at the embassy the next day, the mobs raised him on their shoulders and hoisted him onto the south wall. There, arms waving, he declared that Imam Khomeini had charged him to support the students.

"This is not an occupation," he quoted the Imam as saying. "We have thrown out the occupiers!"

And Khomeini himself formalized the demands made by the students: the Americans would be freed only if the Shah were extradited or expelled from the United States to stand trial in Iran.

The Western press screamed that the Iranians were uncivilized, that they had broken the most sacred trust of international law — a nation's obligation to protect foreign embassies and their staffs. In shocked prose and stark headlines, people everywhere were reminded that *even* the Japanese during the Second World War had respected the sanctity of the American embassy and that all during the war the American embassy and its staff were protected, while technically under house arrest.

Many Iranians too were dismayed by the takeover of the American embassy. Others, like Sadegh, thought it was a symbolic gesture and would last only a few days. Sadegh and others who believed as he did knew the action was wrong but they felt the United States was at fault, too. Not for one minute did they really believe the Shah was ill. And even if he was, medical care in Western Europe was equal to medical care in the United States. Why couldn't the Shah have gone to Germany or Switzerland, they asked.

But there were other Iranians who knew what the embassy's occupation was costing Iran. Prime Minister Bazargan was one of them. He came to the meeting of the Revolutionary Council demanding action.

Ayatollah Beheshti was adamant. "You," he said to Bazargan, "must be firm and take control of the crisis and the embassy. We don't know who these people are."

Sadegh turned on Beheshti. "Of course we know who they are. They're Moussavi Khoeini'a and his gang of students from the university. They are certainly not the Fedayeen or the Mudjahedeen."

Beheshti deliberated, then insisted, "All the more reason to take firm control. We don't really know Khoeini'a, do we? We have to stand our ground."

Bazargan interrupted in a fury. "What madness are you talking? This is an international crime. Our government is obliged by law to protect foreign diplomats. I have given my assurance as prime minister that we shall do so. And you talk about dealing with a bunch of students who are breaking the law! Khomeini must order them out. We must! Or we are no government."

"It may not be that simple," Beheshti offered.

The debate stormed on.

When Beheshti left, Sadegh took Bazargan aside. "Don't listen to Beheshti," Sadegh advised. "Khoeini'a and his students are extremely strong. Don't try to oppose them. You have to take the occupation over, then you can control it. Don't forget, the population is all for the students, and so is Khomeini."

Sadegh knew that to sound doubtful or negative about the correctness of the seizure now would be fatal: Khomeini would turn on anyone who reacted in that way. In any case, Sadegh was not truly worried. Khoeini'a had assured him the takeover of the embassy would be brief. When the fever cooled, Sadegh felt, he could make Khomeini realize that the Americans could not under any circumstances send the Shah to Iran, that even to expel him was politically unthinkable.

Sadegh was once again overconfident, and in two days, his optimism was shattered. Faced with civil disobedience condoned by the Imam, Bazargan resigned. The government dissolved.

Sadegh was appalled. And furious. Bazargan had submitted his resignation twice before to protest the shackles placed on his gov-

ernment. But on those occasions he had gone personally to see
Khomeini. In principal, Khomeini always accepted resignations.
"If they don't want to work," he would say, "we don't need them."
But, rare as a flower in sand, Khomeini harbored a personal affec-
tion for Bazargan, and on the two previous occasions he had asked
him to remain in office. But this time Bazargan insulted Khomeini.
He sent his resignation by letter delivered by an insignificant young
relative.

Incensed, Khomeini accepted it. In a last meeting, Bazargan tried
to explain. "You are weak, sir!" Khomeini hurled back snappishly.

*   *   *

Around a long oak table on the other side of the world, the presidential advisers were grim. Jimmy Carter said nothing as he entered
and took his seat at the head of the table.

One of the men passed a note to Hamilton Jordan that said: "I'm
waiting for the president to say, 'I told you so.' "

To his credit, President Carter did not say it. "With Bazargan
gone, who does that leave us to deal with?" he asked without
preamble.

Peering over his glasses, Cyrus Vance replied, "Ayatollah Khomeini."

They discussed alternatives, then decided to send former attorney general Ramsey Clark to try to open a dialogue with the Iranians.
Clark had served under Kennedy and had been an outspoken critic
of the Shah's regime. Moreover, he had actually met the Ayatollah
in Neauphle. Hamilton Jordan rolled his eyes heavenward. In his
opinion Clark was a fringe human-rights activist whose choice of
causes and positions was anti-American.

As he left the meeting, Carter paused at the door. "By the way,"
he said, "I'm tired of hearing those bastards holding our people
referred to as students. Jody, you and the rest get together and
figure out what to call them. Terrorists or captors, or something
that accurately describes what they are."

"Yes, sir," Jody Powell, the president's press secretary, agreed.
After the president left, Powell turned to the rest and said, "How
about Islamic thugs?"

*   *   *

With Bazargan's resignation, the Revolutionary Council became
the official provisional government of Iran. There was considerable

maneuvering by all factions and individuals to ensure no one person or group gained more power than the others — though few at this point realized just how dubious power was. Sadegh actually convinced Bazargan to return to the council — unity of the moderates was now more vital then ever. Yazdi, however, was excluded by unanimous vote.

Bani Sadr was unanimously voted to the Ministry of Finance, and before anyone could speak Sadegh proposed that Bani Sadr also be named minister of foreign affairs. The moderates, he knew, must control the negotiation line to the Americans, and Bani Sadr was more acceptable to the rest than he himself was.

As always, Bani Sadr looked at Sadegh with suspicion. Why did Sadegh want him to be minister? So he could sink into the mire of the hostage crisis?

"No, I'd rather not," Bani Sadr said, refusing the post.

"But you are the only one who can," Sadegh insisted. "You're known overseas. You speak French. You have to take this on."

Bani Sadr smiled a sardonic little smile, amused in spite of himself. "You're known overseas and you speak French and English. You do it. I'm not going to be foreign minister for a nonexistent government. Where does policy come from? Us? Who voted for us? No, Sadegh, you go right ahead."

Sadegh was exasperated. He insisted again, and finally they agreed on a bizarre solution: Sadegh would be a sort of shadow minister, while Bani Sadr would be the official minister until the end of the hostage crisis. Then Sadegh would officially take over the Foreign Ministry.

A few days later, in the comfortable surroundings of his friend Alef's home, Sadegh brooded in silence while other guests discussed the appalling situation at the embassy. Alef looked at his friend helplessly. Sadegh withdrew more and more into private reveries, shutting others out.

Sadegh had reason to brood. Had God set up obstacles to test his perseverance and faith in God, his revolution and Khomeini? The others had turned on Khomeini so quickly! But Sadegh had not. He wanted to protect the Imam from all those lying bastards in the clergy. They were the ones behind it all. They pushed Khomeini into these actions. And then there were Bazargan and Yazdi, both ready to sell out, he figured. And Bani Sadr, playing his own game. How could he rescue Khomeini and the revolution from these turbaned plotters? The mullahs were now the *taghooti*—the devils. What irony! Sadegh felt as if he were battling a many-headed dragon. And he was.

* * *

Fereidoun Hoveyda, brother of the murdered prime minister, had once been the Iranian ambassador to the United Nations. Now he lived permanently in New York, where he wrote books on the Middle East, the Shah, Islam and the revolution. He was also a painter. I visited him in his gracious apartment on Park Avenue.

We sat together in his studio, surrounded by walls of books and the clutter of paintings he was working on.

Hoveyda showed me the *Shahnameh, Book of Kings,* the central book of Persian legends.

"Look at these pages. Legends of fathers killing sons. We Iranians always have a father." He sighed. "Taleghani was a great *wa'ez,* a great teacher, but he was not of the rank of *marja e taqlid* — the supreme religious authorities, the experts on Shi'a law. There were only six of them, and the father has to be one of them."

"Khomeini," I finished for him.

"Khomeini. Once the Shah had lost his stature as father, once he weakened, Khomeini could kill him as Faridun killed Zahhak, the Cannibal King, in the legend. Khomeini will kill his sons, too, as they do in the legends. The young must die to protect the power of the old."

I shivered. Hoveyda was not the only scholar who pronounced this bleak judgment on his country. I burrowed through the pages of the *Shahnameh,* entranced by the exquisite painted miniatures that illuminate its stories. These illustrations glowed with rich colors, fantastic faces in clouds and rocks, jeweled saddles on war ponies, wonderful faces of warriors and gods and lovers, peasants and guards and mullahs and all manner of great adventures and daily banality. The pages were a revelation of Persian life. These pictures and stories contrasted sharply with the dour puritanism of Khomeini and his minions.

"Khomeini," Hoveyda warned, "hates anything Persian. If it is not Islamic he will destroy it."

So there it was. The Shah wanted to bring back the pre-Islamic days, and Khomeini wanted to kill history before Islam. But the country was a magnificent melding of the two — so well blended that total destruction could only follow the amputation of either half.

I read the two tales in the *Shahnameh* that Hoveyda had mentioned. I read them with interest and foreboding, for I, like many others, believe that folklore often represents certain deep truths about a people.

In the Persian legend the young Zahhak made a pact with the evil demon, Ahriman. Ahriman tempted the young man by promising to kill his father and make Zahhak king.

But, when this was done, the demon afflicted Zahhak with a pair of hungry snakes that grew from his shoulders. In order to appease the serpents, who needed regular servings of human brains, Zahhak sacrificed to them two youths each day, and thus he became known as the Cannibal King.

His people lived in fear of this monstrous king until Faridun rose to lead them in revolt. Faridun's army triumphed and Faridun captured the monstrous Zahhak, whom he had chained to the summit of Mount Damavand, and left there exposed to the elements, so that his brain might chafe and his agony endure.

For the revolutionaries the Shah was Zahhak, the Cannibal King, in this first tale. And I saw Khomeini as Faridun in the next.

Faridun, the hero who vanquished Zahhak the Cannibal King, and became King in his stead, had three sons, tall as cypresses, swift and powerful as elephants and with cheeks like spring. In his love for them, Faridun refused to tempt fate by assigning them names.

Instead, he determined to test them. He sent his young sons to Yemen, to marry the daughters of the King Sarv, and when the sons were journeying home with their pearl-like brides, they were suddenly met by a dragon, waiting for them in the rocks of the mountains.

It was an enormous beast, long and black, and thick and sinewy, with strong legs and massive paws full of thick white claws. Its eyes glowed red and gold with a blue pinpoint, and it breathed golden sulfurous fire. It was Faridun in disguise, transformed by his magic into a dragon.

When they came upon this monster, the three young men were horrified by its terrible aspect. The horses reared and snorted.

Scattering dust clouds and bellowing, Faridun charged his eldest son, who retreated in terror, remarking that no sensible man fights dragons.

Faridun then turned upon his second son, who drew his bow menacingly and boasted that it made no difference whether he fought a raging lion or a cavalier.

The youngest son, confronted next, cried, "Be off! You are a mere crocodile; beware of lions! If you have heard of Faridun, you will not dare fight us, for we are his sons and each of us is a warrior like him!"

Knowing their characters now, Faridun met them at the palace in his human form, and gave them names according to their hearts.

And he divided his kingdom among them.

But there was a difference. Khomeini *was* the dragon-monster. Only Sadegh the son could not see that this was his true face. It was his fatal Persian flaw.

* * *

As soon as Bani Sadr was named foreign minister, I called him for a long-distance interview. By this time I was working in the central newsroom in Toronto on the international desk, sifting through the global gloom.

Bani Sadr was dancing on hot coals. One moment he said he was in charge of the matter, the next he was hedging his bets and claiming that the fate of the hostages was "in the hands of the people and the United States, who could solve the affair by handing over the Shah to Iran."

"You don't seriously believe the United States can do that?" I asked.

Over the long-distance line came an answer that, unknown to me at the time, would set the tone for the next fourteen months. "Whether I do or not, it's a question of human rights," Bani Sadr replied.

Nonsense, I thought. Double-talk.

I talked long-distance to Sadegh every few days, but I could not express any of my thoughts freely. As usual I assumed the line was insecure. There were so many questions I wanted to ask him. In particular, I wanted to know who was behind the students. Everything I knew about Iran, and the politics of the Middle East, told me this was no mere student escapade.

Sadegh, too, was careful. "We may have a breakthrough soon. Don't worry. When are you coming?"

"Not yet. I'm chained to this desk," I answered, thinking how much more I wanted to say, and how much I wanted to see him. I wanted to tell him I missed him, but I couldn't. I didn't want to miss him. I resisted his power over me. I tried to involve myself with others, to shut him out, banish him to my outer reaches, and to his Iran, his God and his Father. Not for one moment did I think he pined for me in monastic solitude. He was considered the revolution's most eligible bachelor, and I was quite certain he took advantage of that. But temporary liaisons were not what mattered on either side.

I said goodbye, knowing I would probably call tomorrow.

Days passed and turned into weeks. Sadegh was caught in a riptide. He tried first to swim with it, then against it. The crisis escalated in a series of waves, each sweeping him farther out to sea.

Beheshti agreed that former attorney general Ramsey Clark could mediate. Then, when Clark was on his way to Iran, Khomeini asked, "Do they think the Spirit of God will converse with such evil characters?"

Clark's mission was now useless. Khomeini had pulled out the rug. Then Khomeini announced that giving up the Shah was only a prerequisite to negotiation.

Yasser Arafat came to offer his services for mediation. But Sadegh was by now convinced that the PLO was, in fact, in cahoots with the students. A few of them had obviously been trained in PLO camps; some of the journalists even recognized them from South Lebanon.

What really aroused Sadegh's suspicions was the appearance of Dr. Peyman, a most unusual dentist. Peyman had been a vocal leader for the Islamic revolution at the university while the Shah was in power. Now, dressed in his white dental coat, he was a highly visible figure among the students. But Sadegh knew he had close ties to al Fatah, Arafat's PLO guerrillas. Although a longtime acquaintance of Arafat's, Sadegh no longer trusted the PLO leader, and when he arrived Sadegh issued a pointed snub. He refused to go to the PLO leader. Nothing came of Arafat's mission.

Move and counter move:

- Trade between the United States and Iran in oil and military supplies was suspended.
- American and British warships maneuvered in the Arabian Sea.
- Bani Sadr threatened to withdraw Iranian deposits in American banks.
- Jimmy Carter froze Iran's deposits in American banks.

Fearful of the level of tension that had been reached, Sadegh and Bani Sadr struggled to lower it. Bani Sadr hit on the idea of releasing the women and blacks among the hostages. It would appeal to Khomeini's sense of righteousness.

"The world will see you are truly a savior of the oppressed," Bani Sadr argued, "and the move will gain us sympathy among women and blacks."

On the floor in Qom, Khomeini nodded.

The release would also signal to Washington that the Iranians were trying to extricate themselves. Bani Sadr did not, however, say this to Khomeini.

Khomeini agreed and thirteen of the hostages were freed. Later, Khomeini was told that the students had kept one black and three women, but he did nothing. Instead, he turned around and threatened America, saying that the remaining hostages would be tried as spies. He made this announcement in an interview with a foreign journalist while Sadegh translated. Aghast, Sadegh relayed what Khomeini had said.

"You did it!" Bani Sadr later shouted accusingly at Sadegh. "You gave him the idea!"

"Why on earth would I do that?" Sadegh replied. "That's the last thing I want."

But Bani Sadr was not convinced. His friends warned him not to trust Sadegh. Sadegh went to see Khomeini alone, they said, and tried to turn Khomeini against him.

"I was translating at an interview," Sadegh went on. "When he said that, what could I do? I had to translate it. I was as shocked as you."

But the old distrust remained between them and it destroyed whatever power they might have had in unison.

Nonetheless, they decided to attempt to defuse the issue of a spy trial by calling for a special session of the United Nations Security Council to discuss the Iranian problem and to hear Iranian grievances against the United States. At the last minute, the United States also asked for a Security Council meeting. Kurt Waldheim, then secretary general, compromised. He called one on his own.

The point was lost in advance. It was one thing to call a meeting, it was another to be summoned to one. Sadegh and the Revolutionary Council decided to cancel the visit, but Bani Sadr was determined to go to New York.

Then the Ayatollah sided with the council against the foreign minister. He order his son Ahmad to announce that Bani Sadr would not attend. When he was told that Bani Sadr might have already left, Khomeini announced, "If he has, I will announce that he is no longer minister of foreign affairs."

But Bani Sadr had not left. Once more he took a helicopter to Qom with the rest of the council to try to persuade Khomeini of the wisdom and usefulness of the UN session, regardless of who called it. It was, he argued, "a golden international forum for our testimony against America and the Shah."

But Khomeini had no interest in justifying his action in the arid niceties of the UN.

"What," he asked, "is the Security Council?"

As they began to explain he interrupted. "You mean the representatives of the aggressor have a veto? Then I don't want anything to do with it."

When Bani Sadr, Sadegh, Beheshti and Ahmad landed back in Teheran, Bani Sadr was livid. Once on the ground, he scrambled out and, in a perfect fury, roared at Sadegh as the wind from the helicopter blades whipped around them.

"Okay, you bastard!" he shouted. "It's your turn now! You can bloody well be foreign minister!"

Sadegh tried to be conciliatory.

"No buts! It's all yours!" Bani Sadr insisted.

"I don't want it."

"That's too bad. You've got it! Everyone told me you wanted me saddled with it just to ruin me. Well, I'm getting out while I'm in one piece. Everyone knows I'm against the hostage seizure, and that I'll fight Khomeini and the students."

"I didn't want to see you ruined," Sadegh protested. "That's a lie."

Beheshti clucked at them, making placating noises, while Ahmad watched with satisfaction.

"It's not a lie," Bani Sadr yelled over the low scream of the helicopter. "You backed Khomeini. You agreed that I shouldn't go to the UN. Who gave him the idea? You. You and that Associated Press story you broadcast about how the U.S. had won, and the UN could censure Bani Sadr in person. Well, didn't you?"

"Yes, but not to ruin you. Can't you see? You would have been ruined at the UN. Iran would have been ruined, too. We'd have been so humiliated that we would never have gotten the hostages out. Khoeini'a would have had his 'spy' trials for sure."

"Horseshit! I've had enough. You are now foreign minister, my friend," Bani Sadr shouted.

* * *

It was November 29, 1979. As I came into the newsroom that afternoon, the international assignment editor pushed through the noise and confusion, waving a Reuters wire at me.

"Guess what? Your buddy's just been named foreign minister."

That night as the new reports came in by satellite, I watched on my monitor. Reporters crowded around the new foreign minister. He looked full of mischief and good humor, not at all like a man who had just taken the helm during an international crisis. He proceeded to give what was perhaps his most memorable quote.

"Are you a hard-liner?" someone asked.

Sadegh smiled engagingly. "No, I'm a nice guy."

When I finally reached Sadegh long distance the next day, he was an insouciant as ever.

"So," I said unnecessarily, "you *are* foreign minister." It was the role I had predicted for him so long ago in Paris. The role he had said he didn't want.

"It's not because I wanted it," he said, as if remembering his original protest.

"I know. But what a ghastly mess to have to take over." Again I felt the need for caution. Our phone conversations were always stilted, always veiled.

"Don't worry. It'll work out."

"Beheshti, I suppose." I was hedging, trying to get some information.

"No, he's the least of our worries. When are you coming?"

"Soon — even if I have to hijack a plane. I'm certainly not going to sit here forever, watching you play a comedy routine. 'A nice guy,' indeed."

"But I am."

"*I* know that, but hardly anyone else does. Oh, Sadegh, what *are* you doing?"

"We'll talk when you're here."

More days passed. Salvation Army Santa Clauses in red suits appeared on the streets of Toronto. Crowds surged through the Eaton Centre and along Bloor Street. The rush hour was extended and Christmas carols filled the airways.

In the Arabian Sea, the aircraft carriers *Kitty Hawk* and *Midway* shifted positions with nineteen other American warships. Soviet and Iranian fighters overflew the massive flotilla. In Iran the new foreign minister announced that any hostages proven not to be spies would be freed.

Sadegh decided to run for president.

In Alef's comfortable living room, words of disbelief and irritation hung in the warm air.

"No!" Alef said, cursing. "You must be mad!" He leapt from his armchair, almost upsetting the tea tray on the table. "Whoever is elected president now is doomed! Stay out of it, Sadegh! Let them wipe each other out. No one but Khomeini will come out on top of this. Keep your head down and be ready when the blood-bath is over."

But Sadegh saw the presidency as a solution. "No, no. That will be too late," he told his friend.

"It's too late already. Khomeini won't help you. The Islamic Republic Party will mobilize all it's got. You'll be torn limb from limb."

"This is my country and these are my people. They love me as much as I love them. When they see how much I care, they'll vote for me. And Beheshti and the rest of the mullahs are already against me."

Alef sighed. Sadegh was still living in the Iran that his mind had fashioned in exile, the Iran that would welcome the ideas of democracy and the rhetoric of Bobby Kennedy. He still underestimated the mosque. And he still believed his spiritual bond with Khomeini gave him a mystical appeal.

"You'll be running against Bani Sadr," Alef reminded him.

"What else can I do? It's the only way to control this mess. Bani

Sadr would be a disaster as president. I wish he would stay with his books and leave the real world to us.''

Alef did not reply. He was not optimistic about Bani Sadr's presidential abilities either, but he knew Sadegh was in no position to win.

"You'll see. I'll win," Sadegh said confidently.

Suddenly Alef realized that part of Sadegh wanted the presidency, not just to save the revolution but for itself, and Alef began to feel the same. He finally agreed to help Sadegh and so did Sadegh's other friends.

Still, the main preoccupation was the hostage crisis. Sadegh wanted the hostages released, not out of sympathy, but because they were becoming a lever for his clerical enemies. The clerics saw the hostages as a way to gain absolute power. The students were slowly releasing documents they had discovered in the embassy revealing American operations, naming liberal Iranians who had been in close contact with them. Some of those named then were National Front people. Sadegh didn't care about some of them, but then the students started using the documents to spread slander. They began falsifying papers to condemn liberal Iranians for their alleged association with the Americans. If all the liberals and moderates were condemned, the clergy could take over everything. It had to be stopped.

Sadegh went to Khomeini to discuss his idea for an international jury to investigate America's past actions in Iran and render the hostages unnecessary. He spoke to the Ayatollah in terms of divine signs and the will of Allah. Khomeini understood and agreed.

Soon after, the foreign minister announced, "American foreign policy is going to be on trial."

I watched Sadegh on television as one American network anchorman interviewed him via satellite. It was a discomforting experience. I could feel the American frustration with Sadegh's smug complacency, and I could feel Sadegh's discomfort as he tried to strike just the right note of genial aggression.

Sadegh felt he had to show the Americans his firm resolve combined with tolerant reason; but to the Iranians and the Imam he had to appear sufficiently anti-American and bloody-minded. The result was calamitous. Political posturing came hard to Sadegh. Some of his charm managed to seep through, as any number of the women in my office who were smitten would testify. But the general effect was monstrous, and it was worsened by his languid drawl.

"Well," he said to me on the phone that night, "did you see the interview?"

"Oh, yes. I saw it."

"How did I do?"

He was like a little boy, asking for praise. "Do you really want to know?" I asked seriously.

"Yes. And any advice you can give me about presentation on TV."

I almost laughed. "Oh, fine. I'm to be your media consultant."

"How did I do?" he persisted.

"Well, you looked like a snake in the grass. Sadegh, I know what you're trying to put across, but that wasn't the way. You have to look as though you're serious. You can't sit there smirking, as if you enjoy having America over a barrel."

"No. It's the only way. We'll talk when you come here."

Our conversation was still truncated for the benefit of hostile, listening ears. But I no longer floundered. I'd grown accustomed to these strange conversations with a strange world.

"Can you go to New York?" Sadegh asked. "If you can, call the Iranian mission at the United Nations. I'm appointing a new ambassador, Mansour Farhang. I'll tell him to see you."

"Should I know anything about him?" Again, I was the reporter.

"He's been teaching in California. He's a professor of international politics. That's all. Just ask him about everything. I'll tell him to see you," Sadegh repeated.

"All right. Take care of yourself. I wish I could say more."

"Just come back soon."

I replaced the receiver. Sadegh went back to the jungle warfare of the hostage crisis and the demands of the presidential campaign, where friends had become enemies stalking each other in the tangled undergrowth.

Sadegh sat in his office considering the few options open to him. To deal with the students, he reflected, was to confirm their power. But as long as Khomeini protected them, he too was stuck with them. He had to barter. The Shah for the hostages. All Iran's legitimate claims had been reduced to the level of cheap goods. It was like trading beads. Damn them all to hell!

Then the voice of the BBC World Service announcer jerked Sadegh out of his thoughts. The Shah, the radio was saying, had reportedly left the United States for Panama, to live in an island villa.

According to the story, he had left voluntarily, accepting the invitation of Panama's president, Aristides Royo, and its ruler, General Omar Torrijos. "It is the Shah's hope," the announcer revealed, "that this will end the hostage crisis."

Sadegh sat back to consider this new development. Then he phoned Christian Bourguet in Paris.

"Have you heard the news?" Sadegh asked anxiously.

"What news?"

"The BBC says the Shah just arrived in Panama."

"Yes. They've just announced it on the radio here."

"Find out everything you can about it. Use Hector's contacts. Find out why they accepted him and on what conditions. Who knows? Maybe I can go there myself and get him. Take him off their hands." Hector was Hector Villalon, a longtime friend of both men and a flamboyant Argentine businessman, whom Christian and Sadegh had met through Nuri Albala in the seventies. Villalon was a volatile character with a penchant for politics and a flare for trouble. He was deeply involved in crusades for human rights in South America. A Peronist in his own country, Villalon's business ventures and political ties often crossed as he negotiated government contracts in other countries for his professional and political friends. He lived in France, prudently away from Argentina's ruling junta.

"I doubt they'll give you the Shah, *mon ami*. But we'll find out everything we can," Bourguet assured him.

"Then be ready to come to Teheran, both you and Hector. I'll call you tomorrow before the council meets."

Sadegh hung up. Perhaps this new development did indeed offer a way out.

When Sadegh phoned the next day, Bourguet filled him in. "Hector Villalon happened to be in Zurich, meeting with a senior representative of the Petroleum Company of Panama," he revealed. "The Petroleum man has gone back to Panama today and will open a dialogue with the government there for you."

Bourguet hung up and began packing to leave for Teheran, where he and Villalon would meet with Sadegh.

13

For years Christian Bourguet and Sadegh had met in tiny apartments or in the lawyer's cluttered Paris office on the Avenue de
l'Observatoire. Now Christian Bourguet and Hector Villalon were
ushered into the palatial splendor of the offices of the foreign minister of Iran. It was a spacious room with high ceilings and rich Persian
rugs. The sofas and chairs were elegant and the windows looked
down on an enclosed garden.

Villalon spoke English and French with a heavy Spanish accent,
but in any language he was authoritative and at the same time
childishly excitable. He was as tall as Sadegh, with thinning black
hair, dark eyes, a sharp nose and a slightly receding chin. In his
impeccable tailored suits, he looked like a large, impressive squirrel.

Bourguet studied Sadegh and concluded that, in spite of his surroundings, his old friend had not changed. If anything, Sadegh
had less hauteur than he possessed on television. But one thing
about Sadegh was noticeable; Bourguet could see that the hostage
crisis and the burdens of office had taken a toll. Sadegh looked
tired.

The three men sat down and discussed the various Panamanian
options.

"The Panamanians are willing to help free the hostages within
the limits of their law. They could arrest the Shah for extradition if
you go through legal channels. But they'll need to know you can
deliver the hostages," Villalon told Sadegh.

"We'll discuss it at the Revolutionary Council meeting," Sadegh
concluded.

Revco agreed that Villalon and Bourguet should go to Panama.
They even agreed to free three hostages for Christmas, as a gesture
of good faith and generosity. But the bigger hurdle was yet to come.
The students and Khomeini had to agree as well.

Then Sadegh was summoned to Qom.

"Agha Khoeini'a and his students were here," Khomeini told
Sadegh. "They say if they let the Christian minister in for Christmas,

150

there will be security problems. I want you to find out about these problems and solve them."

Sadegh could hardly control his exasperation. "That's ridiculous. They're at the embassy. People go in and out all day, and security is looked after day in and day out."

Khomeini made an indeterminate noise.

"The students must not block the Christmas visit," Sadegh insisted. "It would be a grave matter if an Islamic government were to be criticized on religious grounds. I know we don't care what the Americans say about us, but on religious grounds we cannot behave like this. We must not, Agha."

Khomeini pondered silently. "I'll tell them to receive the Christians," he finally agreed. He sounded tired and even bored. Khomeini hated dealing with such details. Then he gave his blessing to the release of three hostages for Christmas.

Bourguet and Villalon headed for Panama, tendering this promised gift and a formal letter from Sadegh in the name of the council.

Again, the rug was pulled out. In Iran one of Bani Sadr's aides told a visiting French diplomat of the impending hostage release. The diplomat seized the opportunity to be in the limelight and released the information to the press. Furious at the premature announcement, the students reneged and announced that no hostages would be released.

In Panama, Bourguet and Villalon were caught off guard, their diplomatic mission revealed and rendered impotent. Sadegh begged them to go to Panamanian authorities and urge the Shah's arrest. "Even if he can't actually be extradited," Sadegh urged. Sadegh did not care about getting the Shah. The point was that the arrest might be enough to enable him to pry the hostages from the students.

It was now absolutely clear to Sadegh that the hostages had to be gotten out of the hands of the students. Otherwise the students could continue to manipulate, and the Imam would say nothing. The Imam, Sadegh believed, didn't know what to do himself. Beheshti and his group were telling him one set of lies while Hashemi Rafsanjani, another powerful mullah and a member of Revco, and his followers told yet another story. Ayatollah Montazeri filled the Imam's head with God knew what, and Ahmad was juggling everyone.

On January 18, 1980, Bourguet and Villalon, with Sadegh's knowledge, met secretly in London with two grave and angry men: Hamilton Jordan, Jimmy Carter's chief of staff, and Harold Saunders, the assistant secretary for Near East and South Asian affairs at the State Department. Representatives of the Panamanian government were there as well. They discussed a wide range of possibilities and opened the first contact between Sadegh and the White House.

Returning to Teheran, Bourguet and Villalon reported to Sadegh. Extradition could be tried, but it was a long legal procedure and, in the end, would probably fail. The Americans wanted the Iranians to toss around some other ideas and gestures "along the lines of Waldheim's visit." Earlier the secretary general of the United Nations had tried to visit the hostages. He held out the possibility of an international commission to investigate American activity in Iran if the hostages were released. But he tipped his hand and was literally chased out of the country before he could see a single hostage.

Sadegh sat in silent thought for several minutes, as though Villalon and Bourguet weren't there. Finally, he said, "What if we had a United Nations commission made up of respected Moslem leaders come here? Any true Moslem leader or scholar will condemn the students and the imprisonment of the hostages on a *religious* basis and that could be the key that would unlock Khomeini."

The others thought they saw the sun breaking through the clouds and agreed that the ploy might succeed in showing the students to be "un-Islamic."

"You go to Bani Sadr," Sadegh suggested. "But don't tell him this is my plan or he'll reject it out of hand. If he thinks I had nothing to do with it, he'll come to me for support. I will, of course, agree to support him. Then we can both go to the council and I will appear to be backing him."

"Byzantine," Bourguet remarked as he half-smiled over his pipe.

They also agreed to telex the Panamanian government asking for the Shah's arrest for extradition.

After three anxious days, Sadegh called Bourguet in his room at the Intercontinental Hotel in Teheran. It was 3:30 in the morning and Bourguet was hardly awake.

"It's decided," Sadegh revealed. "Torrijos called. They'll arrest the Shah at 7:00 in the morning. Should I announce it right away?"

"No. Wait for confirmation," Bourguet advised. "Telex Panama and ask for telex return to confirm."

"I have to go to Mashhad at 7:30," Sadegh announced. He explained that because of the hostage crisis he had done hardly any campaigning for the presidency and could not cancel his appearance in Mashhad, a key center.

"Be sure you leave precise instructions, then," Bourguet cautioned.

At 7:00, the Iranian Foreign Ministry announced the arrest of the Shah in Panama in Sadegh's name.

But in Panama, General Omar Torrijos blanched as he heard the news. He was just going to his own meeting to have his cabinet ratify his decision. Although accustomed to rubber-stamping his decrees, the cabinet would draw the line at acquiescing to a fiat already made public. The scheme was scuttled.

Sadegh was wild with anger and frustration. "It was the last chance! It's hopeless now!"

Having breakfast at the Intercon when he heard the news, Christian Bourguet cursed silently. Sadegh had spoken with him at three in the morning, and he had been so sleepy that the time Sadegh gave him for the arrest did not register. Of course, the Panamanians had meant 7:00 A.M. Panama time, not Teheran time! Miserably, he blamed himself for this disaster.

Christian felt inadequate. The waters were far too deep for an ordinary French lawyer. But they were all just ordinary people in an extraordinary situation, he reflected.

When he returned to Teheran from Mashhad, Sadegh consoled his old friend. What was done was done.

The mullahs were delighted and declared that Ghotbzadeh had lied, there never had been a deal with Panama. They dubbed Sadegh Charlatan.

Sadegh shrugged. "We'll get Torrijos to back up my claim. But it doesn't matter. There's no chance of the presidency for me now."

Sadegh had believed that a solution to the crisis might carry the election. Christian was not so sure, but in any case, Sadegh was now determined to free the hostages come hell or high water. "Or those bastards in turbans will take over the whole country," he said.

Bourguet and Villalon worked out with Sadegh a step-by-step plan they called "the Scenario." If Jimmy Carter would agree, a UN commission would lead to the release of the hostages in this carefully choreographed deal. Sadegh sent Bourguet and Villalon to the White House with the scenario.

In his White House office, Hamilton Jordan read the CIA reports on Bourguet and Villalon. He groaned. Bourguet was a left-wing activist lawyer, and Villalon was a dubious wheeler-dealer who had once been arrested for an Italian political kidnapping, though he'd been later exonerated.

Jordan decided to see the two men anyway. They were his only link to Teheran.

When they arrived, Bourguet handed him a tape of a Revco meeting with UN secretary general Waldheim, as proof he was a bona fide negotiator with high connections. Then the two emissaries from Teheran proceeded to outline the Scenario: Iran would call for a UN commission to look into its grievances against America. The United States would object but acquiesce. Iran would seem to have won a victory. The UN commission would go to Iran and find the hostages being held in conditions unacceptable in Islam. The Ayatollah would release them. The commission would report on America's past abuses.

Jordan and his colleagues were dubious. There were the frozen assets, a thousand complications. But they decided to try it. For two days they all hammered out this face-saving political dance. And in Iran, the presidential election took place.

On January 25, 1980 Bani Sadr was elected first president of Iran with 76 percent of the vote. His nearest rival, Admiral Ahmad Madani had 15 percent. Habibi managed 4 percent. Sadegh's vote was not even 1 percent.

The mullahs were furious. At the last moment, the candidate of their party, the IRP, had had to withdraw: Djalalodin Farsi was disqualified because his father was Afghan, not an Iranian citizen. Habibi had hurriedly taken his place. I barely noticed Farsi's name. Only much later would I discover he was a deadly enemy.

The Mudjahedeen leader Radjavi had been disqualified too, because he had not voted for the constitution. His disqualification eliminated the huge vote of the Mudjahedeen organization.

When he returned to Teheran, Bourguet found Sadegh sunk in ineffable sorrow, as a man in mourning for a lifelong friend. Embracing Christian, Sadegh motioned him to sit on the long sofa in his inner office while he settled slowly into the capacious armchair in one corner. Sadegh sat in silence in the presence of his friend, somewhere between thought and meditation, running the beads of his *tasbi* through his fingers, his face a mask of grief.

"Sadegh, what is it?" Christian asked gently.

"The Imam," he said brokenly. "The Imam. He spoke during the presidential election. But not for me. He finally spoke and it was for Habibi. Habibi! How could he? What has Habibi ever been to him? Ever done for him? Ever done, period! Made a dirty little deal with Beheshti. And then, the best of it all is, everybody thought when the Imam made his speech about the faithful voting for the worthy candidate of the true line he meant Bani Sadr! Isn't that great? Bani Sadr was elected by mistake!"

He was like a man with a fever eating him. Bourguet tried to soothe him but it was no use.

"Ever since my eyes first saw him, I have been his disciple. I gave him my faith and accepted him. Maybe I wasn't his first follower, like Ali was the Prophet's first convert, but he was *my* prophet. And now, it's like Ali, isn't it?"

Bourguet gestured helplessly.

"While Ali wept and mourned the death of the Prophet, the others usurped his place as leader. And while I've consecrated myself to trying to save us from this hostage disaster, Habibi and Bani Sadr and all the others took my place. God knows what they've been telling Khomeini about me."

Both Sadegh and Bani Sadr had been appalled to find their old friend Habibi used dirty tricks against them in order to help the mullahs' party, the IRP. For his part, Sadegh was puzzled. Had he made such a bad impression? What could he have done differently? The rejection hurt, but he buried the pain inside.

"I can't keep you on as foreign minister," Bani Sadr told Sadegh.

"Why? What are you talking about?"

"For God's sake, Sadegh, you helped get us into this mess. You're responsible for the hostage crisis."

"Me? What are you talking about?"

"You put the television and radio at the disposal of the students. You backed them. You destroyed me in the Foreign Ministry with that little coup of yours about my UN trip. That was our last chance. And now you've cooked up this international tribunal. It's crazy! It just encourages the students to string it out and ask for more."

Sadegh wouldn't explain his need to cajole Khomeini, to win him over with loyalty. But to be out in the cold again, with no way to put things right—it was too much. Exhausted, Sadegh looked at

Bani Sadr. The ruins of the revolution lay at their feet. Sadegh wept with anguish.

"It's not all true. I'm not responsible. Not for everything. In the beginning I let myself be taken in by Khoeini'a and the students. Keep me on. I'll do everything I can to end it."

Bani Sadr contemplated Sadegh's offer. Sadegh was infuriating and difficult, but he was still sincere and ultimately loyal. Finally, Bani Sadr told him he could stay as foreign minister.

Sadegh was still weeping. "I'm not crying for myself," he said softly. "I'm crying for Iran."

*   *   *

January 29, 1980, almost a year to the day since the catastrophic, triumphal return to Teheran and nearly three months since the hostage seizure at the American embassy, I sat on the other side of the world, in the New York office of the newly appointed Iranian ambassador to the United Nations, Mansour Farhang.

The outer reception room of the Iranian mission to the UN had been stripped of all imperial paraphernalia. Pale rectangles on the walls showed where portraits of the royal family had once hung. The only decorations now were Koranic texts that had been put up here and there, and a scowling portrait of Khomeini. The magnificent rugs and a large blue picture of Isfahan survived, but that was all that was left of the former regime. Secretaries in black scarves demurred to the men. Tailored diplomats of the ancien régime and stubble-faced envoys of the new worked in uneasy tandem.

Together with the camera crew, I was ushered into the ambassador's inner office. The office appeared unscathed, an inoffensive assembly of modern plush in beige and brown tones, and a dubious modern painting on the wall.

Mansour Farhang settled his long frame with dignity on the sofa. He had a pleasant face and unruly gray hair and was impeccably dressed. He looked and spoke like a professor, which was exactly what he was.

As he had been avoiding the press, he was cautious and resentful at first. But he had been ordered by his foreign minister to see me, though at first he agreed only to a brief conversation and refused to appear before our television cameras.

Weeks earlier, I had been in New York interviewing a CIA defector about the agency's relations with SAVAK, and I had buttonholed the Iranian chargé d'affaires outside the UN building, with our cameras rolling. I posed a few unwelcome questions about the hostages, then asked him if Mansour Farhang would have any new proposals.

"Who?" he had responded.

"Mansour Farhang, your new ambassador. I gather he hasn't arrived yet."

"Who told you this nonsense?" he snapped.

"Your foreign minister, actually."

"Oh," he replied, utterly undone. "I don't know. I haven't heard anything." And he scurried off. Later I learned that the UN mission was often the last to hear the facts from Teheran. I gathered that the chargé d'affaires as well as Mansour Farhang were still confused by their foreign minister's unorthodox ways.

But Farhang warmed up after a few moments and, unaware that another bolt of lightning was about to hit Iran, extemporized rationally for two hours on the sources of the revolution and on the Shah's regime. He emphasized the difference between the Shah's kind of Westernization and the revolutionaries' concept of modernization in harmony with Islam. Like Sadegh, he wanted the hostage crisis ended. He confided that the secretary general of the United Nations would soon announce a new initiative. I found myself liking him.

Finally, Farhang agreed to repeat a few of his comments for the cameras. We were in the middle of filming when an urgent phone call came through for me. It was the Toronto desk.

"What are you doing now?" the voice on the other end of the line asked.

"Interviewing the ambassador," I replied, totally mystified.

"Good. Now keep a straight face. Ken Taylor, our ambassador, just escaped from Iran with six Americans from the U.S. embassy. He's been hiding them all this time. Hit Farhang with it with the cameras rolling."

Taken by surprise in the glare of the television lights, Farhang stumbled, but quickly marshaled his thoughts. The affable, logical human being vanished as the diplomat mouthed words about the dire consequences of Canada's actions. The human being was relieved that at least some of the hostages were safe, and he was genuinely worried about reprisals from the extremists in Iran. But the diplomat had to guard his rear. And his front.

In Teheran, Sadegh did the same. He angrily threatened that Canada would pay for its crime, and for its "duplicity and cheating."

"The Canadian government," he declared, "will be responsible for any harsh treatment meted out against the hostages. Everyone was talking these past couple of months about the violation of international laws by Iran. But now Canada has permitted itself to forge the passports and stamps and to send out some people."

The drama took on the absurdity of Pinter or Waugh: American diplomats sneaked about in disguise; Sadegh, of all people, railed about forged passports; students and priests chanted "Death to Canada," a shocking consummation for a nation that thinks of itself as a political virgin.

And meanwhile back in Washington, Bourguet and Villalon were in Hamilton Jordan's office when the news came through. Bourguet immediately called Sadegh, who confided, "Between us, I'm glad and I understand. In no way does this change my commitment to our discussions. Besides, if *I* make dire threats, the students will probably do nothing — just to make me look like an idiot. Did the Americans know some of their people were in the Canadian embassy?" he asked.

"No," Bourguet replied. "They're as flabbergasted as anyone." Actually the Americans had known, but had lied to Bourguet.

"I suppose we have to bring Bani Sadr in on this now," Sadegh suggested.

It would be hard to do otherwise, he *is* the president," Bourguet replied.

"So he is," Sadegh acknowledged. "Prepare for the worst, and come back to Teheran."

* * *

Emerging ten days later from the trauma of the Canadian escapade, our newsdesk decided to send a full crew back to Teheran. Mr. Ghotbzadeh had announced an official visit to several European capitals. I was ordered to Paris to meet the foreign minister and then return to Teheran with him.

As soon as the hotel porter deposited me in my room at the Hotel Marignan, in Paris, I called Farhang in Geneva. We had talked several times since our first meeting, and each time more congenially. He was to be part of the foreign minister's party in Paris and had told me where to reach him in Geneva. He had gone there on other business first.

"Oh, I am so glad you called!" he said fervently. "Where are you? In Paris, I hope."

"Just arrived."

"Good. Look, can you do me a favor? I arrive tomorrow at Orly airport just before Ghotbzadeh. The nitwits at our embassy are in complete confusion, and I'm not sure anyone will meet me. I have to find the VIP lounge Ghotbzadeh is coming to, and I don't speak any French. Could you meet me and take care of getting me there?"

The absurdity of the situation harmonized with the overall insanity of recent events.

The next afternoon I found Farhang at the airport. He was considerably agitated, since I had been sent to the wrong gate and had missed his arrival. The ambassador of the Islamic Republic of Iran to the United Nations had been wandering disconsolately in the halls of Orly airport, trying in vain to communicate the concept of a VIP lounge to surly French functionaries.

I managed to get the directions to the lounge, and Farhang and I rushed to the adjoining hall. Outside the lounge, the local and foreign press corps had gathered in a fevered crush. They were held back by a rope barrier and several gendarmes. A couple of old Paris colleagues of mine called out, then looked in puzzlement as I waved, then swept past them with Farhang. We were ushered briskly inside by the gendarmes.

Inside, under the ghastly glare of fluorescent light, a dozen or so dignitaries were gathered, seated on the deep couches and in armchairs. The gentlemen from the Quai d'Orsay, the French Foreign Ministry, smoked cigarettes with the nitwits from the Iranian embassy, as they all nervously awaited the arrival of their old adversary, the dreadful Ghotbzadeh.

Farhang introduced me to an aged man sitting apart from the others. He was Shamseddine Amiralai, Iran's new ambassador to France. He chatted amiably with me for some time, then asked politely, "What office are you from?"

"I'm a journalist with Canadian television."

The ambassador gaped, horrified, like a man who had just discovered the log he is sitting on is, in fact, an alligator.

"A what? What are you doing here? Who let you in?"

"It's rather complicated, actually." I gestured toward Farhang.

The ambassador called Farhang over for explanations, but at that moment a flurry of activity signaled the arrival of the foreign minis-

ter's plane. Farhang left with Amiralai to greet Sadegh on the tarmac. And as he left, Farhang whispered in my ear, ''I'll warn him
you're here.''

I nodded gratefully, since I had not had the opportunity to contact Sadegh before he left Iran.

Moments passed and the chatter around me grew more distant.
I was lost in a mixture of apprehension, anxiety and anticipation.
Even though Sadegh and I had talked almost daily, it had been a
year since we had seen each other.

And suddenly he was there. Sadegh, the elegant bear.

I stood in a kind of oblivion in the middle of the room, seeing
only him. He walked straight toward me, ignoring the diplomats,
who dangled uncomfortably as protocol was thoroughly breached.
Taking my hands, Sadegh took me to sit on a couch in a remote
corner of the room.

''I could hardly believe it when Farhang told me you were here,''
he said, shaking his head.

''They're finally sending me back to Iran. With a crew,'' I said.
''If the foreign minister will give us visas,'' I added.

''No problem. Right away?''

''I'd like to fly back with you. The crew will follow.''

''And you will stay in Iran?''

''I hope so, but you know television.''

He squeezed my hands, then got up to attend to the waiting dignitaries. ''Stay here,'' he whispered. ''Then come in Farhang's car
to the ambassador's residence.''

Since the cat was well and truly out of the bag, I readily and happily agreed. It was typical of Sadegh to flout the rules and flaunt
me. He was clearly as determined as ever to march to his own drum.
The danger in this was palpable, but caught in the euphoria of the
moment, I pushed it to the edge of my consciousness.

After brief formalities with the assembled gentlemen, preparations were made to open the floodgates and let the press pour in.
Flanked by Amiralai and Farhang, Sadegh sat in the center of a
long couch facing a pair of large sliding doors.

Sitting to one side, I found myself for the first time on the receiving end of an assault by my crazed colleagues. As the gendarmes
loosed the barrier, dozens of wild animals suddenly spilled into
the room in a hubbub of jungle noises. Reporters pushed and shoved
and gnashed their teeth in a savage competition to set up cameras

and to get close to the quarry. Leaping over an armchair, a soundman caught an elbow in the solar plexus, and went over backwards, landing upside down in the overturned chair, pinned there by his equipment, his arms and legs waving in the air like a turtle's.

Through it all, Sadegh sat with the bemused air of a dignified father indulging his rowdy children.

After the press conference, as we drove back into Paris in the cortege, motorcyle escort ahead, Farhang and a representative of Iran's London embassy and I discussed the PLO's efforts to assist in the hostage crisis. It looked like a dead end, but the conversation was still guarded.

The residence of the Iranian ambassador is on the rue Fortuny in one of Paris's finest neighborhoods. The cars entered through a grill gate and drove under a wide portico sheltering the front entrance. Inside, a lushly carpeted stairway swept up in a graceful wave to the main salons. In one of these, Sadegh was already ensconced in an elegant chair of gilt and brocade, holding court. Others were fanned out in a wide circle, each sitting in brocaded splendor, sipping tea and munching cookies. I joined the circle, choosing a chair far from Sadegh and between the man from the London embassy and someone from the Quai. Sadegh was making small talk in English about revolutionary trivia, addressing the group at large.

Looking around at the ornate luxury of gold, crystal and Bourbon antiques, Sadegh remarked with a grin that he and his friends had stayed out of government during the Shah's reign because they hadn't wanted to be bothered with the housekeeping. He added that the new enthusiasts at the Agriculture Ministry had thrown out all the furniture and were using cushions on the floor instead of chairs. He laughed and added with a sweep of his hand, "No wonder!"

There were easy laughs from those who knew Sadegh, and polite but uncomfortable titters from those unsure of which way the wind was blowing.

After an interval during which I asked harmless questions of the London man and wondered what was expected of me, Sadegh got up and motioned me into an adjoining room. It was small, with a settee, a desk and a few chairs for private meetings. Closing the door, he sighed deeply, pulled me to him and held me close and silent, my head on his shoulder.

I worried about the raised eyebrows and wagging tongues outside, but he wanted just a moment of peace. Let them wag, I thought.

There was relief as well as love in his arms. To be with someone who was simply a friend and not part of any Byzantine betrayal or plot was, I learned later, something Sadegh had longed for.

Then he stood back.

"I have to file a report," I told him honestly.

"Promise you'll come back for dinner."

I nodded and we returned to the tea party. Soon after, I left to head back to the CBC Paris bureau.

I had promised myself I would keep a professional distance from Sadegh. His life, I believed, now could not possibly include me. As a result of that vow, I had not made any confession to my superiors. But the promise I'd made myself dissolved instantly in his arms. I could no more deny Sadegh than change my soul. Still fighting his Persian armor, I was passionately, furiously in love with him.

I arrived at the CBC Paris office on the Avenue Matignon in my own electric storm. Fortunately, the place was deserted at that hour.

I filed a report, which was, no doubt, utterly inane. Then I finished some other work at the bureau, and stopped by my hotel to change into a low-necked but relatively modest silk dress I considered appropriate for diplomatic soirees. By the time I arrived back at the ambassador's residence, dinner had already begun.

When I was ushered into the dining room, I stood utterly appalled. I'd been expecting a New York- or Washington-style diplomatic dinner: high embassy staff, some officials from other embassies, a few hand-picked journalists and some French dignitaries. But sitting around an enormous oval table debecked with fine china and shining silver there were only men. Iranian men, murmuring in Persian.

This was a private embassy dinner. The soft murmurs stopped, and all eyes turned to me as I was ushered to an empty seat beside Sadegh.

I whispered to Sadegh that he must be mad, but he politely welcomed me, introduced me to the table, and ordered the staff to serve the late arrival. Then he turned and, picking up where he had left off, went on talking to Amiralai, Iran's ambassador to France.

Beside me, the Iranian diplomat from London mercifully rose to the occasion and engaged me in conversation about ancient Persian culture. Two chairs away, Farhang looked at me and then at Sadegh. He seemed to alternate between amused resignation and angry disapproval.

If I had been feeling less reckless, I would have been mortified and made an effort to be invisible. But in this situation I mirrored Sadegh, reveling in high mischief, enjoying every perverse moment. The paintings, the dinner, the faces and the conversation took on the bright glow of the illicit, and I met Farhang's gaze with happy defiance.

Then suddenly Amiralai was yelling at Sadegh, pounding the table and pouring his heart out in a long, impassioned speech. But it wasn't Khomeini, the hostages, censorship or executions that troubled him. It was the embassy decorators. Just before the revolution, the embassy had contracted for extensive renovations, and now Sadegh was refusing to pay the bill. Let the Shah pay. No Foreign Ministry of his was going to spend money on something the Shah had wanted. Left holding the bag, Amiralai was furious.

Gradually, some kind of order was restored and everyone took long swallows of orange juice.

Excusing myself as the meal ended, I went to the main salon to make a scheduled call to the Toronto desk to fill them in and tell them to arrange for the crew to follow me to Iran. Across the Atlantic it was early afternoon.

It was a long conversation, and as I hung up, Ambassador Amiralai approached in his white tie and tails, looking more like a butler than an ambassador. Bowing, he announced, Jeeves-like, that His Excellency was waiting for me in the other room. He proffered an arm. Thinking Sadegh was rather rubbing it in to the old fellow, sending him to fetch me, I went with him, expecting after-dinner coffee with the others.

We walked down a small hallway and the ambassador opened a door to a tiny elevator. Surprised, I stepped in. As we rose slowly, I asked how long he had been there and where he had learned French. As usual I wondered what was happening. When the elevator stopped, the ambassador stepped out and showed me to an open doorway. Inside a luxurious room I saw an enormous bed and Sadegh's jacket hanging over the back of a chair.

I turned in dismay.

Amiralai looked at me sadly and said wistfully, "It's rather lonely here. Me, I'm all alone." And he left, whirring away in the elevator.

Aghast, I stepped into the room. It was green and gold, predictably ornate, with a kind of masculine magnificence. It was empty. Another doorway led into another room. The second room was pink plush, and had a baroque divan and a creamy dressing table.

I went back to the first room and leaned against the door to think. But at that moment Sadegh came through a mirrored door in the other wall, drying his hands on a towel.

"Isn't this just a little bit intimate?" I asked sarcastically, folding my arms.

"Nice, isn't it?" he smiled innocently.

"Nice? Sadegh, are you out of your mind? The rest — this afternoon, this evening — was indiscreet enough, but this is crazy!"

Suddenly, Sadegh became serious. "I've been discreet all my life. I'm tired of it. I fought all my life, hiding, being followed. Now I'm foreign minister and I have to be discreet? I'll do what I want for once."

I felt torn and confused. I closed my eyes and shook my head. "It's *because* you're foreign minister that we have to be discreet. Oh, Lord. Sadegh, you know that. You know how dangerous it is. It's dangerous for me, too."

"Come here."

I paused, then went to him. The damage was done.

He grinned. "It's a chance that can't be passed up. I'm told this was the Shah's bed when he stayed here." Sadegh stretched out, still smiling.

"Was Farah next door?" I asked.

"Maybe. Anyway, this bed doesn't know how to do anything else." He laughed.

I laughed too, even though the Shah was then dying, Farah was in agony and Iran was in flames. Whether or not the bed had really been used by the Shah, Sadegh believed it had. For him, sleeping in the Shah's bed was joyful revenge, a way of savoring victory. For me, fantasy was reality and reality fantasy. Only Sadegh was real.

I looked into his dark eyes. "Can we keep the foreign minister and the journalist out of here and away from us?" I faltered. "The journalist has a few bones to pick with the foreign minister about the revolution, but I'm not the journalist right now. I love you,

Sadegh, just you. Do you understand that? Do you believe me?''

He did, but he said little. We were together again and the world disappeared.

There is a Persian custom: a beautiful mirror is placed before the bride during the marriage ceremony. It is a lovely piece; the mirror is encased behind small exquisite doors in a frame elaborately carved in an arabesque shape and delicately painted with colorful flowers, birds and figures, which are intricately intertwined with lacy scrollwork. At first, the bride is not allowed to see her intended. She kneels with her back to him, reading the Koran. But as he recites his vows, she may look at him in the mirror. And as the vow is made, he may approach to kneel beside her. As they exchange rings and give each other a spoonful of honey, they see themselves in the mirror. They are two souls united by the light of the candle that glows beside the mirror.

To be with Sadegh, even in this reprehensible situation, was for a fleeting moment to see him in the mirror. He suddenly allowed me a brief glimpse of the soul that might join with mine. But in another instant he closed the doors of the mirror and the image vanished like a ghost. Again, he retreated into his Persian opacity.

Later we once again became the foreign minister and the journalist, and we talked about the maelstrom in Iran, the hostages and Beheshti. Sadegh still refused to regard Beheshti as a serious threat, believing stubbornly in the Master, Khomeini. The executions and the repression had become a second priority in the face of the threat posed by the students at the embassy. In any case, in his heart he believed a certain amount of ruthlessness was inevitable and necessary.

Tired, happy and looking forward to tomorrow, I left Sadegh. An embassy car took me to my hotel.

As we had talked, a mysterious young man had disembarked from a private jet at Charles de Gaulle airport. His features were hidden by a hat and scarf. On the tarmac a limousine waited. He climbed inside, and it spirited him away as the watching eyes of the Renseignements Generaux, the French security police, registered his presence.

At 4:30 A.M., Christian Bourguet arrived at the house on Rue Fortuny.

"I'm expected," he told the night guard.

A big man came out of the house and slid quickly into Bourguet's car. His collar was turned up and his hat pulled down. It was Sadegh.

"Is everything going as planned?" Sadegh asked Christian.

"Let's hope so. As far as we know, all's well so far."

Meanwhile, the young man who had arrived at the airport also secretly slipped into an anonymous-looking car with two other men and a woman. They drove in a circuitous route, doubling back at the Bir Hakeim bridge, and circling round till they came to a pair of huge doors at an address on the Avenue du President Wilson. Silently they entered and took the antique hardwood elevator to the sixth floor.

Christian and Sadegh also drove in elaborate circles until they came to the same address. They knocked quietly at the door on the sixth floor, and Hector Villalon appeared to welcome them to his home, motioning them into a room on the left, where the young man and his companions waited.

Sadegh shook hands with Hamilton Jordan.

The two men faced each other over a vast gulf. Yet they were oddly close in spirit.

Jordan was young and green, freely admitting he was utterly out of his depth in handling the monumental crisis. He was still enough of a novice in international affairs to have been goggle-eyed when Christian Bourguet picked up a phone in Washington and was connected directly to the Iranian Foreign Ministry. Villalon had had to dissuade Jordan from wearing an absurd wig and makeup to the secret rendezvous. Despite Jordan's naiveté, Sadegh felt certain he was someone he could talk with. Each man sensed in the other a readiness to try the unorthodox, to speak without the flummery of diplomacy.

At the earlier secret meeting in London, Jordan had been prepared to go to Iran to meet Sadegh, but Bourguet and Villalon had dissuaded him. "It's too dangerous. You'd just give them another hostage, a presidential adviser at that."

Jordan had joked, "Well, if the hostages aren't released, I won't be a presidential anything."

Bourguet was impressed with Jordan's uniquely American way of seeing, doing and feeling things. He was intensely personal and sentimental — qualities one did not find in French diplomatic circles. "I'll talk to Ghotbzadeh," Bourguet promised.

But Sadegh, too, vetoed a trip to Iran. "Set it up for Europe when I travel there," he told Bourguet.

Now Sadegh and Hamilton Jordan were at last face to face. They retired alone to an inner drawing room, where they talked for several hours.

Hamilton Jordan's main concerns were the hostages, the effect of the crisis on Carter's reelection and the possibility that Iran was vulnerable to Soviet penetration.

"Putting aside your government's feelings about the Shah," Jordan said, "how does it benefit Iran to hold these Americans?"

Sadegh exploded. He had just spent over an hour telling Jordan about the revolution, about Khomeini and about the Shah and the Shah's horrendous crimes against the Iranian people. "The Shah *is* the reason for the hostage crisis!" he shouted. Then, the outburst over, he shook his head. "There is no 'putting aside' our feelings about the Shah."

Jordan seemed to understand. "How can we end this crisis quickly, honorably and peacefully?"

"Kill the Shah," Sadegh shot back.

Jordan was aghast at the suggestion. "That's impossible."

Sadegh shrugged. "I'm only asking you to do to the Shah what the Shah and the CIA did to thousands of innocent Iranians over the past thirty years."

"It's totally out of the question," Jordan replied.

Sadegh smiled. "You asked me how to resolve the crisis quickly." Once again, Sadegh wondered how he could make the Americans realize that the hostage crisis was hurting Iran more than it was hurting them. "I want to remove this thorn from your side, as much as you want it removed," Sadegh told Jordan. "But we want it ended for different reasons. You want your citizens home and your president reelected. I want to refocus the attention of the Iranian people on the revolution and keep the United States and the Soviet Union from subverting it."

They returned to a discussion of the commission that would investigate the Shah's crimes. Sadegh asked Jordan to have patience and ask Carter not to threaten Iran further. He assured Jordan that the Imam had approved the idea of the commission, and that, with patience, the hostages would be released in weeks.

Again, Jordan promised to keep the meeting absolutely secret, and the two men returned to eat the magnificent meal that had been prepared by the Villalons. Then, confident that a working base had been established, Jordan left.

"The mullahs will have you for breakfast if they find out about this meeting," Christian warned.

"The hell with the mullahs," Sadegh responded.

The next day, a French reporter announced to the world on Radio Luxembourg, one of the largest French stations, that Iranian Foreign Minister Ghotbzadeh had met secretly with White House Chief of Staff Hamilton Jordan.

At the airport, besieged by questions about the alleged secret meeting, Sadegh assured the press he had never heard of Hamilton Jordan and added that certain members of the French Communist party had started the rumors to make trouble for him.

It was only half a lie. Sadegh believed the secret meeting had been betrayed by Nuri Albala, the old friend he had once worked with in Paris who was now a member of the French Communist party. Sadegh and his allies argued over the advisability of trusting Albala after he joined the Party. The Party, of course, had it's own men in the Renseignements Generaux, the police assigned to Jordan.

At the time, I did not know of the meeting with Jordan. Nor would Sadegh have told me. He would never have handed me such an explosive conflict of interest. If I had known of the meeting I am not sure that I would have reported it. For me, journalistic responsibilities did not include jeopardizing the solution to a crisis, especially when the fate of the hostages and the political figures involved hung in the balance. But it was not always easy to judge the degree of risk, a fact my colleagues and I would face many times throughout the nerve-racking crisis.

As the plane took off I joined Sadegh in the forward cabin, and we talked of the great dilemma. Then we sat in weary silence as the clouds fell beneath us, and we flew toward Iran.

14

February 1980. The phone in my room at the Intercon rang at seven in the morning. I was groggy, having crawled into bed only five hours before. After a moment of resistance, I answered the diabolical thing.

"Hello, Miss Jerome?"

"Yes," I answered, silently cursing.

"We're calling from the Nest of Spies. We are calling you —"

"Oh, for Christ's sake," I muttered, angry at the practical joker on the other end of the line. I slammed the phone down and turned over, only vaguely worried that the joker might be a komiteh agent in the hotel who had something against me.

The phone rang again. I reached for it irritably.

"Look —" I started.

"Miss Jerome. This is the office of the Student Followers of the Imam's Line. We are calling to tell you to be at the gate of the Nest of Spies at nine o'clock for a press conference. Will you be there?"

Nest of Spies? Oh, Lord, the American embassy. I woke up. "Yes, of course. What's the conference about?"

"We have important revelations," the male voice answered.

"I'll bet you do. Can't you tell me any more?"

"No. Be here at nine."

"With my camera crew, I trust?"

"Yes."

I heard the phone disconnect on the other end so I, too, hung up. I reached for my note pad and recorded the fact that the students clearly knew the names of all the members of the press arriving in Teheran. I wondered if a list was provided by the airport or the hotel. As usual, almost all of the press were lodged in the Teheran Intercontinental.

The rest of the CBC team had arrived the day before in time to report on the riot that occurred weekly in Freedom Square. As usual the Mudjahedeen and Fedayeen fought with each other, and both were attacked by the gunslinging, club-wielding Hezbies.

This time in Iran, I was acting as field producer for our daily TV news reports. In television, this job can involve everything from directing the shoot to fetching sandwiches for the crew, supervising the satellite feed and getting the reporter out of bed. How much of what is done by whom depends on the individual reporter and producer.

The on-camera reporter on this trip whom I will call "Dick," in case he has to go back to Iran, was a senior prima donna who took umbrage at the idea of working with a junior female producer. This created a dynamic that made a difficult situation exasperating. On the other hand, Dennis and Bill, our crew, were superb professionals and also close friends who helped balance the difficult working conditions.

Toronto had asked me, in addition to acting as field producer, to supplement the daily news with some of my own longer feature reports. In this case, I acted as reporter, too.

I roused the crew and Dick and gave them the happy news that we had received a personal invitation to the Nest of Spies.

To cross the cordon around the nest of spies, or den of espionage, as it was sometimes called, journalists showed passes issued by the Ministry of National Guidance, referred to in our ranks as the Ministry of Truth. The Orwellian aspects of the revolution grew more sinister every day, and the press, in turn, grew more cynical.

At nine o'clock, the four of us showed our passes and were waved through the barrier of sandbags. We walked the fifty yards or so to the gate, down a corridor framed on one side by the embassy wall and on the other side by the crowds that pressed against the metal bars of the barrier. A few other invited journalists joined us, and together we waited for an hour in the bitter February cold as a light snow fell.

At ten o'clock the students from inside the embassy unlocked the now-famous gates. Taking us into a hut immediately to our right, they silently searched our equipment and us. We were then led across the paved yard into one of the smaller buildings, formerly the marine guards' office, and now festooned with banners and pictures of revolutionary martyrs. Here, the students had set up a couple of tables facing rows of chairs to create a conference room. We waited for another cold hour with the dozen or so other chosen reporters, talking cautiously or reading the morning edition of the local English-language newspaper, the *Teheran Times*, which had been reborn as a revolutionary daily.

The students finally filed in. They seemed a motley lot, sour and surly, even defensive. As I watched them through their interminable presentation of incriminating documents found in the embassy, it struck me how joyless they were. There was no spark of enthusiasm, no flash of spontaneity. They were supposed to be victorious guerrillas, but they behaved like lifeless androids. Absurdly, I found myself wondering why their revolution couldn't be more fun. Here they were, allegedly giving life and freedom to the nation, but their revolution seemed like a black rite. Does Islam condemn a smile or a cry of joy? Is there nothing to laugh about? Did Mohammed laugh or allow a smile? Does God demand a frown and Allah a scowl? The laughter of children at play, the love I shared with Sadegh, were to me closer to the divine than these grim specimens of the Imam's Line. I studied them more carefully. Some were young and slightly awkward, novices learning their roles. They were probably genuine students. But others had that ineffable air of the professional; these had been trained at PLO camps in Lebanon, according to colleagues from the press corps in Beirut.

The revelations of the morning were like others before them — not really that revealing.

I arranged to visit the family of the late Ali Shariati, the Lenin of this revolution. I accepted, hoping that I would find some of the original light that had lit the revolution. Shariati had, before his premature death in London, been the intellectual beacon of Sadegh's progressive Islam. He had also been a friend and mentor.

My depression, however, increased as soon as I entered the Shariati home. It was a large, spacious bungalow furnished with chairs and cushions. Shariati's mother, a small, plump woman with lines of great weariness on her face, was gently welcoming. But then I saw with dismay a young woman enter, wearing the same grim scarf, tunic and dour expression as the students at the embassy. She was Shariati's sister.

Certainly there was cause for sorrow in this home, but there was something else as well — an almost puritanical restraint. Even if Shariati had lived, even if the revolution had gone as they had meant it, there would have been little gaiety here.

Shariati's family was circumspect about discussing the current political situation, but it was clear they were bitter. Shariati's mother, her eyes full of anxious pride, rather shyly pressed copies of her son's booklets on me. In that moment, she was like any bereft mother, and I felt the bottomless tragedy of the lives around me.

I returned to the hotel in a cloud of anger and sorrow. I thumbed again through the pages Shariati had written and I pored over his writing and speeches. His ragged scholarship was infuriating, full of unfounded generalities and wild assumptions. He announced that "Medieval Europe had declined due to the influence of Aristotle's analogical reasoning," a sweeping series of wrong assumptions that left me breathless. And he wrote only of the benign things to be found in the Koran. But what of the strangulation of all logical and metaphysical inquiry by some of the caliphs in the name of Islam? What of the violence that can be justified by the Koran's verses on fighting for the faith? The Koran is a poetic maze. For every verse prohibiting violence, there are more that order it in the name of the faith.

I found myself torn with anger. How could Sadegh believe all this medieval quackery? Everything in me rebelled against the religious and philosophical basis of it all. For me, religion that puts its faith in the scribblings of mortals — be it the Bible or the Koran — and takes them literally as the word of something they call God is a negation of intellect. For me, divine grace was present in a rose petal, a beautiful day or a Mozart concerto. I had rejected organized dogma at the age of thirteen. Word of God indeed! Who said so? No, I needed no priests or other mortals yapping about God's law, killing the rose and silencing the music. But here I was in the middle of a society that was being torn apart by yet another version of religious fraud. I threw the booklets down in disgust.

But still I could not bring myself to confront Sadegh with this awful chasm between us.

*   *   *

At two in the morning my phone rang. A deep male voice spoke. "Mr. Ghotbzadeh sent me. I'm waiting downstairs in the lobby."

"Who are you? What are you talking about?"

"Here is his number. Call him."

I sat up in bed and dialed the number.

"Sadegh?"

"Hi. Where are you? I'm waiting for you," he answered cheerfully.

"Sadegh, it's the middle of the night. I can't come to your home in the middle of the night." I wondered what on earth he was thinking about. Then, to add a note of practicality, I added, "I'm exhausted."

"You won't come?"

He sounded surprised by my refusal. "No," I repeated. "Can't you see how it would look?"

"Okay. I'll send him tomorrow night at midnight."

He hung up and I looked at the receiver, trying to comprehend his invitation.

Should I have gone? I cursed my cowardice, wishing I had run to him. But who was the man in the lobby? Could Sadegh trust anyone? No, I had done the right thing. And in truth I was too exhausted to stir, even for Sadegh. I fell into a well of sleep.

The next night the deep voice called again from the lobby. When I went downstairs I was greeted by a well-dressed thickset man who introduced himself as Shin.

As we drove in Shin's Mercedes through the dark, empty streets of Teheran, I sat in fearful silence. Was this man really to be trusted? Although alert to the awful possibilities, I was still young enough to enjoy risking my life, for it was no less than that.

Glimpses of shadowy men, armed and ready to kill, passed in the night like bat's wings. Near the Niavaran Palace, as the car swung up into the hills above the city, I saw a brief confrontation illuminated in a pool of light from a dim streetlamp. Armed figures grappled with two others. We didn't slow down, but turned and then climbed up the last slope, passed through a gate and into a treed yard.

Inside the house, Sadegh was waiting. He was dressed in a long white *aba*, a robe. It was the first time I had seen him in this garb, and it was a small, pleasant shock. This was another Sadegh, at ease in his skin. Had the Western dress been a mere costume? I decided not. But oddly I was more comfortable with this oriental Sadegh, perhaps because he, too, was now closer to himself. We settled side by side on the sofa, his right hand on mine, his left clicking a string of *tasbih*. He was quiet, tense, and seemed preoccupied.

Beside Shin was another man in a shirt and slacks. He had laughing eyes, and Sadegh introduced him as Alef. The house was comfortable, furnished in a spare modern fashion with two portraits, one of Taleghani and one of Shariati, on the wall in the dining room.

As we sipped strong, sweet tea, Sadegh and his two friends spoke in Persian, sometimes paraphrased for me, or we spoke English, with Shin translating for Alef, or Alef and I spoke German while Sadegh pondered at length, smoking his pipe.

A lot of the conversation concerned the operation of the Foreign Ministry, which was now full of adherents of the Islamic Republic Party, the IRP, who had been wished on Sadegh by Revco. The hostages, I realized, were not the only problem. As Sadegh worked, birds of prey watched and waited over every doorway.

Alef soon departed, and as we all retired for the night, I looked at Sadegh. Here, in Iran, I felt I was finding him for the first time. Yet he also was farther away. He was peremptory now, almost commanding me, an Iranian man sure of his ground, and I resented it even as I obeyed, following him to our room.

He put his Thompson gun and his heavy black Llama .45 pistol on the bedside table.

I toyed with the heavy pistol. "Are you sure having me here is such a good idea? They" — I meant his enemies and I knew there were many — "want any excuse to get you."

"They won't do anything. Let me worry about that."

It was his revolution, his country and his judgment. It was wrong to risk all three — and my own skin, for that matter — but he did and I did.

Wordless, incoherent with love and fear of him, I watched him undress, wondering how to reach out to him across this new gulf. Only when we touched, loved and held one another did the barriers dissolve.

"I was afraid I had lost you," I said, "to Iran, to this awful mess."

"No," he replied. "I'm just me, my beauty."

He had never called me that before. Did he bestow this endearment on other womenfriends? I felt idiotic and angry worrying about romance when his life's work, his country and his people were in chaos. I put my arms around him as if to hold some of the chaos together.

"When this is over we'll go live in Quebec," I joked, retreating to our mutual fantasy. "That's a million miles away, isn't it?"

Over a breakfast of flatbread and goat's cheese we discussed the talks I had had with some of the CIA men who had run the Iran desk for the past twenty years. I told him the agency people were angry at taking the blame for "losing" Iran, and consequently some were ready to talk to the press. They claimed to have warned their supervisors of what was coming in Iran, and to have appealed for years for funds to infiltrate the mosque. One of their reports allegedly said the Shah was a megalomaniac out of touch with reality.

The agents said they were subsequently informed that this was not the sort of thing the U.S. president wanted to hear.

Though some of this information had appeared in the press, I gave Sadegh names, dates and other information I had been given.

"The Americans still claim you're a KGB agent," I added.

"That's what the Israelis tell them," he replied with a shrug.

Sadegh took some notes as he finished his breakfast. Then he picked up his pistol and put it in his belt, checked the Thompson and slung it over his shoulder, kissed me goodbye and left the house with his brawny bodyguard. They slipped quickly into a blue Mercedes and Sadegh went off to another day as foreign minister.

A few minutes later I left with Shin in his car.

"I think," I said carefully, "I shall never understand why Sadegh loves Khomeini so much."

Shin smiled briefly. "Khomeini is a good man with a good heart."

"Well, he certainly hides it well."

"It's because he is Iranian. We don't show our emotions on the surface. But believe me, he's got a very big heart. It's the others who are so bad. They just want power. They aren't men of God like Khomeini, they're politicians."

"All of them?"

"No, but too many."

"Is the revolution lost to you?"

Shin stared through the windscreen of the car. "Yes," he said, after a moment.

We drove down Pahlavi to the Shahanshahei expressway, then into the choking city traffic. How could they all believe that under his cold exterior Khomeini had a good heart? Couldn't they see that the exterior was the reality, not a disguise? They believed the lie and denied the truth, they believed Khomeini's mouthings in Paris and denied his writings on the *faghih* and Islamic dictatorship. They believed he was warm, when he exuded a frigid cold.

I thought again of the Iranian folktale from the *Book of Kings*. "They needed to believe that their father loved them," Fereidoun Hoveyda had told me. "Only, just as in legends, for the father, power comes before love. You see, in the West you have a central myth of the father, that is the Oedipus myth. In it, the son kills the father and takes his place. In our myth, it is the opposite. The father kills the sons. Myths are a kind of paradigm of society. They are not an absolute, determining the pattern — nothing so rigid — but

they do provide keys, and they do show what is traditionally acceptable. In the West, sons don't literally kill their fathers, but sons do
replace fathers, and that is how your society regenerates itself. But
in ours, the father often eliminates the son in one way or another.
Do you see?''

Back at the Intercon I found Dennis and Bill tucking into breakfast in the coffee shop. Dick, they told me, was in his room on the
phone.

When they asked where I had been, I lied, saying I had gone to
tell our driver to pick up our translator. I hated lying to the crew. In
the field, a television team is a little life-support unit, utterly depend-
ent on each other, and ''my boys'' were also my friends. I wanted
to tell them about the situation, but the fewer who knew the better.
Besides, if I did get into difficulty, they could truthfully say they
knew nothing about my nefarious dealings with the foreign minister.

* * *

The Foreign Ministry was in turmoil, turned upside down by
Sadegh. He was one of Khomeini's feared lieutenants, yet he did
not proceed like the other new ministers of state, who swept their
ministries clean with a theological broom. Sadegh dismissed the
elite *taghooti*, followers of the Shah, but he kept others who were
manifestly liberal-minded. And though he himself was devout, he
defied Khomeini's orders on more than one occasion. He did not
make the women who worked in the ministry wear a *hejab* to cover
their hair; he refused to close the office for noon prayers, saying
there was too much work to be done: and he stubbornly refused to
change the ministry letterhead by removing the royal crest and
replacing it with the sign of Allah, as Khomeini had ordered. The
staff could not discern precisely what was in the air. And to add to
the confusion, the three Americans who had been at the Foreign
Ministry when the American embassy was stormed were still there.
Held in protective custody, they read, exercised and watched television in their reasonably comfortable prison above Sadegh's office.

Of all the things that caused friction, however, the matter of the
ministry's letterhead loomed largest.

''I order you to change the letterhead!'' Khomeini was hoarse
with anger. ''This is the seventh time I have ordered you to change
it.''

Perhaps Sadegh was testing. Perhaps it was just his innate stubbornness, but he still refused. He had the printers invert the crown

on the insignia, and looked at the result with a satisfied smirk.

Again Khomeini summoned him and castigated him. "This is the eighth time! I order you, and you disobey! Why? Do you want me to command you publicly?"

The picayune matter had assumed the proportions of an ideological rupture, a crisis of principle.

"Agha," Sadegh said, "in religious matters, you are my master. If you order me for religious reasons to do anything whatsoever, I will do it, even kill myself if you want. But in political matters you are not my unconditional master, and I have the right to disagree with you. You can force me to resign by using others to push me aside, but you can't force me to obey you. And if you attack me publicly, that's what I shall reply, publicly."

Khomeini puffed out his cheeks like a cobra before a strike. "I order you in the name of Islam to change it."

They continued to spar, but in the end, more out of prudence than fidelity, Sadegh bowed to Khomeini on this and other matters. He had to choose his battles with care. He was under attack from many sides. The students at the embassy were mounting another offensive.

Using the radio as their weapon, the students ordered Mr. Ghotbzadeh to hand over the three American diplomats held in the Foreign Ministry.

Sadegh replied in an open letter to the Imam that there was no religious or political reason to transfer the Americans and that, as the foreign minister, he was fully responsible for the American spies. Then Sadegh sat back secure in the knowledge that Khomeini would do nothing. Khomeini would not tempt fate and take on his foreign minister over this matter.

For Khomeini the matter of Allah on the letterhead was crucial since it was a question of symbolism and purification. But the transfer of the hostages from the Foreign Ministry to the embassy — from Sadegh to the students — did not interest the Imam. The hostages were simply not as important to him as the letterhead, they were a mere detail. Thus the three hostages in the Foreign Ministry languished in a diplomatic reception room upstairs. And Sadegh won the round.

*   *   *

After many delays, the United Nations commission was constituted and ready to leave for Iran. It was the first step in the Scenario. The commission included Adib Daoudy, political adviser to Hafez al Assad, the president of Syria; Mohammad Bedjaoui, the Algerian ambassador to the UN; Andres Aguilar, Venezuelan ambassador to the United States; and Henry Jawardene, a civil-rights lawyer and the brother of the president of Sri Lanka. Their mandate was vague — to investigate the Shah's human-rights record and the role of the United States in Iranian affairs. They were also to visit the hostages, who had by then been held for 111 days. The rest — negotiations, settlement and release — would follow, Sadegh hoped.

As the team flew toward Iran on February 22, 1980, Sadegh reflected on the chances of success. It would have been better had they all been Islamic, but he was confident that Khomeini would listen to men of their stature.

Then a television announcement caught his ear. A decree from Khomeini declared that the hostage issue would be decided by the new *madjiles*, the Iranian parliament, which was to be elected in May.

Sadegh stared at the screen in utter shock. Those sons of bitches! They had put Khomeini up to this! It was Rafsanjani, Beheshti and the rest of the *karamzadeh*, bastards, in the IRP. Once again, the rug had been pulled out from under a possible solution to the hostage crisis.

Now it was more important than ever to get the hostages out of the students' grasp. They had to be freed whether Khomeini liked it or not.

Sadegh went to Qom.

"Agha, the revolution is in danger if we allow this to go on. If we allow the students to take power from the government, anyone can."

"The students are as much a part of the revolution as the council. They are followers of the right path," Khomeini intoned.

"Yes. But we cannot have two governments. A body can have only one head, one heart."

Khomeini sighed, and Sadegh believed he had made his point.

*   *   *

Dick and the crew and I now had an interview with the foreign minister. The four of us piled into the huge, finned, white Chevrolet with the electric-blue interior. We drove down the hill where boys washed cars in the dirty water that ran along the ditches. We passed huge modern banks and government buildings that flashed white with glass and steel. Then we drove by blocks and blocks of tacky little office and shop buildings. Many were held up by metal supports, and had only corrugated tin doors. Most shed plaster dandruff. People bustled down the streets carrying bags and baskets. Then the scene changed again and we were on the quiet, treed streets where the residences of the prime minister and president nestled behind protective walls. Across the shaded road there was a villa that had been the home of Ashraf Pahlavi, the Shah's twin sister. Next came the modern sweep of the tall senate building and then, farther on through more busy streets, the austere yellow brick bulk of the Foreign Ministry.

We arrived and set up our television gear. Sadegh ensconced himself in the leather armchair in the outer office, a portrait of Khomeini and a large globe behind his shoulders. He somberly answered Dick's questions.

Sadegh seemed once again in control. As Dick pressed the interview, Sadegh handled the questions with a deftness and assurance that belied his distress and anger. The UN commission *must* see the hostages as the council had agreed, he said.

Would he use force?

"Let's not speculate now," he soothed.

And what about the three hostages in the ministry?

"They're up there," he said, raising his eyebrows slightly and smiling. "Jogging. They're better off there. No, I won't hand them over."

When will the visit to the hostages take place?

"Tonight that will be decided by the council, but even after the hostages are transferred to the jurisdiction of the council, parliament will most probably decide what to do."

Sadegh motioned me into his inner office. This luxurious room was by now familiar to me. Each day I came here to discuss the day's events. Sadegh now told me the students had put Khomeini up to the business about the parliament.

"He doesn't know who to believe," Sadegh told me.

"Are you sure he didn't set it up?" I pressed, ever cynical about his damned Imam.

"No, no. You don't understand."

"I don't," I said. But in truth I did. I understood all too well.

On February 23, the five men of the UN commission arrived in a flurry of media shouting, television lights and optimism. Their first stop was to be the Foreign Ministry to meet Sadegh.

When the commission arrived, they found Sadegh with two men. But Sadegh did not introduce Hector Villalon and Christian Bourguet, nor did he reveal to the commission that the two were already deeply involved in trying to negotiate the crisis. The five commission members, already offended because Ghotbzadeh had kept them waiting, were further alienated. But the Syrian, Adib Daoudy, thought it best to indicate the commission's optimism that the Scenario might work. To his astonishment, Sadegh said, ''There is no Scenario.''

Sadegh was hedging his bets now. He hoped the commission would go along with the change in script. Khomeini's announcement that the parliament would decide the hostage crisis meant that he could no longer carry off the scenario worked out with Hamilton Jordan. Surely they could see that. But he could not say so in so many words. All he could do was say there was no scenario and hope for the best.

But the commissioners were appalled. Was this all a trick?

They left to talk to Bani Sadr, who assured them there *was* a scenario. When they got back to Sadegh, he replied, ''Bani Sadr can say what he likes, I don't depend on him.'' It was an extraordinary reply from the president's foreign minister. But it was typical of these two: as usual, Sadegh had been acting on his own. Bani Sadr was furious at his secret meeting with Jordan.

Discouraged, the commission retired to their hotel. At least they were still being told by all members of this bizarre government that they could see the hostages. Only Daoudy doubted this. With his greater insight into the politics of the Middle East, he saw that even the liberals on the council were split and could not be counted on to vote together. And he had met Beheshti and had concluded that until Beheshti was firmly in power there would be no solution to the crisis.

The poor commission was lost in the looking-glass world, where things worked backward: judgment first, then investigation.

The media dogged the commissioners' footsteps even though we all saw the writing on the wall. The commission had become a football for the various factions. They listened to victims of SAVAK, but were not allowed to see the hostages. The students said they could talk to the hostages, and then the next day changed their

minds. Sadegh railed against the students, calling them communists and zionists. Khomeini said the commission would see the
hostages, and Bani Sadr announced that the final decision would
be up to the Revolutionary Council.

Sadegh was beside himself. Just when they had seemed to be
getting somewhere, Bani Sadr decided to use the hostage crisis,
too. Beheshti blocked a solution until it could be *his* solution, and
now Bani Sadr was doing the same. Couldn't Bani Sadr see that
they had to get out of the hostage mess *now*?

In the meantime, we journalists milled about the lobby of the
Teheran Hilton, drinking innumerable cups of strong coffee or tea
from huge brass samovars, eating little cakes and waiting for the
UN spokesman to hand us the day's few crumbs of information
and double-talk.

For days Khomeini wavered. The students took full advantage
of the time by refusing to allow the commission to see the hostages
until *after* it released a report to the UN damning the role of the
United States in Iran.

At last Khomeini stirred.

"The Imam wants the council to take full responsibility for the
hostages," Sadegh announced as he arrived at Bani Sadr's office.

"He told you this?"

"Yes, just now."

Bani Sadr raised an eyebrow. "Did he tell you he'd already suggested once that the president be responsible?"

"No, he didn't," Sadegh replied warily.

"Well, he did," Bani Sadr insisted. "And then, when he saw
from my acceptance that I thought it would do me a lot of good to
solve the crisis, he reneged. He had thought that solving the crisis
would ruin me. He's ready to use any opportunity he sees to erode
us."

"I don't believe it."

"As you like, but it's the truth. So now he wants to saddle the
council with it. All right. But he'd better let us solve it."

After Sadegh had left, Bani Sadr called Ahmad Khomeini, who
confirmed that his father wanted the council to take over the hostages. They were to be handed over to the foreign minister.

In the silence of his office, Sadegh ruminated, softly clicking the
beads of the *tasbih* over and over while Christian Bourguet and Hector Villalon listened.

Then, looking around thoughtfully, he said simply, "We'll have to get everything here ready for the hostages' arrival."

"Do you really believe they'll hand them over?" Hector asked.

Sadegh shrugged. "Who knows. But I'll do everything in my power to make them. We can't let the students keep them forever. It's not America that's being held hostage, it's Iran. They're hold-ing *me* hostage!"

It was true, Christian reflected. That's exactly what the students were doing, whoever they were.

Sadegh had the ministry prepared. Cots and armchairs were brought in, the halls were cleared and the windows painted for privacy and protection. "I want five helicopters, some decoys," he ordered. "And cars to leave the embassy as decoys, too."

As Christian and Hector helped Sadegh prepare, they hoped it would not all be in vain.

The next day, as they put on the finishing touches, a young bearded ruffian appeared at the foreign minister's office. Christian and Hector turned to watch as Sadegh greeted the young man stiff-ly. The young man, unprepossessing as he might appear, was now one of the most powerful individuals in Iran. Sheikoleslam was a representative of the Student Followers of the Imam's Line.

"Well?" Sadegh said.

"Everything is ready for the transfer, but we must have a letter from Mr. Bani Sadr as president of the council confirming the order to hand over the hostages, even if it was Khomeini's order."

Sadegh exploded. "It will be done regardless of any damn letter."

The student grew rigid. "You are appointed by the council only to act as a liaison for the transfer. We want a letter from the council president."

Sadegh looked at him with helpless loathing. He would have to get the letter: if he went to Khomeini the Imam would waver, won-dering why he and Bani Sadr couldn't just write a simple letter. The delay would be dangerous. Every delay was dangerous.

When the student had left, Sadegh called Bani Sadr, who agreed to send the letter. But an hour later the letter had not arrived at the Foreign Ministry. In a white rage, Sadegh called Bani Sadr again. Shouting every imprecation he could think of, he threatened to go to the Imam with details of Bani Sadr's manipulations against car-rying out an order.

The letter arrived almost immediately. But it was too late. Sadegh turned to look at the television: thousands were demonstrating against him and against transfer of the hostages to the ministry. He sank into his chair.

"It's too late," he muttered. "If we try to transfer them, they might be killed. And when Khomeini sees this demonstration, he'll back off the transfer. The council itself will have to take the hostages into custody."

Later, at the Intercon, Christian learned with horror that there had been no such demonstrations. The students had edited footage of old marches and broadcast it. But now they announced that the transfer had never been approved by Khomeini, and that Sadegh had tricked them. From the wall of the embassy, Khalkhali, Judge Blood, shouted that the students must not give in to liars and deceivers like Sadegh.

When the council convened again, the revolutionary leaders had to make their way through the crush of reporters lying in wait for them in the corridor that led to their meeting chamber in the old senate building. I buttonholed Sadegh when he entered. Our cameras were rolling.

"We understand the students don't like the idea of handing the hostages to you, that it's you personally they object to," I suggested.

He stopped and said with cold anger, "I don't give a damn if they do or not. They have to."

Sadegh was always so wonderfully quotable. The rest of the reporters scribbled his remarks down. One murmured, "Frankly, my dear, I don't give a damn."

"Would you agree to someone else taking custody?" I asked.

"Frankly," he replied with more of his old insouciance, "I was never so keen on seeing these guys after all they have done," he said of the beloved students. Then he added, "If someone else goes, I don't care. But they have to obey. About that, there are no ands, ifs, buts or maybes." With that, he strode down the corridor to the elevator.

The press settled down the hall to wait while the council met. Some journalists sat on the blue carpet while others leaned against the wall. Some had brought hot dogs and Pepsi. The guards, Pasdaran most of them, objected to our picnicking and ordered the hot dogs removed. But as a Pasdar commanded me to either cease eating or leave, I suddenly and irrationally grew defiant. I was tired of their constant and obstreperous tyranny. I made my stand over my hot dog. The Pasdar unslung his gun and pointed it at my stomach, yelling furiously while other reporters tried to calm him. I ate my hot dog as he twitched his trigger finger. When I finished, he simply left. But later, when I climbed on a chair to see over my colleagues' heads after the council had emerged, the same Pasdar returned and snatched the chair out from under me. I fell on the floor, marveling at the infantile lunacy of it all.

Jon Randal of the *Washington Post* looked at me briefly and said, "There's only one thing I'm sure of in Iran: whatever I write, it's going to be wrong." Then he turned and went back to pacing.

When the council members finally emerged, Bani Sadr announced that the council was giving the students twenty-four hours either to turn the hostages over or to allow the UN commission to see them.

I saw Sadegh and the black look in his eyes. "Mr. Foreign Minister, does this mean the government has folded in front of the students?" I called out.

His head jerked up. "No, no. We'll be able to work it out. The council has made a decision and it must be implemented."

He was prevaricating and I knew it. Sadegh had lost the battle in council. I felt guilty, trapping him with an unfair advantage, but I had a job to do and he knew it.

That night at Shin's, Sadegh looked at me with reproachful admiration.

"That was nice. I thought I was going to get through the reporters without anyone asking me that question."

I shrugged. "It seemed the obvious thing to ask. Revco's folded, hasn't it."

"Revco?" he said questioningly.

I smiled, "That's what the press calls the Revolutionary Council. And you're the Big G, or the Great Ghot to the Brits."

"The Big G? Really?" He was pleased. Sadegh appreciated the press's black humor.

"What about Revco?" I pressed.

"Yeah. They're finished. The government's finished and Bani Sadr is finished because he's too weak to grab the bull by the horns."

"If Revco is finished, that means Beheshti is having things his way, yes? He and whoever else is in his camp," I surmised.

"I'm still not sure Beheshti is really behind it."

"Who, then?"

"I don't know. All of them, but . . ." He stared into space, lost in thought, and running the *tasbih* through his fingers.

"Did they set you up to take the hostages while planning to have the students refuse?"

"No. Well, maybe. I don't know how much control they have over the students."

"Are they students?"

"Yes. Don't forget the Organization of Moslem Students is big and powerful. There are others at the embassy now, but the student organization itself is strong. It has been for decades, remember that."

"Then you're really cooked. Sorry, I should try to be supportive and optimistic, but . . ."

"Never mind." He leaned back and again sank into thought. There was something unreachable about Sadegh. I wondered if he kept his colleagues in this half-light.

Ahmad Khomeini called Sadegh the next day. "Father will announce that the transfer cannot take place until the UN commission makes its report."

Sadegh was again stricken. "Who tricked him into this? Ahmad, he mustn't do this! We had an agreement with the United Nations, for the love of God. Our word will be worth nothing. His word will be worth nothing!"

"That is father's decision," Ahmad answered without emotion.

Knowing there was no point in arguing with Ahmad, Sadegh hung up. The only chance was a resolution from the council. When the council refused to meet for a special session, Sadegh went to see the Imam.

"Agha, we gave our word. By all the laws of Islam, we cannot break it."

"Breaking a promise to the Western satan does not break divine law," Khomeini answered.

Sadegh could have wept with frustration. So often before he had been able to make the Imam understand the global political realities. He had even gotten him to grasp the fact that the Americans could not return the Shah. But here he was defeated. He could not conjure up the arcane arguments of Islamic theology that would change Khomeini's mind. He wasn't Beheshti, nor was he a mullah.

When I spoke with him on the phone, he was candidly grim. It was now or never. If they lost the UN commission, the government lost its last shred of authority.

"Sadegh, will you talk like this for the cameras?"

"No. It's too late."

"We can be there in ten minutes."

There was a doubtful pause. "All right. Be here as soon as you can. I'll wait."

Dick and the crew were out shooting some late footage. I grabbed a British cameraman and we raced to the Foreign Ministry.

We set up lights and a camera in the outer office. I settled myself opposite Sadegh as the cameraman focused on him and rolled.

"This okay?" Sadegh asked.

"Better if you sit up a little straighter," I suggested.

"And keep the answers nice and concise," added the cameraman. "You tend to wander a bit."

For the next forty minutes we conducted an interview whose political candor would have been rare anywhere, and was unprecedented in the Islamic Republic.

"The government is not in control," Sadegh admitted. It was all mostly the fault of the Americans for making wild statements and threatening drastic measures, he said, then quickly added that the fault belonged partly here in Iran among the Iranians, as well. He didn't care if the students objected to him personally, what mattered was that they obey the council. He continued to talk of his preoccupation with freeing the hostages and the need to end the chaotic situation. "The least the UN commission can do is stay and give it another chance," he said. "If they leave now, they will destroy everything."

"I've never heard you talk like that," I observed when we were alone.

"I never have," he answered. "You should interview me yourself more often."

In the studio, colleagues watched the tape in fascination as the network decided to satellite the full forty minutes of this new and ingenuous Big G.

Back and forth it went. Finally the UN commission packed its bags. At the airport, one of the students from the embassy rushed out on the tarmac, clutching a huge bundle of documents from the

American embassy. He shouted that they were valuable evidence of American crimes in Iran and he tried to thrust them into the hands of one of the diplomats. The diplomat refused the indignity and disappeared into the aircraft.

As the plane rolled down the runway, Sadegh and the student stood on the tarmac shouting furious insults at each other.

15

At the Iranian Ministry of Justice, a dozen learned magistrates labored to assemble a massive document: Iran's formal demand to the Panamanian government for the extradition of the Shah. Christian Bourguet and François Cheron assisted them, and in this effort even Ayatollah Beheshti was cooperative.

After enormous difficulties and lack of cooperation from Ambassador Amiralai on the translation process in Paris, Christian flew to Panama with the 400 page document on March 21, 1980.

When Hamilton Jordan arrived at the home of General Torrijos, he was surprised to find Christian Bourguet. The three men discussed what was now their mutual problem: the fact that the Shah wanted to leave Panama. Kissinger and David Rockefeller had advised the Shah to travel either to Egypt or the United States.

"Not to the United States!" Bourguet said. "The students will kill the hostages."

Torrijos took the cigar from his mouth and announced excitedly, "I can keep the Shah here, but I will not do it unless the hostages are transferred from the militants to the government. Tell that to your friends in Iran. Tell them they have twenty-four hours or the Shah will leave."

They then discussed the extradition ploy. Torrijos could not extradite the Shah because Panamanian law stated that no one facing the death penalty could be extradited to a country that had capital punishment.

"He could still be extradited," Bourguet said thoughtfully. "Supposing Iran announced a special law guaranteeing there would be no death penalty. Then Panama could deport him to Iran after all."

"Theoretically, yes," Torrijos agreed.

Jordan cautioned them. "You have to understand we don't go along with actual extradition. But if an arrest would help alleviate the crisis, there's no harm."

It was dawn in Teheran on Sunday, March 23, when Christian called Villalon at the Intercontinental. "Torrijos says the Shah will be extradited if the hostages are transferred to the government. Tell Sadegh he's got twenty-four hours to do it."

Sadegh shook off his weariness to grasp this new opportunity. He called Bani Sadr, but the president was unavailable, as were the rest of the council members. It was Iranian New Year, and they were away on holidays.

Then Sadegh called Jon Randal of the *Washington Post*. Randal was well acquainted with the dark intricacies of life from the Middle East to Capitol Hill and Wall Street. An article duly appeared in the *Post* that day reporting that the Iranian foreign minister accused Henry Kissinger of trying to stop extradition proceedings against the deposed Shah, thereby further endangering the hostages. Kissinger, it said, had visited Panamanian president Aristides Royo on the matter.

In Paris, François Cheron picked up the phone. It was Henry Precht, head of the State Department's Iran Working Group, calling from Washington.

"Monsieur Cheron, we need your help. The Shah is going to leave Panama. Can you help us? We need you to contact Iran."

"If you insist, but what can I do?" Cheron asked.

"Call Ghotbzadeh and Bani Sadr. Get them to make some sort of positive gesture so we can delay the Shah's plane."

Cheron could not believe his ears. "What kind of game is this? I'm just a French lawyer, and you are the representative of one of the two most powerful nations on earth. If you want to stop the Shah, stop him."

"Please. It's not that easy. We aren't the only representatives of America in all this," Precht said dryly.

Still disbelieving, Cheron agreed to do what he could. He realized that the other representatives Precht was referring to were not the hostages' families or lawyers, but Kissinger and Rockefeller. But what kind of gesture could be made? It was absurd.

All day Cheron, Bourguet and Villalon relayed messages between Panama, Paris and Teheran. It was not until eight o'clock that night that Villalon and Sadegh tracked down Bani Sadr. They met in Bani Sadr's office in his residence, where they also found the doyen of French correspondents and a close contact of Bani Sadr's: Eric Rouleau, of *Le Monde*. Bani Sadr was in his pajamas and was barefoot.

Placidly, Bani Sadr said he did not believe the Shah would leave Panama.

Sadegh argued that they had to get the hostages away from the students. If necessary, they should use force.

It would not be decent, Bani Sadr argued.

"Decent! Decent!" Sadegh raged. "What kind of coward are you? This isn't a book or one of your damn theories. This is our last chance."

Sadegh's tirade was interrupted by a phone call. Sadegh listened in silence, then turned to Bani Sadr in a cold fury.

"The Shah has left Panama," he said.

Bani Sadr shrugged indifferently. He had never believed in it all anyway. He went back to bed.

Sadegh was still fuming when Bourguet called him later that night. Henry Precht had assured him the United States would stop the plane in the Azores—if the hostages were transferred. Desperate, and grossly overstepping his authority, Hamilton Jordan gave the order to delay the plane in the Azores if. . . .

Perishing from exhaustion, Sadegh called Bani Sadr.

"He's asleep," said his guardian, "with orders not to be awakened. For anything, or anybody."

Sadegh had Villalon call Bani Sadr. To no avail.

In a final act of desperation, Sadegh had Bourguet contact Eric Rouleau to rouse the president, but Bani Sadr's guards were adamant. And so while Bani Sadr slept on, the Shah slipped into Egypt and out of their grasp.

As he fell into a defeated sleep, Sadegh's mind was wrapped in coils of frustration. Across town, I, too, fell into a deep sleep at the Intercon. I had been to a press conference with the Panamanians, covered some street stories, and made the midnight satellite feed. My own thoughts reeled in confusion as I sensed the myriad enemies surrounding Sadegh. My own dreams could have been his, or were they his?

The monster rose over the edge of his consciousness. A fabulous thing, black and breathing sulfurous fire, it sneaked up over the rocks of revolution to confront Sadegh. Six hairy legs with white claws carried its dark, scaly form, as its eyes of red and gold pierced the nebulous gloom where mortals looked, unseeing. Sadegh smiled at the heaving animal, unafraid, for this was his father, who, like Faridun, had changed himself into a dragon to test his sons and know their souls' courage. And as he dreamed, the dragon melted into the folds of black cloak and turban, peaceful now, no longer

*breathing fire. Sadegh went up and knelt before his father, who
reached out to touch his shoulder. As he touched, the son felt a
sharp pain of penetrating ice, and looking, he saw that his father's
hand was the hairy paw with white claws. Raising his head, the son
saw the red and gold eyes blinding him.*

* * *

Every day the press chafed in frustration. Afraid we might miss
some new development concerning the hostages, we were obliged
to stake out the American embassy almost constantly. Finally, the
members of the press agreed to pool resources and have only one
crew at the infamous gate. This left the rest of us free to go in search
of the revolution.

If a crew missed an important event elsewhere because it was
filming "embassy wallpaper," as we called the embassy stakeout,
it would be supplied with the footage of the missed event in time
to have it edited and fed to the "bird," the transmission satellite,
that voracious jabberwock in outer space.

In the northern section of Teheran I visited great mansions now
taken over by the komiteh and converted to orphanages. The former mayor of Teheran had been caught and executed and his family had fled. Now a wrinkled old peasant woman sat hunched in a
lawn chair by the empty swimming pool, smoke curling up from
the pungent cigarette in her brown hand. In one bedroom teenaged girls wrapped in delicately flowered chadors were praying
before a portrait of Khomeini and a leftover picture of Brigitte Bardot.

Normally, outsiders would not have been allowed to see, let alone
film, the girls at prayer, but our crew had gained their trust. When
the shrouded figures finished their prayers, they removed their
chadors to reveal Western dresses and laughing faces. They were
like any gaggle of schoolgirls. As a reporter, I was ecstatic: this was
what I wanted to show the audience in Canada. I wanted them to
see the common humanity in this looking-glass world.

When I returned to the hotel, I found my colleagues in their customary attitudes of depression and confusion. There were now
about three hundred reporters, photographers, producers, cameramen, sound technicians, translators and other media support staff
from all over the world lodged in the Intercon. All of them seemed
harassed and stupified. It was simply not possible to know what
was happening in the several corridors of Iranian power. As report-

ers gathered in small groups to trade their meager "factlets," it was clear that we were witnessing an internal power struggle of epic proportions, but it was unclear who was allied with whom.

Ayatollah Beheshti held a press conference in the Ministry of Justice each Wednesday morning. Sitting at a great desk under a clock, in a richly paneled office, he clearly enjoyed acting as master-of-ceremonies to the media crowd who answered his summons. He gravely stated the government's most recent conditions for the release of the hostages, then he hinted at a pending agreement. More often than not, he contradicted the president's official statements or simply altered them.

If one of us pointed out the contradiction, he would smile and say, "Mr. Bani Sadr may say what he likes," and carry on.

To Sadegh, Beheshti was, strangely, more generous. He defended Sadegh's premature announcement of the Shah's arrest in Panama. "I can state," he intoned, "that the minister of foreign affairs was induced to error by the government of Panama. They let him understand that by having the Shah under security guard, they meant he was under arrest. In that sense Mr. Ghotbzadeh declared correctly that the Shah had been arrested."

What was Beheshti's game? Why was he covering that particular flank? Was he, too, caught in a trap of his own making? Did he, too, now want to end the crisis? No, I decided. If he did, he would have worked with Sadegh when the UN commission had arrived. And *that* he had sabotaged.

As we left, I smiled bleakly back at Beheshti, who blinked like a lizard on a hot rock. He had every reason to preen. According to the remaining local newspapers, his Islamic Republic party was well on its way to sweeping the first round of elections and thus dominating the new parliament. The foreign press had trudged to some of the polling stations dotted about the city to cover the proceedings, but they returned unenlightened as to either the legality or the efficiency of the system. The only consistent fact appeared to be the presence of a mullah at each polling station.

Each day reporters attempted to simplify and communicate the complex developments to their faraway public. But no simplification could suffice. We felt we were madly flinging pieces of a jigsaw puzzle into the void with every news transmission. But since we didn't have all the pieces in the first place, we could never assemble the picture.

Part of the problem was our relative unfamiliarity with the terrain. Only one correspondent spoke Persian, and few in the press corps were experienced in the internal workings of the Iranian Shi'a mosque. American intelligence had, of course, encountered the same problem before the downfall of the Shah. Among the press, even the old Iranian hands were freshmen. The press tends to follow world events in deciding priorities, and Shi'a fundamentalism had not even been on the list when the crisis took shape. Moreover, foreign correspondents can scarcely be expected to speak the language of all the countries they wake up in. There is a basic arrogant assumption that we of the West can quickly grasp the essentials of these exotic boondocks. So here we were, working with translators, learning how to say *baleh* (yes), and *khahesh mikonam* (please), while learning the modalities of Shi'ism over breakfast.

When I complained to Sadegh that the press had to spend most of its time chasing false leads, he smiled wryly and said, "You have to learn that we Persians are expert at only one thing: starting rumors."

Once, as the poet Byron wrote, "The antique Persians taught three useful things — / To draw the bow, to ride, and speak the truth."

If SAVAK and its forefathers had taught them to fear speaking the truth, Islam had taught them to disrespect it. Ali himself, son of the Prophet, gave lessons on the art of the strategic lie, to protect Moslems from persecution. This dissembling is called *taqiya*, and is at the heart of the mosque. The end result was the suspicion, treachery and chaos of the modern Persia around me.

Khomeini believed *taqiya* weakened Islam. Instead he sanctified forthright betrayal, when he ordered fathers to turn in their sons, children to turn in their parents, if they were guilty of anti-revolutionary "corruption on earth." It was his New Year's message.

All the press's inadequacies were compounded by the Western media's insatiable appetite for action. If the day had been dull and insufficiently photogenic, television in particular was up a creek— but never without a paddle. "Well," said one network producer over the phone to the New York desk one night, "there was only the usual little dust-up at the embassy, but don't worry. We'll make it look like a war." And with judicious editing, he did.

Television crews and satellite transmissions cost each network upwards of $100,000 a month from locations like Teheran. And for that kind of money, New York and London want to see something every day. Pressed from all sides, journalists in the field go numb. Typically, this is the way it went as one field producer directed his videotape editor in a hotel suite.

"Okay. Give me ten seconds of Beheshti, a bit of the embassy wallpaper, some of the mobs there, then fifteen seconds of the slaughtering of the camel in the street, then John's stand-up. Say, did anybody see the Big G at Revco, today?"

"Nope."

"He's probably fed up. Me too. Let's get this thing done. Bird's up in half an hour."

Between the Iranians and the media a kind of symbiotic manipulation prevailed: supply met demand. At the embassy the crowds soon learned to rant and rave only when the cameras were rolling. On night shoots they would come to life as the lights from the sungun on top of the camera swept over them. Local entrepreneurs set up stalls in the avenue and hawked checkered PLO *kaffiyehs*, headscarves for the ladies, electric-colored socks and John Wayne brand blue jeans.

Many of the demonstrators were trucked to the embassy in shifts from factories and offices. Many were bona fide enemies of Washington, but the overall atmosphere was oddly festive. And everyone loved being on TV.

Inside, the students were deadly serious, but they too performed. They paraded regularly, and ostentatiously performed their daily prayers as a media rite. Without the cameras and the press, everything would probably have been conducted differently, but the two were trapped by a mutual dependency: the media and the participants — like the chicken and the egg — created each other.

From El Salvador to Beirut, journalists traditionally turn to alcohol in the evenings in order to relieve tension. But we had consumed the last of the Intercon's store — all that was left after the Hezbie enthusiasts poured all the evil spirits down the gutter in another media spectacular. So we were reduced to Coke (Château Khomeini Red) and Seven-Up (Château Khomeini White). Bootleggers supplied Johnny Walker at fifty dollars a bottle and some restauranteurs discreetly served "cold tea."

Seated at a table in one such establishment with my British cameraman friend, I ordered for us both.

"Will that be hot tea or 'cold tea'?" the impeccable waiter inquired smoothly.

Before I could reply, my uninitiated companion cried out, "Cold tea? Whatever would we want cold tea for? We want it hot, man, hot!"

Aghast, the waiter vanished. It took considerable effort to repair the error.

Reporting in Iran, like reporting in Beirut or El Salvador, became hard work punctuated by whatever fun we could dig out of it. There were dumb jokes and the typical cynical humor that belied the danger of the situation.

But cynical or not I saw American reporters weep in bewilderment as Iranians burned the Stars and Stripes. I had also seen them moved to tears by the victims of SAVAK, and I would later see them sickened by the spectacle Iran made of the American dead. Beneath the cynicism most journalists harbored a deep patriotism and a commitment to human rights. The black humor and hard shell usually protected a very compassionate, caring person. Good journalists invariably do care.

One of those who popped up regularly on televisions in living rooms around the world was the regular spokesperson for the students. She was a dour young woman with a horsey face that looked out from under a homely scarf. She acted as translator. She told us her name was Mary. When I asked her where she learned English, she replied, "Here, in Teheran."

That was a lie. My translator arranged for me to meet Mary's mother at her home just outside Teheran. Mary's real name was Nilofar Ebtekar and she had been a genuine student who had spent long periods of time in Pennsylvania.

Looking at Nilofar's hunched form and her miserable rabbit-like demeanor, I wondered what moved her. What stirred in her heart? What made her happy or sad? Did she laugh or cry? Did she believe in this twilight zone of bombast and righteousness? Had she ever had a teddy bear? A favorite dress? Did she write poetry, or like horses? Where was her humanity?

Mrs. Ebtekar, too, was a dour little cabbage. She spoke in the same soft but determined tones as her daughter. In her large, gloomy living room, she said she was sure that Nilofar was carrying out God's will as she had always taught her to do. America, Iran, all were in Allah's hands.

When I returned to the hotel, I learned that ABC had reported Mary's true identity that afternoon. Another futile day.

Almost every day I would find a phone message at the hotel desk from "Mr. Ghotbzadeh." The messages invariably read, "Mr. Ghotbzadeh asks you to please call." Ghotbzadeh, I might mention, is a most uncommon name, and Sadegh never hesitated to make certain he was fully identified. He was indiscreet as ever, flaunting and flouting.

I had not seen Sadegh in several days. A few times I had run into Christian Bourguet in the hotel. But even with Christian I was wary, distrustful of everyone when it came to Sadegh's safety. Worse, I was even distrustful of Sadegh. Surrounded by intrigue, I began to wonder if I, too, was being used. Rumors abounded of the amorous exploits of the handsome foreign minister, and I found myself looking at his secretaries at the ministry and wondering. When he asked my beautiful translator to help him with work one night, I fell into an angry turmoil. Vowing to break Sadegh's hold on me, I went to the more than welcoming arms of my British cameraman friend, my guilt increased by the fact that I was genuinely fond of him. Later, my translator sighed and told me Sadegh's invitation had been part of the Persian man's way of dominating by instilling doubt. She had refused his request. It was not a game I wanted to play. I hated loving Sadegh.

But when he called, I went to him like a cat to cream. Back at Shin's one night, I sank exhausted on the couch beside Sadegh with my head on his chest. We sat in silence. Knowing the burden of his thoughts, I had no wish to add to the weight. I left the journalist and the jealous female on the doorstep as much as possible these days, and avoided pressing him on events. But still there was a change in him, here in Iran, that tied my tongue and choked my thoughts. It was not the brutal streak I knew he had, the ruthless side of the revolutionary. It was a change that resulted in remoteness, a withdrawal caused by his awful dilemma and the collapse of his dream. Now, that chasm could not be closed even when I held him at night.

The Shah and the UN commission had both slipped through his fingers. I looked at him. He was so stern, yet so vulnerable, and I wanted him to understand I had no illusions, so I joked. "I love you even though you're a gangster."

He looked at me with a small knowing smile. "No, you love me *because* I'm a gangster."

The next day I was called back to Toronto. It was mid-March, the situation was mired again; the newsdesk felt it might go on forever.

Sadegh and I talked over breakfast.

"Will you come back?" he asked.

"Almost immediately, I imagine. The Americans are bound to try something drastic now. They can't leave the hostages to the tender mercies of the new parliament."

"They'd be crazy to try anything."

"What choice have they? I'll see you then. Meantime try to be more careful of the mullahs. I know you pooh-pooh Beheshti, but he's lethal."

Sadegh was somber and resigned. "Call me when you get back."

* * *

In the White House, Christian Bourguet sat despondently with Hamilton Jordan and Henry Precht. Christian was miserable. The Iranians were threatening to try the hostages in retaliation for the Shah's having "escaped" from Panama. Hamilton Jordan took Christian to the White House map room, a small room where the president sometimes held meetings.

"Welcome to our hero," Jimmy Carter said, arms outstretched.

They took a seat on a small sofa, and Carter listened as Christian launched into a long explanation of the political climate in Iran. He emphasized the fact that in Iran there was a struggle for power and that the hostages were caught in the middle of that struggle.

Carter could not understand why the Iranians wanted to punish the fifty-three Americans for what the Shah had done.

"Mr. President," Hamilton Jordan said, "Christian is planning to return to Iran immediately. Do you have any message for him to take?"

Bourguet shook his head at the naiveté. The Americans would never understand. As he left, Carter scribbled a note and gave it to him to take to Teheran. It said:

a. The United States wants the captors released unharmed — quickly.

b. When desired, the United States wants normal relations with Iran under the existing government, recognizing the results of the revolution.

c. The United States wants Iran to air grievances through the UN International Court of Justice or the media.

Bourguet handed Hamilton Jordan the president's note to read while he was on the phone to Hector Villalon, after he and Jordan had left the president's office. It was then that Jordan noted the president's error. In irritation, Jimmy Carter had written ''captors'' instead of ''captives.''

Then Hector Villalon decided to be creative. He wrote a letter that purported to be from Carter, acknowledging America's ''past mistakes'' in Iran. He sent it with a covering letter over his own signature to Sadegh. Sadegh showed it to Ahmad Khomeini, who immediately turned it over to the press.

The Americans were furious. Carter threatened more embargoes and expulsion of Iranian diplomats if the hostages were not transferred.

Bani Sadr threatened to arrest Villalon because he was ''a crook, liar and con man.'' ''Albala told him that Villalon was an agent of the CIA and the Argentinian Junta,'' Sadegh told Cheron when he arrived from Paris.

Cheron looked at Sadegh, ''Nuri doesn't like Villalon, but he did it to discredit *you* by association, for the party. Moscow doesn't like you.''

Villalon insisted that what he had written did in fact represent Carter's sentiments as relayed to him by Jordan. But the whole matter blew over and it was now Bani Sadr's move. He proposed to put François Cheron and the Swiss ambassador in charge of the American embassy. Cheron was helping Bani Sadr on the legal and financial ramifications of the crisis. But he was still Sadegh's friend. The absurd scheme was stillborn when Washington rejected the idea.

Following that, Khomeini was supposed to go on the air and make a mildly conciliatory speech so the Americans could respond in kind and ease the atmosphere for negotiations. Instead, Khomeini made another speech about the satanic American president. Fed up, Cheron and Bourguet both returned to Paris.

Hamilton Jordan called Paris. He, Bourguet and Cheron were all linked in a conference call. ''Are you both saying there's no hope for these negotiations? You won't keep on trying?''

Christian concurred miserably. There was no point. The Americans would have to try a more direct route to the IRP. Sadegh and Bani Sadr were helpless.

''Then it's war,'' Jordan said simply.

The words sent a shiver of tingling fear through the Frenchman's veins. Despondently, Bourguet agreed to make one more effort.

But it felt so useless now. They were all out of their depth. French lawyers had no business in these echelons. For that matter, none of them had. Sadegh and Bani Sadr were utterly new to the game. And Carter and Jordan were almost neophytes themselves. It was amateur hour, and the mullahs were masters of ceremonies. They'd been at this sort of thing for over a thousand years.

Carter finally decided to break diplomatic relations and impose a formal embargo on American exports to Iran. Summoned to the State Department, the Iranian embassy diplomats told Henry Precht that America was making a mistake. "The hostages were well cared for," said one of the Iranians, and "under the control of the government."

Precht looked coldly at the man. "Bullshit," he said, and left.

The men in the White House were desperate. Reluctantly, Carter admitted diplomacy wasn't working. How could it with this bizarre cast of characters?

Bourguet and Villalon looked more like a hippie and a riverboat gambler then credible mediators. No, that was unfair. They had both risked their lives to help. But the Iranians! A cranky old priest, a dithering president, a bunch of students. How could he believe a word they said? And they were always shifting positions. Bani Sadr was uncertain, nothing very presidential about him. Sadegh Ghotbzadeh was gutsy and had taken a bit of personal risk, seeing Jordan and all. But he was as quirky as the rest.

On April 11, Carter called his top advisers together. They would attempt to rescue the hostages.

In case all else failed, a rescue plan had been in preparation for some months. On April 16, the men in the Situation Room at the White House studied the maps, reviewing every aspect of the operation to be carried out by Delta Force, a unit of hand-picked and specially trained commandos.

Cyrus Vance watched his colleagues in angry misery. The plan was too risky and too explosive. He opposed the decision and told Carter he would resign if they tried it.

Carter himself had second thoughts. He decided to find out if there was any remaining hope of going the diplomatic route. Once again, he sent Hamilton Jordan to meet Sadegh, who was on another official tour. Shortly after Sadegh arrived in Paris, he and Jordan met once again at Hector Villalon's apartment. Sadegh was somber. There was nothing of the ebullient spirit that had characterized their first meeting. Both men knew that time was running out.

"A lot has happened since we last met," Jordan said, as they began their conversation.

Sadegh gave a grim smile. "Actual preparations were made for the Foreign Ministry to receive the freed hostages. We came so close." Then he sighed. "But not close enough." Before Jordan could say anything, Sadegh continued. He was deeply troubled by events, and he wanted to make sure Jordan understood the implications of the action taken by the United States. "It was a big mistake for the United States to break diplomatic relations with Iran. You have left Iran open to the Russians. My country will soon be filled with KGB agents." Sadegh was not trying to frighten or threaten Jordan. It was the simple truth as he saw it.

"What else could we do?" Jordan asked. "This mess had gone on for five months. We're sick and tired of —"

"I understand your frustration," Sadegh interrupted, holding up his hand. "I understand that President Carter is running for reelection. But once countries break diplomatic relations, it's very difficult to reestablish them."

Jordan had not come to Paris to discuss long-term problems caused by the current crisis. He wanted to discuss the hostages. "When do you think they could come home?" he asked bluntly.

"There's no chance of your people being released now before the new parliament is elected and organized. The Imam has left the decision to the parliament and that's that."

"How long will that be?"

"Months. The second round of elections, as you know, will be on May 16. It will take four, maybe five weeks after that for the parliament to organize." Sadegh understood the American's position. "We're doing all we can. Believe me. Don't do anything rash like attack Iran or mine our harbors."

"President Carter is not a militaristic man," Jordan replied quickly and convincingly. But he was uncomfortable. He didn't like lying to the man in front of him.

They parted, both knowing that the deadly game was going to enter a new phase.

Sadegh was planning to continue his tour with an official visit to the new revolutionary government of Nicaragua. In July 1979, only months after the Iranian revolution, the Sandinista Liberation Front had finally overthrown the American-sponsored dictator Anastasio

Somoza. But Sadegh's plans were altered when unidentified gunmen tried to assassinate Shahpour Bakhtiar, the former Iranian prime minister, near his home in exile in Paris.

Sadegh was visiting with Christian Bourguet at the Avenue de l'Observatoire when he heard the news. "Already some of the opposition are saying I'm behind it." He shook his head, weary of the tiresome, predictable turn of events. Then suddenly his mood changed, "Those idiots!" he exclaimed.

"Which ones?" Bourguet inquired.

"What's the point of killing Bakhtiar?" Sadegh asked. "Bakhtiar is nothing! This attempt just makes us more problems." He hit his fist on the chair in anger.

"You'll have to stay here," Bourguet said philosophically. "It would look bad if you went to Nicaragua."

"I know," Sadegh admitted.

But he did leave. The next day, Sadegh left for Teheran in the foreign minister's private plane. It was a relic of the imperial era, a sumptuous affair with cushioned alcoves and ornate plumbing.

As the plane approached Mehrabad airport, antiaircraft fire suddenly spurted up at it from below, narrowly missing the wings. The pilot screamed at the control tower over his radio and the firing stopped. The plane rolled to a stop on the tarmac and a ministry car pulled up beside it. Sadegh quickly descended the steps and slipped into the big car to join Shin, who had come to meet him.

Shin looked at Sadegh anxiously. "The airport authorities apologized. They told me it was mistake; they didn't realize it was your plane."

Sadegh raised an eyebrow, but said nothing. The car swung out and headed for the city.

"They are determined to get you one way or another," Shin said. "All of them, from the clergy to Tudeh. I just want you to realize that, and be especially careful."

The next day Shin joined Sadegh in his office at the ministry.

"Who tried to kill Bakhtiar?" Shin asked.

"Maybe it was staged," Sadegh suggested. "Then used to make trouble for the PLO."

Shin nodded. He was not surprised by the idea. They had once planned to stage a similar attack on Sadegh. It would have been used as an excuse to step up security, ostensibly against assassins, but in reality against the Pasdaran. It would have been good publicity, too.

Sadegh sat back in his chair, sinking into another long silence, smoking his pipe and clicking his *tasbi* beads between his fingers.

As they sat there, Jimmy Carter ordered the Delta Force into Iran. Eight huge Sikorsky RH-53 helicopters took off from the aircraft carrier *Nimitz,* and six C-130 Hercules transports roared off from an airfield in Egypt as part of Operation Blue Light.

PART FIVE

THE DEATH OF A DREAM

16

In Toronto the snows of winter had melted, the days had grown longer and the smell and feel of spring were unmistakably in the air. Tulips, iris and gladioli broke through the earth and created a profusion of color in the city's many parks. The hibernating populace were once again in evidence, brown-bagging their lunches on benches and soaking up the weak spring sun.

Near dawn on April 25 the telephone rang beside my bed. It was the newsdesk. "The Americans have crashed in the desert near Teheran. We're sending you back on the first flight."

I had told my superiors at the CBC of my dubious relationship with the Iranian foreign minister, but they gave me a vote of confidence and elected to send me back in, if I was willing. I was, in truth, frantic to get back.

Reporting on Sadegh's revolution was a professional dilemma and a personal problem, of course, especially now when I did not want to put in danger his efforts to free the hostages and end the internal crisis for the moderates. But he accepted the fact that I had a separate job to do, and that I would continue to point out the dark side of the revolution in my reports. The desk in Toronto seemed satisfied that I did not simply parrot Sadegh's views. Indeed, when one colleague later asked me about the potential for propaganda, I replied "Who do you argue with most? The one you love, of course."

Sadegh never tried to influence a report. On occasion, he gave me information, or made statements, that I was obliged to broadcast: he was the foreign minister, and what he did or said was news. Sometimes I wondered if he were using me to start a public rumor, but in fact he never did. When I made doubtful noises about one story, he looked at me straight in the eye and said, "I have never lied to you, have I? And I never will." It was the simple truth.

This sort of personal involvement by journalists has always been more common than people realize. Two of my senior colleagues in Ottawa were at the time living with powerful women in the government, with no fuss from the desk, or the public. This does happen with human beings, and it is trusted that we maintain professional distance whatever the personal proximity.

"But we crucify politicians for peccadilloes," said one colleague.

Not always, we don't. Most journalists know enough about the bedrooms of the capitals to mortify governments. But we often don't use this information. Dallying with paid enemy prostitutes or accepting payment for services under the table are conflict of interest. Love, on the other hand, is a universal conundrum.

* * *

In a few hours Americans would wake up and hear the grim news on *Good Morning America* and the *Today Show*. The whole world would learn that eight of ninety American commandos sent to rescue the hostages had died in a freak accident in the desert near Tabas. Three of eight helicopters had malfunctioned in a sandstorm. Reduced to a minimum force, the on-site commander scrubbed the mission. But as they prepared to lift off to return to the aircraft carrier *Nimitz*, anchored in the Arabian Sea, one of the choppers veered into a C-130 Hercules transport plane. The rotor blade slashed into the plane and both craft burst into flames. As the rest took off, five air force men and three marines lay dead in the sand at Posht e Badam, the spot they had designated as Desert One, 250 miles southeast of Teheran.

Gloom descended over the White House while the news media worked overtime to get all the facts.

Hamilton Jordan received a dawn phone call that morning, too. It was the Iranian foreign minister.

"Mr. Jordan?"

"Yes."

"What's going on?" Sadegh asked.

"We tried to rescue our people, but we failed," Jordan said quietly, ashamed of the failure. "It was not a military strike, and no Iranians were hurt. It was simply an effort to free the hostages."

"How stupid!" Sadegh exploded. "How stupid of your country to try this! You are going to get the hostages killed!"

Jordan was furious. "Stupid! The stupid thing is your government holding innocent Americans! The mission that failed should be a lesson, we're losing our patience. And let me warn you that if any harm comes to the hostages, Iran will pay and pay dearly!" With that, Jordan slammed down the receiver. He never spoke to Sadegh again.

Sadegh was appalled at what he saw as the Americans' duplicity and, indeed, stupidity. How could they? he asked over and over. In the middle of his own strenuous efforts to extricate them all from this horrible trap, the Americans had tried a dumb stunt, one that could easily get the hostages killed and send him to prison.

While Bani Sadr visited the scene of the crash and made ironic remarks about Carter's lack of respect for international law, Sadegh lashed out with genuine anger. He made a preemptive verbal strike aimed at mollifying the students. He did it to defuse any thoughts they might have about retaliation.

"It is an act of war!" he proclaimed on the radio. He threatened to set all the oil tankers in the Persian Gulf ablaze if the Americans made another attempt. It was all he could do. He hoped the students would contradict him, as they always had.

The students issued angry statements, but contented themselves with crowing that the American failure was a sign of God's pleasure with their actions. The hostages were dispersed to secret hiding places around the city.

Sadegh decided he could go ahead with his plan to tour other Middle Eastern countries, to mend fences and build alliances. He left just as I arrived in Iran with the film crew to cover the aftermath of the Tabas disaster. I had been sent back with Dennis and Bill. This time our on-camera reporter, whom I'll call Alvin, was only somewhat less difficult than Dick. Sadegh had approved our visas.

We arrived at the Intercon from the airport in time to join our friends from CBS in their suite as they screened the footage they had just shot. The videotape showed the charred bits of the dead Americans displayed in the embassy compound by Judge Blood. The Iranians had gathered up the corpses and pieces of bodies in clear plastic bags and then held a press conference. Judge Blood, Khalkhali, held up the gruesome evidence and poked at the bags on the floor. Presiding over it all was none other than Archibishop Hilarion Capucci, archbishop of the Greek Orthodox Church in Jerusalem and one of Christian Bourguet's old clients. The prelate had once been caught by the Israelis with a carload of PLO firearms. Christian had been called in to defend Capucci, and, predictably, he lost. The Pope had finally arranged a dispensation and Capucci was released from prison.

Capucci had originally come to Teheran to see what could be done to save the Christian schools. Now he was back to handle the matter of the American bodies. Both sides had agreed he should act as middleman, turning the bodies over to Eric Lang, the Swiss ambassador, who would in turn have them returned to the United States.

Hardened reporters turned in nausea as Judge Blood made his repellant display while Capucci looked on. Both men were adorned in their priestly robes. As we watched again and again on the monitor, the CBS producer wept. I asked myself what men of God are these? What sickness inhabits their souls? Their action went beyond ordinary vengeance and spleen, beyond politics, beyond religion. Their pleasure was a dark mystery.

I longed to be with Sadegh and to speak with him. I wanted to unburden my soul, hoping he could bring some light into this darkness. But Sadegh was in Kuwait.

* * *

Kuwait is a paradox, a city built in an essentially uninhabitable place, a city built with oil revenues. Many of Kuwait's population remember the days when drinking water was brought to the capital, Kuwait City, by barge from Iraq. Many more remember when the city was a tiny huddle of houses surrounded by a crumbling wall. But today it is a mixture. Gleaming new buildings contain apartments, stores and businesses, while the old city, with its typically Middle Eastern squat houses, tunneling bazaars and beautiful mosques, hovers in their shadows.

Sadegh's motorcade proceeded slowly toward the great Al Saif Palace on the waterfront. Suddenly, gunfire cracked across the front of the car. A Kuwaiti security agent reeled as he was hit. The driver leaned forward and stepped on the gas.

Arriving at the palace, Sadegh was hurried inside to meet a relieved Sheik Jaber al Ahmed al Sabah, the emir. But the assassins were not finished. As Sadegh prepared to leave the palace some time later, another car roared up to the front steps. The Iranians turned in horror as the car bore down on them, then hit them with a ghastly thud. As the car tore off, the tires screaming, guards rushed for the men.

The assassins had missed their real target. At the last minute, Sadegh had paused on the stairway in conversation with the emir. The car had hit two of his bodyguards, who now lay in agony on the pavement. Sadegh remained long enough to see that his men received proper care, then he went on his way.

When he returned to Teheran, he told his compatriots at the ministry, "It was nothing. Forget it."

The newspapers duly reported the attempt on Sadegh's life. The Iranian Press Agency claimed that the gunmen had disappeared into the Iraqi embassy in Kuwait, but the Iraqis denied the charge.

I heard the news of the assassination attempt and Sadegh's survival simultaneously. I was concerned but far from shocked. It seemed almost normal, part of the whole bizarre run of things.

I called Sadegh at the Foreign Ministry the day after he returned to Teheran.

"I'm so glad you're here," he said. "Can you come over right away?"

Our driver drove me through the hot, crowded streets then down a leafy avenue and deposited me in front of the Foreign Ministry. Guards in the cavernous entrance hall inspected my purse then escorted me upstairs.

When I saw Sadegh, I discovered he'd been through another metamorphosis. First, the exile had become a native. Second, the victorious novice had become an experienced victim, and now this proud and chastened man was returning to himself. He no longer hid behind his masks of Persian male or foreign minister.

We sat alone in his beautiful inner office at the Foreign Ministry. He told his secretary to block all calls, so we were uninterrupted during the hours we talked. And if he was more himself than he had ever been, I too was myself. At last I felt comfortable as journalist, friend and lover.

I sat on the sofa and Sadegh sat in the armchair. He finally spoke of his doubts, fears and profound pain. "I've never been lonelier in my life," he confessed as he looked down at his *tasbih*. "All this" — he gestured at the ornate office — "and it's the loneliest place in the world."

Once, long ago, he had been afraid of power, of holding office, of being in the government. I thought about that now. "But it isn't the loneliness of command, is it?" I asked. "It's the intrigue and betrayal. Sadegh, isn't there anyone you can trust?"

"No, not here. No more than Khomeini can. Actually there are a few I can trust. He has even fewer."

"Don't tell me you still trust Khomeini!"

"It isn't his fault. He doesn't know what's going on. They all lie to him."

"And he believes them because they're his religious brothers from the mosque. I gathered as much from Beheshti over a year ago. Sadegh, does Khomeini still have faith in you? Does he listen to you?"

"Yes. But I can't do enough."

In my mind's eye, I still saw bits of charred bodies in plastic bags waved around by the ghoulish Khalkhali. I told Sadegh about it. "It was horrible. It was sick. What *are* these people?"

Sadegh shifted in his chair. "Everyone is upset over eight Americans. No one cared for thousands of Iranians who suffered at SAVAK's hands."

"Oh, I know, I know. But that isn't the point. The point is the gruesome way they reveled in it."

"I know. But I can't do anything about that."

"Talk to the Imam."

"It's too late."

I changed the subject. "Who tried to kill you?"

"Who knows. It could have been anyone."

"Not the Americans, please. I can't stand any more 'American-plot' paranoia. Beheshti told us it was U.S. agents. Pretty funny from him."

Sadegh shook his head. "No way. Not the Americans."

"And not the Israelis," I offered. "They wouldn't have missed. How about the Tudeh?"

"I don't know. I really don't. But it doesn't matter. Probably Tudeh. Or maybe Qaddafi's people. Or the Moslem Brotherhood. Any of them." He shrugged again.

"Qaddafi? The Moslem Brotherhood?" I said in surprise. "Why them?" I knew Sadegh was close to the Syrians, especially to Hafez al Assad, and I knew that others like Beheshti were closer to Qaddafi, who was Syria's arch-rival in the area. In fact, the press corps had taken to calling Sadegh and his friends "the Syrian faction" and Beheshti and his friends "the Libyan faction." But it wasn't taken too literally because of the changing alliances in the Middle East. The term "shifting sands" is more than a literary metaphor, it is a political reality in the Middle East.

But the Moslem Brotherhood? The Moslem Brotherhood, or Ikhwan e Muslimi, was an Islamic fundamentalist organization that had been born in the prisons of Egypt in the 1920s, another reaction to repression and alienation. Yasser Arafat had come out of its ranks.

"Why would the Moslem Brotherhood want to kill you?"

"It's a long story," he answered vaguely.

"Because they're in it with Moscow," I suggested.

"Partly." He turned, suddenly disgusted. "Everybody's in it for themselves."

"What about Tudeh? What are they up to? They must hate you as much as ever."

"More than ever," he pronounced. Then came his most surprising conclusion. "And they're behind the hostage seizure. They'll cut us off from the States, then they'll destroy me and the revolution."

We parted and I returned to the Intercon to prepare for the satellite feed. But I was thinking how much the Tudeh and Moscow must have hated Sadegh. Sadegh's hostility toward the Soviet Union had if anything increased since his student days. He had watched as the Tudeh made a cynical alliance with the clerical party, the IRP, claiming suddenly to be devout and faithful. The Tudeh leader, Noureddine Kiannouri, appeared regularly on the university grounds for Friday prayers; the Tudeh helped the clergy organize SAVAMA, son of SAVAK, to help the mullahs destroy their common enemies: both the Mudjahedeen and the moderates like Sadegh and Bani Sadr.

And Sadegh had continued to incur their wrath. When the Soviet Union marched into Afghanistan in December 1979, Sadegh denounced their action. And as foreign minister of Iran, his denunciation carried some weight. In January he had attacked them again, pledging to do everything possible to help the Afghans.

The Kremlin cared a great deal about its reputation in the Third World, especially in the Middle East. It did not like to see its carefully constructed image as the champion of local aspirations trampled in the political mud. Relations between the Iranian Foreign Ministry and the Soviet embassy deteriorated, reaching a nadir when Sadegh expelled Moscow's first secretary as a spy, accusing the Soviet Union of unwarranted interference in Iranian affairs.

Relations did not improve when Sadegh met the legendary Soviet foreign minister Andrei Gromyko at the solemn occasion of the funeral of Yugoslavia's hero, Marshal Tito, in Belgrade. Seeing

Ghotbzadeh in the throng of dignitaries in the great hall, Gromyko arranged to be introduced.

"Don't forget," he said suavely, "We are your friends and neighbors along hundreds of miles of mutual border."

"Oh, I know. Just like Afghanistan," was the reply. "Don't worry. I never forget our neighbors."

It was later, in May that Ghotbzadeh became more a danger than a pest for the Kremlin. He took his crusade against the Soviet Union to the Islamic Conference in Islamabad. The white-robed and gray-suited representatives of the Islamic countries filed into the enormous conference room in Pakistan's capital. Saudi Arabia, Kuwait and Morocco presented a draft resolution condemning "American military agression against Iran."

There were stirrings when Sadegh arrived with a group of anti-Soviet Afghan guerilla leaders, listed now as members of the official Iranian delegation. When his turn came, Ghotbzadeh stood, and in an urgent, powerful voice exhorted the conference to condemn American aggression in Iran *and* Soviet aggression in Afghanistan, equating the two as classic imperialistic forces. Beyond that he called on representatives in the name of Islam and the laws of the Koran to stand up against the Soviet infidel who transgressed on Moslem land.

Everything he believed in hung on this vote. This was the test of his faith in the possibility of Moslem unity. Here in Islamabad he had worked without rest to achieve it, calling in all his past cards, counting on the friendships and alliances he had forged over the years in every corner of the world. And the cards came in. One of the most frequent visitors to his hotel suite was Saud al Faisal, the Saudi foreign minister whose vulpine good looks so resembled those of his great father. President Zia al Haq came, the ministers of Bahrein, Kuwait, Syria's foreign minister Khaddam, by now an old friend, and Sheikh Sabah from Kuwait.

Only Qaddafi's minister did not come to call.

The others listened and responded. Here, for the first time, was an Iranian leader prepared to join wholeheartedly in the Arab world. One who was flouting America, the Soviet Union and Israel in one grand design.

Washington and Tel Aviv looked on in vast displeasure as Ghotbzadeh emerged at the head of this consensus.

Moscow's observers watched aghast as the conference brought

in an unprecedented unanimous vote in favor of the Iranian resolution. Even their erstwhile Arab allies in the Rejectionist Front had been swung by the Koranic argument.

On July 9, Gromyko responded to Ghotbzadeh's assaults with a formal memorandum of protest from his ministry, a message of terse displeasure and barely masked menace.

Sadegh pondered the memorandum from the Soviet giant, and wrote a reply that did away with diplomatic niceties. He knew it was likely to end up on the ash heap of history but it needed to be said. He called it ''A Precedent for Revolutionary Candor in Diplomatic Correspondence: The Historic Letter of the Islamic Republic of Iran's Foreign Minister Sadegh Ghotbzadeh to the Minister of External Affairs of the Union of Soviet Socialist Republics Andrei A. Gromyko.''

The astonishing letter informed the Soviet leader that Iran remembered previous Soviet efforts to subvert Iran, its use of the Tudeh, its cynical collaboration with the Shah.

The Soviet Union, he said, was no less satanic than America.

He accused Moscow of supplying arms, satellite photos and money to Kurdish rebels in Iran.

He accused it of using agents in the Tudeh to sow discord in Iran.

He suggested that the motive behind Moscow's refusal to recognize Iran's abrogation of a 1921 treaty between Iran and the Soviet Union, by the terms of which the Soviet Union could intervene in Iran if the government in Teheran was threatened, was the Soviet Union's plan to use the treaty as a pretext for aggression.

He attacked the Soviet Union for its invasion of Afghanistan — adding that American protestation of support for the Afghan resistance was so much hot air. Washington and Moscow, he said, had made a deal, divvying up the world.

He demanded Soviet withdrawal from Afghanistan and an end to espionage and subversion directed by the Soviet embassy in Iran. He demanded accreditation of the same number of Iranian diplomats in the Soviet Union as there were Soviets in Iran, adding that if this demand were not met, he would close one of the Soviet consulates.

He ended his letter on a cordial note:

> In conclusion, once again I cordially hope that questions raised in this letter will be taken into consideration by the government

of the Union of Soviet Socialist Republics. It is in this manner that the way for the development and consolidation of bilateral relations can be paved.

With the assurances of my highest regards.

Sadegh Ghotbzadeh
Minister of Foreign Affairs

Gromyko was not pleased with this "revolutionary candor." Ambassador Vinogradov replied with righteous indignation. And, true to his word, Ghotbzadeh expelled over a hundred members of the embassy and closed the Soviet consulate in Rasht.

The Tudeh stepped up their efforts against both Ghotbzadeh and Bani Sadr. They brought their secret organization into play, using those whom they had prudently kept underground, including those in the armed forces who made up their military council. Their officers spread rumours against Sadegh through the ranks of soldiers and made public speeches against Bani Sadr.

Kiannouri, the secretary general of the Tudeh, went to Bani Sadr to whisper in his ear that Sadegh was a CIA agent. Bani Sadr told the communist leader to get out of his sight and warned him that anyone who thought, as the Tudeh apparently did, that they could use the mosque was dreaming. "It will be the other way around," Bani Sadr predicted.

When I talked about it with Christian, he smiled. "Oh, yes," he said laconically, "Moscow has it in for Sadegh all right. Especially after Islamabad. But I think the thing that upsets him most about all that is Nuri's betrayal."

I decided to find out just what Nuri Albala had been up to. Christian said he had informed reporters of the meeting in Paris with Jordan. One of those reporters was an old friend of mine, Christian Malar, from RTL radio. I called on him to find out if Nuri had been the source of the leak.

"Oh yes," he affirmed. "Albala called me to tell me Sadegh was meeting with Jordan. I told him I already knew, from my own American sources."

"You're sure it was Albala?"

"Absolutely."

The benefit for Moscow in revealing the Jordan-Ghotbzadeh meeting was obvious: scuttle talks, compromise Ghotbzadeh and the other moderates, cut off another avenue for the Americans, keep them mired in crisis.

As I was writing about it all so many years later, I decided to simply ask Nuri Albala.

He received me in a luxurious office on the rue de Rivoli. I recognized at once the tall, languid figure, the prominent eyes in the handsome face.

"So," I asked, "Why did you give away the Jordan meeting?"

He affected righteous disdain. "I had nothing to do with that."

Why did he choose to deny, rather than take credit for, what he did? After all, he had been openly a member of the French Communist party, and had performed a valuable service to his party. But he had since dropped his membership. Maybe the answer was there.

"Why did you break with the PCF?" I asked.

"Oh," he replied easily, "I've never broken with them. I'm not a member of the party anymore, that's all. In fact, I got in trouble with them because I was always a staunch friend of Sadegh's and defended him. They hated him. Moscow did. Or at least Moscow's men in Iran, in the Tudeh party, especially Eskanderi. He was the head of the Tudeh before Kiannouri."

"I know."

"Well," he went on, "I met Eskanderi once, and he was wild on the subject of Ghotbzadeh. Wanted him eliminated if possible. Kiannouri is less rabid about Sadegh, but they all hate him. And so did our party, the French I mean."

I said little more, thinking this over. At least Albala confirmed my belief that Sadegh had indeed earned Soviet hostility for his years of work against them. Now why on earth didn't the Americans figure that out? Because, I hypothesized, the Israelis told them the opposite, and the Americans believed them. The Israelis, of course, knew the truth, but Ghotbzadeh represented a grave danger to them: he was a *pro-Arab* Iranian leader. More than any of the others, he would take Iran on a course that would lead it away from its traditional working agreement with Israel, and into cooperation with his Arab friends in Syria and Lebanon and everywhere else. Carter's people apparently didn't believe anymore that Sadegh was an enemy agent. But others highly placed, did.

It was in the middle of this mortal combat Sadegh fought with Moscow that John Connally, former Texas governor announced that "a foreign government" informed him that Iran's Ghotbzadeh was in league with the KGB" or at least a marxist." I could only deduce that the informers were Israeli, as before. Connally refused my calls.

After the satellite feed, Alef came to pick me up at the Intercon for the long drive through the darkness to Shin's. For safety, Sadegh varied his residence. Usually we stayed at Shin's. Alef was despondent as he told me how Sadegh was surrounded by sharks in the inky waters of the revolution.

Later we sat having tea. Tension was etched on Sadegh's face. He seemed moody and withdrawn. He'd been playing a role these last months; he'd performed, acting out amateur bravado, for the Americans, the students, perhaps even for the Imam. But tonight he seemed to be more himself. He was facing the battle head-on on familiar terrain.

To lighten things up, I asked, "Is it true that the mullahs still indulge in temporary marriages?"

"They're the worst ones." He laughed. "Business is booming in Qom."

The practice of *sigheh* was a time-honored tradition of sanctified fornication by which the gentleman in question married the lady in question for half an hour, or a night, or a weekend, or a month, or whatever duration was desired. The arrangement automatically meant he became her provider and any children were protected.

While prostitutes were arrested, flogged and sent to be re-educated, *sigheh* flourished. Prostitutes were women of independent means, so to speak; *sigheh* preserved male supremacy. The mullahs liked it; they muttered pious platitudes about protecting the female, while fearing and loathing her and their needs for her in their bitter groins. The mullahs availed themselves freely of *sigheh*. As I lay with Sadegh, held him, loved him and was loved in return, I thought of the grim priests who would lash us and murder us for this, they who killed with such fierce devotion and hypocrisy.

* * *

Press coverage in Iran had become an elaborate game of hide-and-seek. The American networks were banned, but, ever resourceful, they sidestepped this obstacle by sending in non-American freelance crews who were accredited to sundry obscure European networks. CBS, for instance, sent in a British crew accredited to Nor-

wegian television. ABC was present in the form of two enterpris-
ing Greeks who pretended to be Greek television. NBC was less
colorful; its coverage was handled by the English Visnews crew.
No network had their star anchorpersons on sight, of course, but
they all got their pictures. This was accomplished by means of an
elaborate theatrical performance at the satellite studio every night.

"Okay," the Iranian controller would call, "who's first?"

"Norwegian television," the CBS man would answer, holding
the satellite control phone. "Hello, Oslo? Are you receiving? Okay,
roll it!" and the pictures would go on their way through the ether
to Oslo — and New York.

"Okay! Athens, you're next!"

And so it went. Sadegh loved it. In his inner office, he leaned
back in his chair, feet up on his desk, and laughed. "They think
we're stupid? Suddenly Greek television has thousands of dollars
to spend on satellites every night. Do they think we don't know
what's up?"

"It is pretty transparent," I answered.

"Of course it is. But we like it this way. It means we get the coverage without having the network heavies around." He grinned,
"It's terrific."

"And easier for the rest of us, too. The competitive fever is a bit
less intense without them. Much as I liked having them around,
it's less of a circus."

"Exactly."

Apart from those filming for U.S. networks, there were a few
Scandinavians, and my pals from Canadian Press and CTV.

Alvin was already badly disposed towards the "Big G," whom
he regarded as "that smug character" he had watched at home on
his television. But he *was* the foreign minister, so once again we
went to interview him.

When Sadegh strode into the room from his inner sanctum, I
could feel the impact he had on Alvin. As they talked, Alvin gradually succumbed to Sadegh's charm. Sadegh spoke with warmth
and strength, but, as was his way, he never reached out. He made
others want to reach out to him.

Perched on the edge of the conference table next to the camera, I
listened with increasing interest. Sadegh spoke in a way I had rarely
heard him speak to others. The interview had begun with a discussion of the crisis at the Iranian embassy in London, where dissi-

dents had seized several hostages, then it had progressed into a discussion of martyrdom.

"What is this great desire for martyrdom?" Alvin asked. "It's something we in the West can't understand."

Sadegh grew almost lyrical. "Exactly. You see, we believe in the way of justice. We believe in heaven and hell. We believe a man continues to live after life. Therefore, the ultimate aim, goal and aspiration of every believer is that his real life, perhaps for thousands of years, will be free and will be happy. Therefore, he is ready to sacrifice the very short time in the period of the history of mankind in which he temporarily lives. It's not the end of it; it's just the beginning, it's just passing by.

"This concept gives us enough spiritual power to accept death — not just accept it, but go toward it, to gain it as a salvation for all time, for eternity." Sadegh's voice echoed in the stillness.

Then he continued, "Since the Second World War, America has acted like a spoiled child that gets everything it wants. When it doesn't get what it wants, it brings out the marines and the guns. But the power of the United States can be resisted if you believe you must die many times. The Soviets are experiencing this kind of resistance from the Afghans now. This is spiritual power. Americans calculate in terms of dollars and cents, we calculate in spiritual values."

"What about the possibility of a major military intervention by the United States?" Alvin asked.

Sadegh waved his arm, an indication of his contempt. "We're not afraid of military intervention. We don't care about it. But we *must* break the impasse. I've said so for months, ever since taking office. People say I'm a hard-liner. I'm not. I know America. I lived there for twenty years, but I was born here. So I understand both countries. We need hard work, perseverance and understanding for a just and honorable solution to the crisis. Problems are the creation of men, and men can solve them."

Sadegh went on to confirm that he had defied the students and been attacked as a result. Then he avowed his undying belief in the priceless core of revolution. "Dictatorship disregards man. If you kill a million, so what? You kill them. In a dictatorship they're part of a machine. But if you create a man who is free, if you create thirty-five million of them, then that country is the richest in the world!" That was Sadegh's dream: to create a nation of free people.

Still struggling with the unexpected seductiveness of the man, Alvin added, almost as a postscript to the interview, "Now really, do you honestly believe in all that stuff about martyrdom?"

Sadegh smiled. "Yes. But I don't want to die in bed with my boots on." He turned slightly and winked at me.

"You are impossible," I said to him as we went into his inner office, leaving Alvin and the crew to pack up.

"I thought I was pretty good," he replied as he took me in his arms.

"You were." But where in Iran are there free men, I thought to myself. Where is Sadegh's vision?

His expression changed to one of sadness, as if he had heard my unasked question and answered it silently. "Oh, my beauty," he sighed, using his pet name for me, and holding me closer. "It's so lonely."

* * *

It was like living backwards. Archbishop Capucci, dressed in his regal religious robes, sitting before the cameras set up in my room, pontificating on divine justice and justifying barbarity; armies of turbaned mullahs with the latest automatic weaponry parading for Khomeini; Iranian air force Phantom jets overflying the city in an absurd show of strength and menace; filming in the slums of Iran where people lived in squalor beneath the shining Shahyad monument and the half-built luxury high-rises; buying a *chador* to wear as protective armor in the increasingly hostile territory; and Ayatollah Montazeri leading Friday prayers with an American M16 rifle. These were only a few of the assaults on our senses.

One night I had dinner at the French restaurant at the Intercon with some colleagues from the BBC and their amiable and intelligent young translator, Bahram Deghani-Tafti. Bahram's father was bishop of the Anglican Church of Iran. We discussed ways of escape for Bahram, who had been threatened by unknown thugs. The next night we came back to the hotel to hear that Bahram had been shot in the head on his way to the hotel from the university he attended. The BBC reporter who filed the story in professional tones broke down in tears as he replaced the telephone in his room. Others who had known Bahram sat stunned beside our BBC colleague.

The Shahyad monument rose straight from its gracefully curling base to overlook a ritual battle in what was now called Freedom

Square. The Mudjahedeen cheered the speakers at their rally, and the Fedayeen moved in to disrupt the proceedings with the Hezbies close on their heels. Suddenly, in the hands of the Hezbies there were rocks, clubs and guns. These they wielded in the name of the Imam and the Almighty.

Separated from my camera crew and caught in the changing fronts of combat, I crawled under a car as the rocks thudded and the clubs met skulls. Then, two feet and a gun butt appeared beside my head. A voice ordered me out, telling me I would be safer yonder.

"No, thank you," I said politely. "I'm just fine here."

"Get out!"

Hairy male arms hauled me through the hail of rocks. I had no idea who my captor was; there were no distinguishing uniforms. He marched me behind a small hut, probably a storage shed for the tools of the park's gardener. He held me at gunpoint to the wall, as a wounded demonstrator writhed and bled on the ground beside us. Three others now came up to us and conferred with my captor. Then one pulled a knife and held it to my neck.

"Let's kill her," he said happily.

"No," said my captor. "We have to have a trial first."

"Then we kill her," the other chimed in.

All of this was said in English for my benefit. The one in command turned on me.

"What do you think of imperialism?" he asked somberly.

On trial for my life, I answered, "It's a very bad thing."

"But what are *you* doing to fight it?" he demanded.

"I'm a journalist. My job is to report to the world about your fight."

"Are you American?" he demanded angrily.

"No. I'm Irish," I said, leaning heavily on distant ancestors. After Ken Taylor's escape with the Americans it was not a good idea to be Canadian. "Oirish, from Oirish Tee Vee. There, see, that's me crew over there." I waved madly at Dennis and Bill, who were barely discernible in the tumultuous mob. I fretted absurdly that if I didn't escape, we would be late for the satellite feed.

"Let's kill her," said the knife-wielder.

"No," said my captor who turned to me. "We'll drive you to your hotel. Come with us."

Fully aware of where the drive to my hotel could terminate, I shook my head. "Oh, thanks very much. But I can't leave my crew.

Oh, there they are! Bye now!'' And I ran, sprinted through the flying rocks, expecting either a tackle, a stone or a bullet to ground me. But nothing did, and I reached the crew. We all tore for our car and screeched away. Our poor young translator had been hit by a stone. He cowered on the floor, clutching his arm and crying.

At the Intercon, we frantically put together a report, adding the riot to other material Alvin had gathered. CBS was late, too, so, carrying their tapes, and with minutes to satellite deadline, I leaped on the back of a huge red Suzuki 1250 motorbike behind CBS's dispatch rider. The rider was a tiny fellow, like a jockey. As the thing roared out into the murderous traffic, I clutched his back. We made the twenty-minute trip to the station in seven minutes.

I jumped off and ran to the door, but a guard caught me across the collarbone with his rifle. Winded, I pulled out my press pass and ran inside to give the tapes to the censor. Ahmad the redhead was on duty tonight. He was young and officious, a revolutionary technocrat in training.

He looked and pondered. Then he put the tape of the rock fight in the bottom drawer.

"That can't go," he announced.

"Why ever not? It's just a riot, Ahmad. It happens every week!" I was frantic.

"It shows Iranians fighting each other," he replied, as he closed the drawer.

Sadegh had his frustrations. I had mine.

*   *   *

And then we had the elections. "A new pinnacle of unabridged anarchy," wrote Eric Rouleau, for *Le Monde*. Preeminent candidates were claimed by two or three parties each to ensure more votes.

The National Front claimed that seven IRP candidates were its own, and both Tudeh and Mudjahedeen announced Radjavi on their lists, in spite of their undying hatred for each other. Bani Sadr was suddenly proclaimed by the National Front, and the IRP hugged Bazargan to its cloaked bosom, after having denounced him as a "pro-American" reformist. With everyone claiming the candidates were theirs, it was hard to tell the exact makeup of the new governing body, causing one American to comment that it was only slightly less confusing than a California primary. The only certain result was that the mullahs had won the parliamentary election and the IRP dominated. In the new parliament, the IRP held 118 of the 229 seats.

Wild at having lost the presidential elections, the IRP had ensured that the parliamentary balloting would proceed differently. First, opponents were libeled in the name of Allah, then on election day voters were threatened, ballots destroyed, and those voting for the IRP got to vote more than once. Khomeini was more than helpful in aiding and abetting this farce. He disqualified the Mudjahedeen from voting altogether.

Bani Sadr's office was deluged with protests over the election rigging. But one testimony he received stood out above the others: ''People [were] forced to vote for IRP candidates through the use of deceit and intimidation. The judge of the Islamic Court disrupted the elections through coercion, mass imprisonment and murder. I am grieved to declare that at no stage in history have acts such as these been perpetrated. People did not expect the Islamic government to act this way.'' The cable was signed by Ayatollah Seyed Pasandideh, Khomeini's elder brother.

The marauding hooligans of the IRP went on a book-burning spree, and the fuel for their bonfires was the writings of Ali Shariati and Ayatollah Taleghani. The campaign against the universities was also accelerated, and Khomeini, who had come to power on promises of freedom for the universities, now declared that ''all troubles afflicting mankind have their roots in universities.'' The Hezbies and the Pasdaran attacked the campuses, tearing up books and burning entire libraries. They pulled the veils off the female students, screamed obscenities at them, then raped and savaged them. They split the head of a girl at Mashad University and as her blood poured over her face, they shouted, ''Kill her! Her blood is *halal!*'' *Halal* means religiously lawful.

Khomeini was destroying Islam itself. He was extinguishing every light that had shone in its halls and replacing it with his own veil of darkness.

That night, I talked with Sadegh about the rapacious mullahs and of course of Khomeini.

''But what about Khomeini? I know he believes in what he does, believes in his Islam. But surely his Islam isn't your Islam,'' I said, wanting confirmation.

''No. It's the man himself I believe in. You can't understand.''

That was the simple truth. Sadegh was a Middle Eastern Moslem male and I an Anglo-Saxon nominally Christian female. And between these two stars lay an eternity of the unknown. I regarded his religion with the eyes and soul of an outsider. I was still intrigued by its mystery and was alternately attracted and repelled by its depths. I always perceived as exotic what to him was a commonplace part of everyday life. Khomeini and Sadegh's relationship tore at me intellectually and personally.

We were alone at Shin's. Sadegh was dressed in his long brown-and-gold robe. He stood up and wordlessly motioned me to follow him to bed. I did as I was bidden. Once we were together there, the barriers were gone. There was nothing between or beyond us. "In all this," Sadegh said, suddenly, opening the doors of the mirror, "you are the only true joy I have known."

As he slept, I wept.

In a strange way, I felt as if I were in competition with Khomeini for Sadegh's heart and soul. I pulled Sadegh toward life, toward the temporal. Khomeini, Sadegh's dark fate, pulled him toward what I perceived as the darkness. How much simpler it would have been to battle another woman for Sadegh's love! That I could have understood, but I could not battle the black prophet of Islam who demanded not only Sadegh's spirit but his life as well.

* * *

It was a beautiful May morning when I left with Alvin and "the boys" for Isfahan, slightly over four hundred miles from Teheran. Isfahan had been the capital of Persia in the splendid days of Shah Abbas the Great. Shah Abbas had rid the country of the Turks in the north and, having done so, established his capital in the more secure city of Isfahan, where he ruled in glory from 1588 to 1629.

As we flew in, our cameraman filmed the spectacle rolling into view: Isfahan appeared out of the desert like an island in the sea, green sprouting suddenly out of the limitless beige plains of sand. In the shadow of an escarpment, row upon row of combat helicopters and Phantom jet fighters lined up on the tarmac at the airport.

We landed and proceeded to tour.

Shah Abbas the Great, for all his benevolent rule, was a man of his time. He ensured his longevity as king by having his sons killed, thus eliminating rivals to the throne. In Iran they tell the story of how he ordered his servant to carry out the ghastly deed. When the sons were dead, the shah ordered the servant to kill his own son, his only child. And the man did.

"That was hard, wasn't it?" the shah is said to have asked.

"Yes, sire. He was my only son."

"Know that if I had a thousand sons, I would kill them all for one more day of power," the shah proclaimed.

Fathers and sons, shadows of power, all seemed to float in the air and lurk in the corners of Isfahan.

At the Forty Columns, a stately palace in a park, I wandered in the antique chambers, discovering the craftsmanship of their architecture, the wood inlay and the beautiful paintings of life in the Persian renaissance. On one canvas two dancing girls in modest embroidered gowns bent like joyous musical notes, their long, braided hair rippling with rhythm. Around them, servants poured wine from long-necked flasks, filling the cups of courtiers dressed in peaked turbans and multicolored robes. Above them, on a low dais, Abbas was splendidly dressed in red, with the imperial peacock feathers in his headdress and a curved saber in his belt. Abbas knelt with his guest, a darker-skinned ruler who holds his hands outstretched to the shah, palms up-turned in homage, as the shah seemed to control a hint of a smile. It is a painting in which gaiety and dignity balance in an eternal rivalry.

Outside the pavilion there are really twenty wooden columns supporting the portico, but they are reflected in the long pool and thus make forty, the magic number of the poets. Another mirror.

In the park our driver, Nassir, insisted on offering us tea and a *narghil*, a cool water pipe. We sat cross-legged beneath the trees on the patterned carpet at the low table and drank sweet tea from glass cups while we smoked the cool, thick tobacco. Both tea and pipe were brought to us by a small boy who saw to these matters. There, in the quiet warm stillness, Iran crept into my heart.

For me, Judge Blood, Ayatollah Beheshti and the pious students holding the hostages — even Khomeini — assumed proportionate places in the great tapestry that had been Persia in the past and was Iran in the present. In this nation I had found the vibrance of past artistry and the generous warmth of people like Alef, Shin and others I cannot name because of the mad cruelty that has woven itself into their nation.

Until now this mirror world had bewildered and frightened me. Even the writing was backwards, strange squiggles going from right to left, silent to my eyes.

Now here in Isfahan, the city they called Half the World, I saw the lyrical beauty of the mysterious writing with plumes like horses' tails. I was beginning to learn this language.

I was beginning to see, not the surreal looking-glass world of Alice, but that of the Sufi mystics, who say that it is "the rays of the soul's mirror that bring the world to view." The Sufis were the other face of Islam, inspired heretics who couched their forbidden beliefs in poems of love. To love a woman was to love God. "To dance in the lovers' circle" was to take part in eternal life.

Here in Isfahan, I saw Sadegh's world, and learned to love it.

It was dinner spread out on a white cloth on the floor at the home of Iranian friends: great dishes of *fesenjoon*, chicken in walnut and pomegranate sauce, and *baghalipolo*, fragrant rice with broad beans and dill, which we enjoyed as we knelt and talked. Iran was driving up the Darband to have *chelu kebab*, mincemeat kebabs with rice, and *dourgh*, a cold yogurt drink, with friends. Iran was Sadegh sitting beside me in his robes, quietly running the *tasbih* through his fingers. And Iran was the blue sunlit silence of the Masjid e Shah, the King's Mosque, placid at the base of the Place Royale here in Isfahan.

To enter the mosque, a woman must wear the *chador*. Overcoming my revulsion for it, I donned my "black bag," as the crew called it, and stepped through the portals of the mosque into an oasis of ancient beauty and sanctity. The delicate turquoise, white and gold mosaics of the arches were dazzling in the sunlight that filled the courtyard. As I walked across the patio toward the central pool, the soft folds of the *chador* billowed slightly in the breeze. It no longer felt humiliating. It felt serene and private, it felt sacred. Inside it, I felt I was individual and inviolate.

I was grappling with this new sensation and my sudden understanding of the appeal of the drapery when I came upon Nassir returning along one of the small, dark corridors behind a prayer hall, having just finished his devotions. Perhaps cherishing notions that Western women are up to anything, he slipped over to my side and grabbed me for a kiss and a feel. And in my sacred bag! As I struggled to get away while holding the *chador* with one hand, the ludicrousness of the scene struck me and I started to laugh. Shamed, he scuttled away, but my reverie was broken.

We drove out into the dry plains and saw in the distance the prefabricated town built for the Russians who worked at the steel refinery a few miles farther out. We continued on to the refinery itself, surreptitiously filming the massive complex from the car window as our translator cowered on the floor, gibbering, ''They are going to kill us!'' A guard fired his gun in our direction and pulled us over. After inspecting our credentials, he ordered us to be off.

On our way back to Isfahan we drove off the main road onto a track that led into the trees and over a small stream into a village of baked mud and plaster houses. Girls rinsed laundry in the shaded stream; men and boys loaded wheelbarrows with bricks for a wall under construction and children ran about us ecstatically.

An old man came up to us; his kind eyes and lined face bore an expression of curiosity. He invited us to his home for tea and a pipe. His name was Amir, and his small house formed a square around a central yard, each room plain and clean. A verandah spread out from the largest of the rooms and there we knelt on a carpet, sipping tea, smoking a *narghil* and eating slices of flatbread and goat's cheese, while chickens clucked in a nearby pen.

The mother joined us with her four young daughters, who were all in full veil. Two of the four daughters tugged at me to follow them to the farthest room. There, a great vertical loom was set. From its base, like a magic garden, threads of hyacinth blue, marigold, fuchsia and leaf-green intertwined in a magnificent Persian carpet that grew on the loom.

The girls sat cross-legged before it and pulled me down next to them. They began lovingly to show me how they made their garden grow. They took one tiny thread at a time, slipped it around the strands of the loom, tied it in a timeless knot and pressed it down to hug the previous tiny thread. They showed me the secret of the Persian knots and we remained there together creating the garden while the others sat on the verandah. The girls laughed as I slowly and ineptly progressed while their fingers sang over the strands like hummingbirds. When I returned to the verandah, the talk had turned to the revolution.

''Khomeini.'' Amir shrugged. ''The Shah.'' Another shrug. ''They pass here like desert storms.''

Amir pressed a sheaf of golden flatbread on us and he and his wife wished us a safe journey and a long life as we left their village.

We departed their home knowing that this too was Iran.

When we returned to Isfahan, I interviewed the local mayor, a pompous religious civilian who spouted Islamic rhetoric, and we toured a textile factory. We went to the home of one of the senior clerics, Ayatollah Taheri, and were chilled once again by the compassionless righteousness of religious bigotry. And we saw and heard the signs of growing calamity, people afraid to talk openly, factories and shops closed.

Away from the eye of the political storm in Teheran, we could feel the revolution here as it was felt everywhere, diffuse but omnipresent.

That night we stayed in a nondescript hotel in Isfahan; the more famous regal one had been closed.

Dennis suggested we go into town to buy a birthday present for Bill, so I voluntarily donned my bag again to go shopping. Having no fastenings, the *chador* obliges the wearer to hold it closed by hand or teeth. This effectively reduces female activity, and the *chador* is thus a subtle tether, which restricts and trips its wearer, reaffirming the credo that the female is meant only for certain limited duties. But as I walked with Dennis across the Bridge of the Thirty-three Arches, and then wandered in the streets peering in the shops and looking at the wares of food vendors, I nestled in it happily. I was unseen and unknown. It was my buffer. Without it I was a vulnerable cipher in Babylon. Still wrestling with this elusive reversal in my own feelings, I went to see Sadegh as soon as we returned to Teheran.

I was leaving for Canada in the morning, called back now that the crisis once again appeared stalemated.

At the ministry, Sadegh worked with a sense of ceaseless futility to outmaneuver his adversaries. We talked of the hostages, agreeing despondently that they were at the mercy of internal politics.

"The whole affair has nothing to do with revenge for America's years in Iran — not anymore," I concluded. "Will the parliament put them on trial?"

"I don't think so. That's not what they want. They want to destroy me and the other liberals. When we're gone, they'll have no use for the hostages."

"They?" I repeated. "The communists?"

"The communists are part of it. But they aren't the only ones."

"But 'they' don't like you much."

"Not much," he said with a wry half-smile.

"And neither does Beheshti and his gang. Are any of them Tudeh?"

"No. Everybody tells stories about Beheshti being a double agent. Don't believe it. Those guys don't need to be agents for anyone but themselves. But Khoeini'a might be Moscow's."

"What about Dr. Peyman, the PLO dentist who is always out praying in the embassy yard with Khoeini'a and the students?"

Sadegh shrugged. "The PLO are getting what they can out of it now."

"I hate to leave you here. But when I'm here I don't know how to help you."

"Just come back as soon as you can."

"I'll be with you in my heart." I reached up to touch his face, brushing his temple. "You're so tough," I said. "It's always strange to find your hair is so soft."

"It's like my heart," he said with a sudden, lighthearted sorrow.

In his classic gray suit, Sadegh was irresistible. He bent to kiss me good-bye. I wanted that moment to last forever. I was afraid it would be the last time I would see him. Pressing my head against his gray jacket, feeling his heartbeat, I feared for his life. Before, he had pretended his enemies were not there, and as a result his strength was an illusion built on sand. Now he admitted they were real, and he was prepared to do battle with them.

The next morning at the airport, huddled on our pile of luggage and gear, I broke down and wept as I prepared to leave Sadegh in the jaws of the monster he had helped to create.

*   *   *

July 27, 1980. Gaunt and ravaged by cancer, sixty-year-old Mohammad Reza Pahlavi, the Shah of Iran, died in Cairo surrounded by his family and friends. The abscess on his cancerous pancreas had hemorrhaged, and the Shahanshah, Light of the Aryans, had succumbed to the darkness.

Egyptian President Anwar Sadat was seemingly the only ruler with the courage of his convictions. The Shah had been his friend, and Sadat had incurred deep hostility by allowing him to come to Egypt.

The worst of the Shah's pain was surely the utter collapse of all he had believed in and all he had worked toward. In his reign he *had* dragged Iran toward the twentieth century. He had improved education, built hospitals, set up land reform, modernized industry and emancipated women. But SAVAK, imperial corruption, militarization and the dizzying speed of it all had canceled out his advances. His own ego had blinded him. Instead of a regal death, for eighteen months he had wandered the world like a pariah, haunted by thoughts of American treachery.

"The Bloodsucker of the Century Has Died at Last!" screamed the Iranian news agency, the VVIR, formerly NIRT. Its new name said it all: VVIR stood for Voice and Vision of the Islamic Republic.

Sadegh was contemplating the irony of the Shah's death when Shin came into his office.

"Any word on who the parliament wants for prime minister?" Shin asked.

Sadegh laughed. "Judge Blood — Khalkhali — thinks he should be prime minister. The other night at dinner he told the Imam, 'If I were prime minister I'd solve everything wrong with the country and set up the economy so there wouldn't be any more shortages.' And the Imam smiled."

"The Imam smiled?" Shin asked in surprise.

"He does, you know. And he said, 'Sure, you'd solve everything by killing everyone. Then there'd be no shortages. You'd have it all to yourself!' Khalkhali was really upset. When I made fun of him he started to cry. He asked me why I didn't like him! He's always like that with me. It's so easy to get his goat."

"Are you sure getting his goat is a good idea?" Shin asked.

"Khalkhali's an insignificant lunatic who keeps trying to buy my approval. God only knows why. He was the one who arranged for me to rent the house. And that was after I said he was an idiot who knew nothing about military matters and should keep his mouth shut."

"So you made him cry again?" Shin asked smiling.

"Yup." Sadegh said with satisfaction.

Sadegh delivered one last broadside against the students in the embassy. He warned the nation on national television that they were not followers of the Imam's Line at all, but communists and Tudeh pawns who were using the hostages to destroy Iran's Islamic revolution by fomenting internal strife and bringing the world's condemnation down on the nation's head.

After much discussion, the IRP forced Bani Sadr to accept their choice for prime minister. It was Mohammad Ali Rajai, a rumpled-looking high-school math teacher whose sole government experience was as deputy education minister for one year. But he had more important qualifications in the eyes of the IRP. His revolutionary record was unassailable. He had twice been imprisoned by SAVAK, the last time for four years.

"Rajai," Sadegh announced to his friends, "is a nitwit. His government won't last two months. I couldn't work one day with him. But it doesn't matter because I'm going to resign. They'd probably remove me anyway."

Shin prevailed on him, "First you have to deal with the attacks on you from our turbaned friends. Montazeri has been ranting again. And the others have made a point of singling out your operation of the Foreign Ministry." Old Ayatollah Montazeri looked likely to succeed Khomeini.

"I know. My ambassadors are idling in luxury, according to them."

"They're after you for wanting to compromise with the Americans on the hostages."

Sadegh sneered. "Montazeri's a moron."

"True, but he's still dangerous. You must make a reply."

"I know. In fact, I'll have to. The bunch of jerks have summoned me to parliament."

Dozens of eyes under curved rows of turbans watched with naked hatred as Sadegh entered the *madjiles*, the parliament. They radiated scorn as for an hour he spoke in defense of his record. Iran's foreign policy under his guidance was based on the teachings of Ayatollah Khomeini, he said. Alef, hearing this, groaned. Oh no. Imam this, Imam that. It was Sadegh's downfall.

Central to such a policy, Sadegh went on, is uncompromising opposition to both the United States and the Soviet Union. The Foreign Ministry had been purged, he said, with 30 percent of its 2,100 employees dismissed. Alef moaned.

Sadegh defended his handling of the hostage crisis, his firmness and patience. But his words were lost in the empty air of the domed room. And there was little left of the press to publish his defense.

Once again I interviewed him long distance for the broadcast we put together on the Shah's death. It was rumored that Sadegh had quit his job and fled the country. But I knew the rumor could not be true.

"No," Sadegh told me in a wary voice, "But I can't maintain any more twenty-four–hour days. Someone else will take the office, but the policies won't change much."

Sadegh sounded spent and sick at heart. I could offer no comforting words from the broadcast studio in Toronto. In our obituary on the Shah, I drew the parallels with Khomeini, his negative mirror image.

On August 18, Sadegh delivered an open letter to the members of parliament. It was a last plea for sanity in dealing with the hostages, a courageous argument to release them. Then he went to the Imam to hand in his resignation. He considered the Imam to be the only true chief executive.

The Ayatollah had moved back to Teheran from Qom after a serious illness complicated by a heart ailment. But he still lived in unpretentious lodgings, this time an uninspired modern apartment building in Djamaran, a neighborhood in northeast Teheran.

Khomeini greeted Sadegh with his customary frigidity. He was displeased with the resignation and tried to reverse his protégé's decision.

"No," Sadegh said, "I can't work anymore with these people. They're all liars and traitors."

"You are talking about my brothers," Khomeini snapped.

"Your brothers! These bastards lie to you and destroy our country in the name of Islam! They aren't your brothers!"

"I forbid you to speak so!"

"You have no right to forbid me!" Sadegh insisted. "It's the truth and you must hear it! Hadj Agha, you must! Before it is too late. I believe in you, you know that! See it; stand up to them!"

Khomeini glowered and huffed.

Sadegh left in angry gloom.

Alef, Sadegh and others of the group rented Sadegh offices on Shah Abbas Street. They decided to begin a newspaper, which they named *Valasr*, taken from a sura in the Koran that warns men to turn to the true faith when they are losing the struggle on earth.

But this effort, too, was thwarted by the mullahs. A committee at the Ministry of Information simply refused them permission to publish.

Then an opportunity to counterattack presented itself. One of Bani Sadr's men was now the deputy director of the VVIR, and he invited Sadegh to take part in a round table discussion the first week in November with other former directors of the network.

When he arrived at the familiar studio, Sadegh found he was the only one so far to accept the invitation.

"All right," he agreed. "We'll record anyway if you like, but don't air it until the others have recorded their parts."

The program was to be a discussion of broadcasting in the revolutionary republic. As the cameras rolled, Sadegh lashed out at the IRP and its imposition of Rajai as prime minister and at its subversion of all democratic process. He denounced the oppressive censorship of the regime and its rigidly controlled programming on the state radio and television. It was at best unbearably dull fare that an alienated population sneered at as "mullahvision," and at worst was propaganda and dangerous lies disseminated by power-hungry clerics. He called on the people to take to the streets in revolt.

When none of the others turned up, the deputy director edited out some of Sadegh's more explosive remarks, and put the toned-down tape into master control for broadcast.

Avoiding his own home, the deputy director went to Bani Sadr's and from there called Sadegh to warn him the interview was about to be broadcast. Angry, Sadegh told him to lie low.

"I know they'll be after our hides, at least for a while. I wanted to warn you," the man said.

Sadegh hung up the phone with a violent slam. "Our hides! Mine, you mean!" He was furious, convinced that this was just another of Bani Sadr's tactics to set him up for complete destruction. Sadegh decided to talk to Khomeini. But it was too late. Almost immediately his own image appeared on the television screen, vilifying the regime, demanding an end to censorship.

Sadegh sat down and waited for the inevitable.

*   *   *

Shin was at home on the evening of November 7 when a friend in the Pasdaran called him. "They've gone to arrest Ghotbzadeh" was his only message.

Shin raced to Sadegh's house near the Niavaran Palace. The Pasdars were already there, arrogant and surly in victory. A few spectators arrived and some television camera teams milled outside. Inside, more Pasdars made a show of searching the rooms.

They ignored Shin, considering him unimportant, though they arrested Houshi, another of Sadegh's friends.

In the midst of it all, Sadegh sat impassive as a stone. When he finally did speak, it was to ask permission to get his Koran and his *sadjdjadeh*, the soft white cloth which is knelt on for prayers. The guards hesitated, then gruffly agreed to this request, which they could not refuse.

The Pasdars watched as their new prisoner went unhurriedly to get the holy book and the sacred cloth. Could they have been wrong about him? Made more angry by doubt, they ordered him roughly to get moving.

The cameras and crowd jostled as the ex–foreign minister and his cronies were loaded into the Pasdaran van. Shin watched in despair as it roared down the road. Sadegh had not said one word.

And when they locked him alone in a cell in Evin, he still said nothing. He held his Koran, his *sadjjadeh* and his silence.

17

It was a cool, gray November day. I was visiting Iranian friends in New York City. The nutlike aroma of rice cooking issued from the kitchen as one of the women turned on the shortwave radio broadcast from Teheran.

I had left the CBC even though they had given me the coveted post of Montreal correspondent. I had tried diligently to drop the revolution and take up Quebec politics, but I longed to get back to Iran. For me it was an unfinished, if ghastly, symphony. I felt I had to see the revolution through.

Suddenly the woman nearest the radio hissed at us all to be quiet. Sadegh Ghotbzadeh, the announcer was saying, had just been arrested for counterrevolutionary activity.

I froze. Everyone was talking at once. I hardly heard them. There was nothing I could do for Sadegh — any effort of mine would endanger him — but I had to go to Iran. I immediately began making arrangements.

First I talked with the CBC and arranged to free-lance there for radio and television. Then I frantically called Mansour Farhang at the president's office in Teheran. Farhang had left his UN post and returned to become an assistant to Bani Sadr.

"We'll instruct our London embassy to give you a visa," Farhang promised. I took the next flight to London.

When I arrived on November 9, the functionaries at the Iranian embassy delayed and obstructed, sending me from pillar to post, from one office to another. I languished on a bench in the waiting room. I had reservations on an evening flight to Teheran. Finally as the hour of departure approached, I grew insistent and shouted at the bearded young bureaucrat who held my passport. At last he stamped it, handing it back to me with a snarl.

"I don't want to allow you in Iran," he hissed. "But I have to follow my orders from Teheran."

"Good for you!" I said in exasperation as I left for the airport.

In Teheran, Sadegh's friends were released after being held only a few hours. It was Sadegh the mullahs wanted. Friends set about pressuring for his release. Powerful *bazaaris* were marshaled. Several thousand people turned out in Teheran and Qom to protest Sadegh's arrest. They denounced the clerics who tried to gag the nation. Khomeini viewed the protest with alarm, but he did not act.

Uncharacteristically, Bani Sadr rose to Sadegh's defense. His newspaper, *Engelaab e Islami*, charged that Ladjevardi and Reyshahri, the Teheran prosecutors who had issued the arrest warrant, had no right to do so. "The country is headed for complete censorship," he declared. Then he announced he would not speak on the VVIR till matters improved.

"My newspaper will be next," Bani Sadr predicted darkly.

Bani Sadr's wife, Ozra, even called Batol, the Ayatollah's wife, to ask her to intercede on Sadegh's behalf. But Batol could do nothing. "Agha says it will do Sadegh good to sit in prison for a while," she reported.

Enraged, Bani Sadr went to Khomeini himself. "If you don't release him," he threatened, "I'll go to Evin and join him! And then you'll have a nice crisis with your president in prison!"

Khomeini puffed out his cheeks and blew. "He'll be released."

But Sadegh was not released till Khomeini had put his disobedient "son" in his place. Two more days passed before he sent Ahmad to Evin prison to order Sadegh's release. But Ahmad had his own ideas. He confronted Sadegh in his cell.

"Father says you're to be freed if you arrange for your family to guarantee you will appear in court," he announced menacingly.

"My family has nothing to do with this. You know that. And I intend to keep it that way. No deal."

Blatantly disobeying his father, Ahmad kept Sadegh incarcerated for another twenty-four hours until his prisoner agreed to his terms.

At the presidential office, Sadegh presented himself to Bani Sadr.

"See," Sadegh said cheerfully. "I knew the Imam wouldn't let them get away with arresting me."

Bani Sadr stared at him with angry indignation. "The Imam! Your precious Imam was the one who locked you up. *I* got you out! If it hadn't been for me, you'd still be in Evin. You'd have rotted there till Noh Rooz!" Bani Sadr went on to tell Sadegh all about his visit to the Imam.

Wordlessly, Sadegh headed off to the Imam's house on Djamaran.

He was ushered into the Imam's living room, and there the two of them regarded one another with suspicion and wonder. How had they come to this?

"I told you," Sadegh said, "that you have no right to order me not to speak. That is a political order. Since when does Islam mean total censorship!"

"I order you, and religiously I have a right to! What I command is to save the revolution and preserve Islam! And you will obey!" Khomeini stormed back.

"I will not! Not such orders, Agha," Sadegh pleaded, "Don't do this. Don't let them lead you to destroy everything."

But even as he said it, Sadegh finally realized it had not been the others. It was and had been Khomeini. The scales on his eyes were the skin of the monster. The beast spoke and Sadegh saw it for the first time.

"I want you to promise me not to attack," Khomeini said. "We need time. There are many enemies. Trust me. Obey me."

Hearing the hollow words, Sadegh nodded. "All right. For now. As long as no one attacks me first. See to it." But in his mind, Sadegh was already planning to fight the dragon.

*　*　*

Dawn was breaking over the desert as our Iran Air 747 entered Iranian airspace.

"Look! Look!" said the kerchiefed stewardess excitedly, as she shook me awake. Outside my window, flying wingtip to wingtip with us in the royal blue heavens was an F-14 fighter. Its sleek murderous lines had a strange kind of beauty. Silhouetted against the growing red-gold glow of the desert and the now lightening purple sky, it looked exquisitely deadly. The F-14 was our guardian and escort. Iran had been at war since September, when Iraq's troops invaded the new Islamic Republic.

As the light increased, I could even make out the face of the pilot of the fighter plane. With a jaunty wave, he suddenly flipped his plane over and sank from sight, only to reappear almost instantly on the other side. He leveled out and again flew wingtip to wingtip with the giant Boeing.

In the distance was Teheran, a cluster of tiny imperfections below the proud slopes of the Alborz range. As we flew in across the oil installations and descended over the Shahyad, the fighter pilot gave a last salute and veered away, disappearing quickly into the distance.

The city was hot and tense. The enormous burden of war had been added to the pressure of the revolution, and the whole populace seemed to be clenching their teeth. In spite of the emotional atmosphere, I found myself happy to be back, breathing the dusty air and being engulfed by the sights, smells and sounds of the city. Less appealing was the Intercontinental Hotel, now purged and staffed almost exclusively by komiteh agents. Visas were now severely restricted, so there were very few journalists.

As soon as possible, I went to see Sadegh. When I entered his elegant modern office on Shah Abbas Street, he held me as he always had. I breathed life again as I rested my head on his shoulder.

"I didn't think you'd come again," he said quietly.

"I wasn't sure I should. Things are so much worse now. The last thing you need is your satanic Western journalist friend." I paused. "But I quit my job, and here I am."

Sadegh looked at me in surprise. "Alone? No crew?"

I shook my head. "No. I'm contracted to do radio work."

He looked into my eyes. "You're very brave."

"No, I'm very stupid. But I had to come back. I had to see you. I wish there was something I could do to help you. But I know there isn't." As usual my thoughts and words were half-strangled and filled with contradictions. Was I a millstone or a life jacket? Did he even want me here? And, again and again, did love mean the same thing to both of us?

"It's so good to have you here," he said, "even though you shouldn't have come. It's not safe." Then he paused. "Not many do come to me now," he said almost to himself.

I realized that Sadegh had been abandoned by fair-weather friends who had been along only for the ride to the top. When the chips were down, they deserted. I knew he was faintly surprised that I had not gone, too. But I had always loved Sadegh, not the foreign minister, and now he knew that. Suddenly I could relax and speak from my heart to the man I loved.

"I had to come to be with you." He put a hand to my cheek as I touched the lapel of his jacket. "When you spoke out, did you expect Khomeini to arrest you?" I asked.

A look of hurt and anger crossed his face. "Yes. He'd already told me not to attack the regime. And I told him I was going to anyway. He doesn't like that."

"And now?"

"Now I've promised him I'll keep quiet. So, no interviews."

"Would he imprison you again?"

"Sure. And worse."

I looked into his eyes and suspected that at last he had seen Khomeini's true face. "So what are you doing?"

"Oh," he replied almost breezily, "instigating things."

We talked at length of all the ghastly developments and of the ongoing hostage crisis.

"Have you any idea who's controlling that?" I asked.

"The communists," he said, shortly.

"In the government?" I pressed. "It's said that Nabawi was, or is Tudeh?" Behzad Nabawi had appeared from out of nowhere to handle the hostage negotiations, which were now being conducted out of Prime Minister Rajai's office.

"He's one," Sadegh admitted.

Nabawi was a short unpleasant-looking man with penetrating feral eyes and a permanent three-day beard, a master manipulator who now gave regular press briefings on the progress of bartering for hostages. We learned he had been a Tudeh party member who served time in the Shah's prisons and emerged from his sojourn there with other enemies of the regime as a bitter firebrand.

I did not know it then, but his closest partner now was none other than Djalalodin Farsi, Sadegh's old adversary from Beirut. These two men now stalked him relentlessly.

"And the rest?"

"We're not certain of all the names yet. But we will be." Again, Sadegh grew opaque and wouldn't give me specifics. "I have to leave the office now. Can you come home with me?"

I had wanted him to ask, but I was still surprised he did. "Sadegh, it was dangerous enough before, but now . . ."

As always, he thumbed his nose at his enemies. "Nah, it's okay. But you had better come in your own car, a while after mine."

I nodded. There was something similar about us, something that went beyond our stubbornness. We faced each other from our separate strengths. As I looked at him, I realized he was my Persian mirror. Mesmerized, I again stepped into his reflection.

A great hulking figure opened the door of Sadegh's house near the Niavaran Palace. He was one of Sadegh's bodyguards, and he motioned me in and led me down the wide hallway to the reassuring comfort of the den. Sadegh dismissed the guard and pulled me to him.

"If I don't get shelled to smithereens at the war front, I'll get arrested by a mullah with a gun for incorrect behavior," I commented dryly.

"Are you going to the front?" he asked.

"That's what they pay me for," I answered.

"I'd rather you stayed here."

"I think it's probably more dangerous here than at the front."

We made love and as we held each other I felt oddly removed from him, even though we were closer than ever before. It was a feeling I had never had before. I had never understood his love for Khomeini, but now that he had lost that love's illusion a wall surrounded him. There was a brittleness about Sadegh that was new.

"I can't do anything, Sadegh, but I love you. That's all I can say."

"I love you. It's all right."

But I felt he was far away, thinking of hate.

Khomeini had lost Sadegh's soul, and I had won. But I, too, had lost. The heart of Sadegh's spirit had been his faith in that terrible father, and I now held in my arms the shell of a soul. Sadegh had to find the heart that was his own. No man or woman could help him in that. He was alone. That loneliness shut me out even as it brought me closer to his life. It was the last time we would lie together, the last time I would feel his life deep inside me.

Later, Alef and the others arrived to visit and plot strategies, greeting me as a member of the family. They entertained me with off-color jokes about the Pasdars in the prison, then they resumed speaking Persian among themselves. I watched Sadegh, hoping he felt the same life from me as I had felt from him. I wanted to smash the mirrors.

The next day when I went to the parliament to watch the clergy in action there seemed little to laugh about. Hodjatoleslam Hadi Ghaffari had set the tone for the chamber in March when he proclaimed from his seat, "We will murder any member opposed to Imam Khomeini's line of thought."

The semicircular rows of the parliament were filled with turbans. Looking down on them from the gallery above I was seized by the unworthy thought that they all looked like so many cowpats. Directly ahead was Hojatoleslam Hashemi Rafsanjani, now speaker of the parliament. He presided over the proceedings from his desk high on the front podium. Rafsanjani was middle-aged, a bit pudgy, and wore his hair in a distinctive fringed style sticking out of his turban. He seemed like a roly-poly schoolboy, as he was the only beardless mullah in sight. They called him *Kuseh*, the Shark, because his cheeks were soft and strangely hairless. Rafsanjani was originally named Ali Akbar Bahrami. He had taken the name of his native village, Rafsanjan, where his family had amassed a fortune by cornering the pistachio market. Rafsanjani's brother, Mohammad Hashemi, was well placed in the Foreign Ministry. There, he had been able to keep an eye on Sadegh.

Before the revolution, Rafsanjani had distinguished himself as a liberal thinker and Islamic revolutionary. He had even written a book on Amir Kabir, who was prime minister under Nasr e Din Shah. Now Rafsanjani wielded the power of the shahs, along with Beheshti and the other doyens of the IRP.

When I met the Shark later that day, he was inscrutable, saurian. It was a classic banal interview, a game of political hide and journalistic seek, held in his tastefully handsome office in the parliament building.

I was sharing the Shark with Mike Wallace and his crew from CBS's *60 Minutes*. The *60 Minutes* crew had just arrived in Iran, and Mike was in effect the first direct contact between Iran and the United States since the severing of diplomatic relations and the subsequent lockout of American journalists.

During my part of the interview Rafsanjani spent most of his energy making a play for my beautiful Iranian translator, concentrating on flirtatious asides to her while giving me evasive answers. He even went so far as to remove his cloak and sit with his chest partly exposed in the clerical equivalent of beefcake. But for the first time, when he talked with Mike, Rafsanjani had toned down his rhetoric and was sounding conciliatory, leaving doors open for a graceful way out of the hostage crisis.

My translator listened with horror as Mike's interpreter re-created every sentence, giving it a hard edge. Wallace grew ever angrier while Rafsanjani looked bewildered. Eventually we interrupted and explained the problem to the CBS producer. Inaccurate translation by unprofessional translators was a constant hazard of reporting in a delicate situation. But translation aside, Rafsanjani's conciliatory attitude did seem to indicate a new rift, this time within the IRP.

None of this, of course, meant that Rafsanjani was either liberal or moderate. As I watched his calculated manner, it was easy to remember that he had been the Interior Minister who presided over the first excesses of the revolution, that it had been he who helped Khodapanahi, Ahmad and Khoeini'a undermine Sadegh at the NIRT, that Rafsanjani rivalled Beheshti for ruthlessness.

In fact, there were now several rival clerical leaders. Hojat-oleslam Ali Khamenei (a lot of them, were not really ayatollahs but had accorded each other the title after the revolution) had from the beginning been a founding power of the IRP and now began to emerge in his own right. A thin ascetic looking man with a fierce mien, Khamenei was a righteous zealot who, like Khoeini'a, combined religious zeal with a puritanical devotion to some of the principles he had learned in early days in school in Moscow. It was an odd, powerful mix. Khamenei hated Sadegh with a visceral passion, both politically and personally. ''Why have we not executed this vile fornicator?'' he raved one night at a meeting of clerical allies. An article had appeared in Beheshti's newspaper linking Ghotbzadeh to a western female named Jerome.

Rafsanjani's enmity was cooler, calculated. If Khamenei and his lot were closer to Moscow, Rafsanjani was willing to deal with the Americans, the alternate route to power over his rivals. He would use the Americans as treacherously as the shark he was.

Then there was Ayatollah Montazeri, a genuine ayatollah, a fat old fanatic who led Friday prayers on occasion with an M16 in his hand. Montazeri was mocked as a bit of a bumbling fool by many who knew him and nicknamed him Gorbehnareh, the Tomcat. But he was nonetheless the likely heir designate to Khomeini, as senior cleric. Montazeri was an islamic evangelist who supported the efforts of their groups abroad, such as the Hezbollah in Lebanon, to spread the revolution by violent confrontation. Sadegh had fought a bitter battle in Revco over this, arguing that any effort to spread the revolution had to be done carefully, through education and diplomatic contacts, not to alienate sensitive Arab neighbours. But Revco's clerics and hardliners voted in the end to let Montazeri supervise a new department dedicated to new islamic victories abroad.

Later, Montazeri opposed some of the worst excesses of the regime within Iran, and even went so far as to help protect Bazargan from annihilation, but he remained an arch conservative.

As I watched the mullahs in action, only one seemed genuinely devoted to his religious faith: Khomeini himself. Arch politician that he was, Khomeini's politics served his implacable view of Islam. For the others, religion served to justify politics and power. As Taleghani had warned in his last speech in the graveyard, it was tyranny masquerading as God.

And the most political animal of them all was the redoubtable Ayatollah Beheshti.

Beheshti, known popularly now as *Rubah e Makkar*, the Tricky Fox, still held court at his Wednesday press conferences. His controlled performance was as elegant and as smooth as ever. As I watched him compose himself while we all milled about setting up cameras and microphones, I fancied he was restraining a smirk of victory. He could taste it.

Beheshti knew the moderates were as good as destroyed. It was time to settle the hostage affair and get on with consolidating power. But he, too, was worried.

Ronald Reagan had defeated Jimmy Carter in the presidential elections on November 5, 1980. He would be inaugurated in January. Beheshti wanted a deal with the Americans *before* that happened. Actually, he had wanted a deal before the elections, while Carter had his back to the wall.

Still, there was a chance that they might force major concessions from Carter. The negotiations were moving now. The Algerian government had volunteered to mediate. The Americans had sent Deputy Secretary of State Warren Christopher to Algiers on November 10, the day of Sadegh's release from prison. The conditions laid down by the Iranian parliament were essentially those Khomeini had listed in September. Sadegh looked at the announcement with bitter irony: they were exactly the conditions he had finally persuaded Khomeini to agree to, after convincing him to drop the idea of spy trials and making him see the futility of demanding that the Americans apologize for their crimes. Now the same four points were laid down by the parliament: return of the Shah's property, the cancellation of all U.S. claims against Iran, a promise to stay out of Iranian affairs, and a release of Iranian assets.

When Christopher met with the Iranians in Algiers, the only real problem was in the financial area. Iran's assets and the Shah's wealth could not simply be handed over while there were claims pending in the courts.

Beheshti was furious. If they settled on these terms, it would be a mockery. It was less than the moderates could have had earlier. He had warned his brothers that they should have made a deal before the election in the United States. Now they had to get out with whatever they could before Reagan took over, because Reagan would give them nothing. They needed time to regroup, but had none. The inner circle of clerics met at IRP headquarters. They would have to get the money.

On December 19, they demanded the frozen Iranian funds be deposited in the Algerian Central Bank and that the Shah's property be returned to Iran.

Washington refused.

Beheshti was livid, and beneath his anger he began to feel a tingle of fear. The tide had turned and he was no longer in control.

* * *

My interpreter and I discussed the negotiations as we walked back toward the hotel. We took our time and strolled down Vesal e Shirazi Street, stopping to window-shop and enjoy some time away from the politicians. For all the revolutionary mania we could still appear scarfless, albeit in demure street clothes. We were happy for a few moments off duty.

The streets were crowded and bustling with people. Merchants whose shops had been confiscated by komitehs set up stalls on the streets. Cobblers shined shoes while fruit vendors and grocers did a thriving business. Young men in black leather jackets roamed aimlessly and young girls tried to find *hejab* scarfs with a bit of embroidery or a spark of color. A great fat woman in a full *chador* held up a huge pair of bright pink bloomers, considering them with a judicious eye. Life went on. Farther up the street, music blared from dozens of stalls selling tape cassettes. American pop music had long been banned, but the strains of Persian folk music blended into Rimsky-Korsakov and the "Volga Boat Song" from Tudeh stalls. The sound of Russian music served as a kind of introduction to the new "Soviet fact" in Teheran.

Tolerance of the Soviet fact was also evident in the pages of the *Teheran Times*, which featured full pages from TASS on the glories of Bulgarian fruit production and the Soviet Communist Party. There were also stories on the Soviet-Iranian steel refinery at Isfahan and other joint ventures with the Soviet Union. It seemed that Sadegh had not been exaggerating his estimate of the amount of ground gained by Moscow since the hostage crisis began. I had no chance to see him, though, before we were to leave for the war front.

18

Forty journalists arrived bright and shining on a clear, cold December day at the military air base on Teheran's western outskirts. The Ministry of National Guidance had called a 7:00 A.M. takeoff to assure us of a full day at the front. Previous guided tours to the war between Iran and Iraq had been tedious affairs involving long hours in buses going to and from the front. This trip was billed as a deluxe return trip by plane, which would have us back in Teheran in time to file eyewitness reports of the carnage and still make it to the Intercon's French Restaurant for caviar before it closed for the night.

The entire press corps, Westerners, Easterners and Iranians, showed up to be informed that our one day would likely be closer to three.

"What? But I only wore my Hush Puppies."

"Jesus, I hope everyone has a toothbrush."

Again, Mike Wallace and the CBS crew were with us, and the Japanese were present in force. Some fifteen of them seemed to have some kind of permanent accreditation. We were joined by some twenty Iranian journalists and Dr. Delavar, our official guide from the "Ministry of Truth."

Delavar, the chief press officer, was a startling figure even in that oddball revolutionary ministry, which seemed to be staffed entirely by bearded teenagers and former bus drivers. He was lumpy in his green fatigues, and he had bulging eyes and a bizarre hairdo of stiff, bristling stuff that sat in clumps on his head. It was, I understood, the result of some surgery or transplant.

"Okay, everybody." He grinned. "Here we go. We'll try to make sure you don't get killed." Dr. Delavar loved saying such things — little blood-chilling remarks to remind us that there was a *real* war going on.

"Our takeoff has been delayed because the Iraqis are bombing the area and we could be hit," he announced with contentment. Then he smiled brightly.

Delavar did not fill us with confidence. He loved to talk about

244 The Man in the Mirror

his Ph.D. in chemistry from Berkeley, but that seemed wildly irrelevant to trips to war zones. With his American slang, crackpot humor and revolutionary outlook, it was like flying off to war with an amiable Islamic Zero Mostel.

After a two-hour flight, we finally landed at a military base in the west. On the ground, we were surrounded by the vociferous inhabitants of the town of Islamabad, which was not to be confused with larger places of that name. Dozens of small boys joined in a chorus and chanted, "*Marg Bar America! Marg Bar America!* — Death to America!"

Didn't they know that those were Iraqi planes that had bombed them? we asked. What's more, someone pointed out, they were Russian Iraqi planes. MIGs. "So what's with this *Marg Bar America*?"

"They say that America is behind the war, that Hussein, the president of Iraq, is an American puppet," army Colonel Behzadi translated for us. Our official guide through military roadblocks and red tape, the colonel looked more like an undernourished Elizabethan poet than a leader of the Persian juggernaut. His dark, sunken eyes had a perpetual sadness that matched his ascetic thinness. He was soft-spoken and sincere, and he worked hard to explain how the people felt.

"But why do they blame America? Why don't they think the Russians are behind it?" someone asked.

Several men answered at once. "We cannot see God, but we know he is there. Just so, we cannot see the Americans, but we know they are there."

Farther on into Islamabad we were shown another pile of bricks that had been a house full of people before it was hit by an Iraqi rocket. The villagers all climbed up on the ruins and arranged themselves in neat rows, like a church choir, to cry, "*Marg Bar America!*"

"At first," they exclaimed, "we thought the parachute of the rocket was a downed aviator and we went to help." Then, with horror, they had realized a rocket was on the parachute and it was death descending in slow motion.

Wherever we went, the chanting continued. But those who sang out did not seem serious. They managed to shout, "Death to America," without apparent malice to any of us. And strangely, they appeared to want our personal understanding and even our approval. Indeed, they seemed to like us — the agents of the Great Satan. The children smiled and laughed for the lenses of the imperialist capitalist press as we boarded the bus.

"*Khoda-hafez*, bye-bye," I called out to them as we pulled out. "Bye-bye," they shouted happily. And now, I thought, there is an entire village in western Iran that drinks Pepsi and sings out, "Bye-bye" and "*Marg Bar America.*"

Doubtless some were sincere in their feeling about America, but on the whole it had all seemed rather festive. Back on the bus, one of the army lieutenants accompanying us, a full-bearded revolutionary enthusiast, tried to start a conversation with Mike Wallace about the evils of Washington.

"It's not Americans we don't like, it's your government, see?"

"Yeah," said Wallace. "Well, I'm not so crazy about yours, either."

Mike's response was voted the quote of the trip, but as he gazed out the bus window the Islamabadians gaily waving goodbye and singing out "*Marg Bar America*" one final time, he turned and said, "But there really is something likable about these people, isn't there?"

We missed the front that day because Dr. Delavar, Colonel Behzadi and the rest of the Iranian contingent had to pray at a local mosque. By the time they had said their last prayer, the sun was sinking. And by the time the buses left for Kermanshah, it was dark.

Kermanshah, when we arrived, was totally blacked out. Not a light, not a soul.

Suddenly a sentry materialized out of the blackness and shot a quick burst from his automatic rifle. The noise shattered the dead silence as our supposedly authorized press bus was fired on.

"It's only the sentry shooting at us," Dr. Delavar said cheerfully. "I'll get out and talk, but don't you move or he might shoot you."

That night we were treated to a press conference with some army commanders, and the next morning we were loaded into the bus at six o'clock in order to find the war which had eluded us the day before.

Sar e Pol e Zahab was not much to begin with, and now it was decidedly war torn. Of the buildings left standing, not one was unmarked. Every one was ripped by shell holes and pocked with shrapnel. The village was completely deserted, except for the soldiers who were stationed there.

We were given combat helmets and loaded into pickup trucks in groups of six. CBS went in the first truck on what we all assumed would be the deluxe tour. Next Peter Bregg and Doug Long from

Canadian Press, some East Europeans and I were loaded into another truck.

"Bye-bye, have a nice time," the soldiers shouted.

"Hope you don't get killed," Dr. Delavar added with a grin.

"Jesus, do these people know what they're doing?" Doug Long asked miserably. He was already looking remarkably long-suffering as we started out across the dry plain.

After a time we stopped underneath some olive trees outside a bungalow that had been shored up by sandbags. "Two soldiers were martyred here yesterday," we were told as our guide pointed to dried blood on the ground.

We were hurried inside the bungalow as artillery began to pound closer. One of the soldiers started to explain how the Pasdars, the Revolutionary Guards, cooperated with the army when one of my colleagues complained, "Commander, it'll be dark soon. Can we please go to the front?"

Almost as soon as he asked, there was a stupendous explosion nearby.

"This *is* the front," the soldier replied.

We were all hungry, tired, dusty and disreputable-looking when we finally returned to the Teheran Intercon. After a hot shower, I knocked on the doors of the fellows from Canadian Press to rustle up some company for caviar.

"The Pasdars have been questioning our translators about you," one said anxiously. "They want to know if you're really Canadian, and if you are, why are you with CBS? They even asked if you are really a reporter."

I immediately called a contact with good connections.

"I've been frantic," he said. "I'm not sure, but from what I hear, they're getting ready to arrest you. They're going to claim you're Ghotbzadeh's CIA contact and get a confession from you," he added darkly.

"I'm just the excuse. It's him they want."

"It amounts to the same thing."

I went directly to Sadegh in his office on Shah Abbas. He blanched when I told him.

"You must leave immediately," he said, his face waxen. "These people have no morals."

I understood perfectly. A confession would be extracted from me, and they would arrest him. "I'll get on the first flight going anywhere," I promised.

"And you must not come back until we've changed the government," he said intensely.

"When will that be? How long will it take you?"

"Two or three months," he answered confidently. "I can't tell you any more and you shouldn't know any more."

"I know, but I've an idea what you're up to. Be careful," I said idiotically. On the wall in front of me was a portrait of Khomeini. "I keep it there," he said, "to remind me who the enemy is."

He took me into his arms and held me. "You be careful and get out of here as fast as you can. If you need help, call me."

"All right. Goodbye, my love, *khoda hafez*," I whispered.

"Call me when you're out of the country."

"Is that all right? Can we stay in touch from time to time? We won't be able to say much over the phone."

"Call my home number. Don't say anything direct."

"I won't call often, but I'll be thinking of you. When I call, I can't say I love you. Isn't that wonderful! Great place you have here." I was talking through my tears now.

"We'll change it."

"Goodbye, Sadegh." I stood nearly paralyzed.

"Goodbye, my beauty."

I turned and left. What price my victory over Khomeini? Sadegh wouldn't leave till he changed the government or died trying.

I hurried back to the hotel, but when I called the airport I discovered all flights were canceled for the next few days. The Ministry of Truth was insisting the press corps all go to the front again. Considering myself in far graver danger alone in the Intercon without my colleagues, I left with them for the relative safety of the southern battle zone.

They took us by double-rotor Chinook helicopter with a fighter escort to the south. We flew over the mudflats and water to the desert outside of Abadan, where the huge oil refinery is. Setting us down on a pad in the middle of nowhere, the big choppers and the fighter escort left us to our fate.

Dr. Delavar shepherded us into a dirty bus and we set off. To our left, white smoke rose from the burning Iraqi refinery at Faw. To our right, black smoke poured from fires raging in the Iranian Abadan refinery. More fire and smoke belched from giant oil storage tanks south of Abadan, and we could see the oil tanks themselves, some blazing, some burned out. They had melted from the heat into eerie shapes and now looked like grotesque amphitheatres.

The photographers and television cameramen came to life and started to gear up.

"No pictures here. No pictures!" Dr. Delavar called out.

"Why the hell not? This is what we came for!"

"Not yet. There's a military installation here. You can take pictures in a minute."

So we drove past the installation. "Okay, you can take pictures now," said Delavar. Then, waiting until the photographers were just about to shoot, he shouted, "No more pictures now!"

The photographers gave up. They wondered aloud if there were any jobs to be had in radio.

"Okay," Delavar announced. "We're going to the front lines now. People get killed up there, you know. So be careful not to get yourselves blown to bits."

We tramped off through a palm forest to the banks of the Bahmanshir River. The Iraqis had managed to establish a pontoon bridge there until they were blown out of the water by the Iranians. Across the river we trekked past the carcasses of Iraqi tractors, tanks and jeeps until we emerged on a plain, just behind an array of Iranian guns and mortars. Across the flats, the flashes of Iraqi guns could be seen as they fired into the refinery.

One young soldier, seated beside his dugout was having his teeth looked after by the company dentist. Another strolled past him, introduced himself as Majid, and talked to me about the conflict.

"I'm a soldier of Imam Khomeini," he said simply. "If I die — if one dies — it doesn't matter. We are all the same. We fight for Islam. It is the greatest thing to happen to Iran. And we'll win."

The roar of a metallic explosion cracked into our skulls, and we hit the dirt as the Iraqi guns trained on our position and mortar shells screamed and burst around us. There was no sandbag bunker this time, indeed there was hardly any cover at all.

Twenty yards away, a soldier was ripped open by shrapnel and bled to death quickly. As bursts of artillery fire shrieked across the plain, we ran back to the forest, falling flat on our faces whenever we heard a dull thud. This made our Iranian guides laugh. "Those are *our* shells — outgoing," they said. "Can't you tell the difference? Why are you so scared? We're not. We live here all day like this."

At the riverbank, another young soldier of the Imam shook my hand and solemnly thanked me for coming. His companions insisted that I pose for a photo with them.

By now it was too dark for the choppers to fly us out. Stuck for the night, we were taken right into Abadan. As we drove in, the city was like a tomb, guarded on one side by the burning oil storage tanks and on the other by the ferocious agony of the refinery, both still under constant Iraqi shell-fire. We were bedded down for the night in a small hotel in the center of the old town, right between the two targets.

The Jam Hotel had not been elegant even in its heyday. It was a dark place of evil-smelling drains and slimy sinks, a battered TV set and a blacked-out salon. We sat at masonite tables eating tins of eggplant, the only food available.

A night of shelling followed, our sleep disturbed by Revolutionary Guards shouting, "*Allah-o-Akbar! Khomeini Akbar!*" and "*La Illaha Il Allah!*" — God is great. Khomeini is great. There is one god only: Allah — as yet another piece of the refinery went to meet its maker. And with the dawn came a sandstorm, a *haboob*, like the one that brought down the American helicopters at Desert One during their ill-fated attempt to rescue the hostages. We waited two more days for it to end, but learned little, as the guards kept us under wraps.

By the time I returned to Teheran, my visa had expired. This meant I could not leave the country without a new one. Sadegh was beside himself, angry that I had not already left. We communicated now only through friends, but he railed at them over my delay. There had been no choice, our friends explained. And now I needed a new visa. "They are going to arrest you," I was advised.

Reasoning that whoever "they" were they would not necessarily suspect I was leaving if I asked for a visa extension, I went to the ministry, where I was taken to see none other than Hashemi, the brother of the Shark, Rafsanjani. He treated me coolly and asked about my work and my opinion of the revolution. The bizarre conversation seemed interminable. At last, with a penetrating look, he gave me the necessary papers, and in yet another office of bureaucrats I was furnished with the precious stamps.

At the hotel I made a concentrated effort to look normal and sound as if I had projects for weeks to come. This was for the benefit of the switchboard operator who listened to everyone's calls, and the new batch of waiters who scarcely knew how to set a table, but whose ears almost flapped trying to overhear reporters' conversations.

Friends pulled strings to get me on the British Airways flight to London the next day. I packed my bags in a dither of misery and fear. I hated to leave and I was terrified I would not be allowed to. I said good-bye to my Canadian Press friends and quietly went to the lobby, where I paid the bill with a normally friendly clerk. It was risky to check out like this, but riskier still to try to skip out.

The taxi ride to the airport seemed to last forever. Despite my sense of urgency I was sad as we passed the familiar streets and sights of Teheran. I knew I might well never see them again.

At Mehrabad airport travelers in various stages of desperation formed three raucous lines that snaked forward to the table where vigilant revolutionaries meticulously searched every suitcase and purse.

Minutes passed with excruciating slowness and turned into unbearable hours. I inched forward. Every second I expected to feel a hand on my shoulder and hear the snarl of a Revolutionary Guard arresting me.

I concentrated on behaving quietly and normally. I avoided catching anyone's eyes, while at the same time watching for any sign of an arrest party of Pasdars. I was still banking that they did not yet know I was leaving. It was a slim hope, but about as good as my chances of slipping out of the country through Kurdistan to Turkey, the way others had. A white Western woman was not easy to hide.

At last I was next. Then an uproar broke out. Foreign-currency export was drastically limited, and the British businessman ahead of me in line had been discovered to be carrying sixty thousand pounds, a serious infraction of the rules. While the inspectors were preoccupied with him, I slipped over to the next table where the guard barely looked at me or my things. He was too fascinated by the drama next to him to pay much attention to me.

At the next stage, a Pasdar girl in tunic and kerchief searched me with polite thoroughness. Suddenly I was seized by a ludicrous impulse. When I had arrived in Iran, my shortwave radio had been confiscated, "so you can't listen to Radio Baghdad," they told me. I had argued that I didn't understand Arabic and only wanted the BBC, but they had taken it anyway and informed me that I could have it back on my departure.

Now there was no time to claim my radio. But whatever the revolution had become, the Pasdar girl seemed luminously honest, a genuine scrupulous revolutionary. I gave her the chit for my radio. If she could get it, I asked if she would give it to my Canadian Press colleagues at the Intercon, who would bring it to London. She assured me she would.

I waved to her as we filed out to the tarmac. As I turned, I was relieved to see the British businessman join us, albeit minus his money.

We boarded and sat in tense anxiety as they held the plane on the tarmac without explanation. I conjured up images of Pasdars boarding the plane and dragging me off.

But it did not happen. The great engines started and the plane rolled down the runway and lifted into the air, rising away from the land where I had left my heart and soul. Sadegh filled my thoughts. I knew absolutely now he would take power, or die trying.

*　*　*

An hour and a half after my plane lifted off the ground, the Pasdars arrived at the Intercontinental to arrest me. When they found my room empty, they left in a fury.

The next day, Sadegh was summoned to Qom to be questioned by Khomeini and his wrathful clerics.

"This should be a pretty good show," Sadegh told a friend when the Pasdars arrived with the order for him to appear. "Come on along."

The clerics lined up before him in the shadows of the *madrasseh*, the school of theology, that nestled beside the soaring beauty of the Hadrat i Ma'suma, the shrine of Fatima, and the A'zam Mosque. This was Khomeini's fortress in the holy city of Qom, to which the Ayatollah had recently returned again.

Here, the mullahs grilled Sadegh on his relationship with the "Western journalist female."

"If you do not stop these wicked games that are against Islamic law, we will dismiss you from the Revolutionary Council," they warned. For the moment they skipped espionage and harped on fornication.

With his usual derision, Sadegh scoffed. "Well, gentlemen, just what do you think I was doing during my nineteen years abroad? Playing with myself?" The damn hypocrites. Not one of them could throw the first stone. Islamic laws, my ass.

"And besides," Sadegh added, "how do you know she isn't my *sigheh*, my temporary wife?"

But then the interrogators learned that their quarry had gotten out of the country. Without a confession from the Jerome woman, their case had no weight. They let Sadegh go home.

"They wanted to bring her in and trap her into handing me over," he told his friend. "But they wanted her for other reasons, too. She'd reported a lot on the role of the Tudeh and the left. They wanted her locked up. They probably actually believe she's a spy."

By then I had arrived in London, and a few days later my colleagues from Canadian Press arrived from Teheran.

"Some girl in the Pasdaran brought this and said to give it to you," they said, puzzled as they handed me my radio. I smiled. The Pasdaran would gladly have thrown me in jail for no crime, but still took the trouble to return my radio.

But there was no respite. Some of Sadegh's legion of enemies had concocted another genial scheme. A French newspaper published a report that Sadegh had received one million dollars from "American officials" for his efforts to release the hostages. A photocopy of the check, marked "Payable to Sadegh Ghotbzadeh" appeared beside the story. Underneath the illegible signature was typed, "For release of the American hostages." The thing was singularly crude. I called Christian Bourguet.

"Ah, *oui*, the check business. It's Amiralai."

I had completely forgotten about Shamseddine Amiralai, the disgruntled Iranian ambassador to France. "What on earth does he have against Sadegh?" I asked. "Besides the fact that he brought me to dinner. I mean what's his ideological grudge?"

"I don't know exactly. If you find out, tell us. But he's done a lot to obstruct Sadegh. Sadegh was rough on him, especially over the business of translating the extradition papers, but there's more to it than that. The clergy removed him from the post of ambassador, of course. He was National Front. But now we can't tell whose camp he's in. Unless it's Nuri's. Nuri Albala is, or was, Amiralai's lawyer, you know."

I thanked Christian and then called Christian Malar, the French reporter who had broken the story of the Jordan/Ghotbzadeh meeting, to see if he knew anything.

"Ah yes. The famous check. That comes from the Tudeh."

"Are you sure?" I asked.

"Absolutely," Malar responded. "They called me and told me they had something important to pass on. We arranged a rendezvous, and they sent two guys to pick me up. I recognized them as two Tudeh members I'd seen before. They blindfolded me and drove me to a house on the outskirts of Paris. And there, guess who was waiting for me?''

''Who?''

''Amiralai. He showed me the check and told me it had come to him in the mail when he was at the embassy. He felt it was his duty to reveal it.''

The bank on which the check was drawn declared it a fraud, the check being of a type out of use since 1972. But that made no difference to Sadegh's enemies. It was immediately reported in the clerical newspaper *Azadegan* and blazoned all over Iran that Sadegh had taken money from the Americans. The damage was done. It was part of a stepped-up campaign by the Tudeh to discredit him and pave the way for the coup de grace.

''I'm suing the French newspaper for a million francs,'' Sadegh told me when I called him. ''Nothing will come of it, but I'm suing anyway.'' Then he paused and asked, ''How are you? What are you doing?''

''I still seem to be doing news stories about you, like this story about the check. I'm also doing reports about the war and the hostages for the BBC and the *Times*. I can't quite seem to get out of Iran.''

''Don't worry. You can come back soon.''

I wanted to believe that, but I was afraid Sadegh was still underestimating his enemies. ''You seem to have an enemy in every camp,'' I said carefully.

''Just about.''

''Well, with this lot against you, you can't be all bad. I just hope you know what you're doing.''

''Don't worry.''

But I did, of course. They were moving in for the kill.

I decided to pursue the trail of Behzad Nabawi, who was negotiating with the Americans about the hostages. Whatever his allegiance, it was clear that the conditions he announced, such as the twenty-four billion-dollar payment, were added on *after* Rajai and the parliamentary committee had agreed to quite different terms.

I wrote the story for the *Times* of London, noting Nabawi's role and previous connections with Tudeh. I also questioned whether Beheshti had been the one who added the impossible conditions and sabatoged the negotiations.

It was a slow news day and the story led the *Times*. It was picked up by the BBC and then the wire services. By the time it reached the *Teheran Times* it had been embroidered and dramatized. The story the Teheran papers told was that Canadian Broadcasting Corporation correspondent Carole Jerome had said that Ayatollah Beheshti was a communist stooge.

"Well," said one of my reporter friends still in Teheran, "there's one of our dear colleagues who won't be allowed back here. Why didn't I think of writing that? A ticket out!"

Beheshti might very well have been a communist stooge, but I was more interested in Nabawi. Over and over, Nabawi was the one who made the statements that blocked progress. On January 15, 1981, he stated flatly that, unless Iran's unencumbered frozen assets were not deposited in Algerian banks by that Friday, negotiations would stop.

The men in the White House were desperate. It was Jimmy Carter's last week in office. He was obsessed now with the release of the hostages. He wanted to have his decisions vindicated. He needed to show that his policy of caution and diplomacy could have results.

Then, without warning, Nabawi withdrew Iran's objections and prohibitive conditions. And none other than Sadegh Tabatabai now worked for him to clinch the deal. Sadegh's old friend was now an intimate member of Khomeini's office. His sister was Ahmad's wife. Warren Christopher handled the last delicate negotiations in Algiers. The deal went through.

The Iranians made sure Jimmy Carter got the point, however. They held the hostages until the very last moment, and it was Behzad Nabawi who was instrumental finally in facilitating the deal, made with last-minute brokering from the Algerians. The hostages were released at the very moment that Ronald Reagan was being sworn in as President of the United States. It was January 20, 1981. Four hundred and forty-four days after the seizure of the American embassy.

I spread the pieces of the puzzle before me. Why Nabawi? What was really going on here? Did he work still for the Tudeh?

How did it all fit together?

In press shorthand Sadegh was part of Iran's Syrian faction because of his ties with Damascus while the hard-line clerics were vaguely referred to as the Libyan faction with links to Qaddafi. Was the answer there? I knew that Sadegh had been involved with Amal, the Shi'a organization in Lebanon. But even when I asked, he did not explain it all. I wondered. Israel, Syria, the PLO and Libya were all deeply involved in the Lebanese violence. Was the answer there?

Confused, and more and more frightened by the implications, I sought the help of Christian and François again. Once in Paris, I went as soon as possible to the old familiar offices on the Avenue de l'Observatoire, and there I learned the story of how the other Imam had vanished.

PART SIX

THE GHOSTS OF BEIRUT

19

Cheron leaned back in his chair and Bourguet relit his pipe. "Mousa Sadr was invited to Libya," Cheron began. "It was August 1978. He'd been asked to come for the anniversary festivities of the Socialist People's Libyan Arab Jamahariya. He'd come in response to a warm and friendly invitation sent by Qaddafi. Wait a minute, I have the entire file on it from the Italian police inquiry."

"Italian?" I said.

"Italian. Here."

He produced an eight-inch-thick pile of folders bound by a canvas strap. The story inside was the key to the mystery of the vanished Imam.

Mousa Sadr went to Tripoli on August 25, with two companions: Sheik Mohammad Yaccoub and Abbas Beddredine, both old and trusted friends. Beddredine was a journalist who had come along to record events. But he was also a confidant. He and Mousa Sadr were the same age, forty-eight. Each day's promised meeting with Colonel Qaddafi was inexplicably postponed.

That night, Mousa Sadr called Sadegh in Paris to make sure he was prepared for his arrival. It was with Sadegh, his friend and ally, that Mousa Sadr stayed on trips to Paris. On a previous occasion, Sadegh had even seen to getting him medical help in the French capital. "More than prepared," Sadegh said happily. "It will be wonderful to see you again. There's so much to discuss."

"Until then," Mousa Sadr replied.

Without telling anyone, Beddredine went to the Italian Consulate in Tripoli to obtain visas for Mousa Sadr and Yaccoub; oddly, he did not get one for himself.

On August 31, three men boarded Alitalia Flight 881 at Tripoli's International Airport bound for Rome, escorted by Libyan officials. At Fiumicino airport in Rome, two of the men waited while the third went to passport control to obtain a temporary transit visa for Italy. The officer checked his passport. It was Lebanese and the name on it read, "Abbas Beddredine." The man stated his destination as Malta and showed his ticket and a reservation for the next flight, AZ490, departing September 1. The officer stamped the passport with a transit visa and asked Mr. Beddredine where he would be staying in Rome. "The Satellite Hotel," Beddredine replied. The Italian official noted that on his forms.

A short time later, the receptionist at the Holiday Inn in Rome looked up to see two "Arabs" arriving. One of them came over and reserved two rooms. He was dressed in European clothes and spoke English, but the woman felt she knew an Arab when she saw one. Paying for ten days in advance, he went to the elevator.

On the seventh floor, the maid noted a tall Middle Eastern man in the long robes and turban of a priest. As she looked at him, another "Arab" emerged from the elevator with the porter. The second man was in European clothes. The man in European clothes stopped to talk with the man dressed as a priest. Then the priestly-looking man went into 702 and the other man entered 701. She had just started to clean when they both came out again. This time both were in European clothes. They took the elevator down.

The next day the maid went into rooms 701 and 702. She found the beds undisturbed and the suitcases unopened. Ten days passed and the suitcases lay unopened on undisturbed beds. The hotel management called the police.

When the police arrived they opened the suitcases and found a jumble of underwear stashed inside, along with a few innocuous letters and documents. And on the night tables, beside each bed, they found a Lebanese passport lying open. One passport held the name Mousa Sadr and the other Mohammad Yaccoub.

I was sitting on the floor of Cheron's office now with the documents in the bundle scattered about me. I asked François what happened next.

"Then all hell broke loose in this office!" Cheron said. "Sadegh stormed in here. He was absolutely frantic, and angry too."

* * *

"We have to do something!" Sadegh announced. "There's no word from Imam Sadr! The Libyans are lying! Qaddafi's saying he went to Rome, but he's vanished."

"Give me all the details you can, then we'll decide what to do," Cheron requested.

"Qaddafi's killed him," Sadegh pronounced.

"Possibly," Cheron replied. "But the first step is to get an inquiry going in Rome."

"No problem. I'll arrange for his son, Sadri to retain you," Sadegh said.

Cheron agreed. "And what are you going to do?" he asked.

"I'm going to see that bastard Qaddafi," Sadegh announced.

As his taxi drove through Tripoli towards the presidential palace, he sweltered and fumed in a hot rage. Qaddafi! Mousa Sadr should never have come here, not with matters as tense as they were in Lebanon.

At the palace, he waited, steaming. But when he was finally ushered in to see Qaddafi, his manner was controlled, even cool.

With his thick black hair and blazing eyes, Qaddafi was a singular figure. Paradoxically, the military uniform he wore made him look less dangerous than he was; it gave him the appearance of belonging to some predictable system. But Sadegh knew how dangerous he was. Qaddafi played his own game and he made up his own rules.

Two pairs of dark eyes fixed on each other. The door closed on Qaddafi and Sadegh.

When he returned to Paris, Sadegh said little about his meeting with the Libyan leader, beyond the fact that Qaddafi insisted that Imam Sadr had left after a happy send-off at the airport and boarded Flight 881.

"He's lying," Sadegh still insisted. "I want the Rome inquiry to go on. You go to Rome and I'll join you there."

The Italian police interviewed the Alitalia crew, the passengers on Flight 881, the officials at the airport and the hotel staff. Each told a plain, clear story. But when the witnesses were shown pictures of Mousa Sadr and Mohammad Yaccoub they all positively denied that these were the men they had dealt with. There was no resemblance at all. And none was as tall as Imam Sadr, who stook nearly six feet, six inches tall. Furthermore, Abbas Beddredine stayed at the Satellite Hotel, and took the flight to Malta.

But they did uncover one other interesting little tidbit, as they explored all avenues. On September 1, the Iran Air flight from Rome to Teheran listed three last-minute passengers, noted only as U.N.K., the official abbreviation for *unknown*.

Qaddafi was now claiming that he had been waiting for Mousa Sadr to show up for an appointment on August 31, and that he had waited in vain. His aides investigated, he said, and found that the Imam had left the country.

Cheron pondered the inconsistencies in the Libyan story. Either Mousa Sadr had gone off on his own and not met Qaddafi, or he had had an official send-off from the Libyan government. They couldn't have it both ways.

And where was Beddredine? Was he in on it? Or had he been gotten out of the way even earlier?

And who were the three unknowns who took the Iran Air flight to Teheran? Certainly not Mousa Sadr and his friends. Were they the three impersonators? If so, why were they going to Iran instead of returning to Libya? Who were they reporting to?

Sadegh arrived in Rome, and he and Cheron pored over the depositions of the witnesses. It was absolutely clear. The Imam had disappeared in Libya. And, oddly, representatives from Amal on the same errand in Rome refused to cooperate with Cheron.

On September 21, four senior Shi'a sheiks confronted Qaddafi in Syria. He was there for the summit of the so-called Rejectionist Front, the hard-line Arab states. The sheiks arrayed themselves like a tribunal, cold and suspicious. Radiating warmth and fraternity, Qaddafi explained to them how he had waited for Imam Sadr and how hurt he had been that the Lebanese leader had left without warning. With great commiseration, Qaddafi told them that the Italian authorities had confirmed the arrival of the Imam in Italy and that he had been abducted, or worse, perhaps by Italian terrorists.

The Arab sheiks regarded him silently in disbelief. The Italians had certainly *not* confirmed Mousa Sadr's arrival. Quite the opposite, and the story had been all over the Italian papers. What kind of fools did Qaddafi take them for?

Suddenly Qaddafi leaned forward. "I have been informed," he said almost conspiratorially, "that Imam Sadr was Iranian. Is that true?"

The sheiks now looked at him as if he were a snake. So this was his game.

To have made a point of Mousa Sadr's Iranian background at an Arab summit, to a group of Lebanese Arab sheiks, was not an innocent remark. Qaddafi had tried to imply that Mousa Sadr belonged to Iran and thus to the Shah. Then Qaddafi had offered them a bribe. Forget the Imam and I'll make it worth your while.

It all made sense. Removing Sadr eliminated the main stumbling block to Qaddafi's policy of violent confrontation in Lebanon. It removed Syria's most powerful ally there. And it removed one of the key figures in the Iranian revolutionary movement. Qaddafi wanted the Iranian revolution to fail, or, more to the point, to develop along his lines. Shi'a Islam was a dire threat to his own pretensions of Islamic leadership. The Iranians were his most dangerous enemies.

"Quite a story," I said, wishing I had listened to Sadegh when he had contacted me with it in Paris. "Just another anti-Qaddafi paranoid," I had thought, dismissing. S. Ghotbzadeh — and his kidnapped holy man — when he had called me so long ago, it seemed.

Discovering the intrigues that made up his life was like peeling an onion. So many layers, and each layer more potent than the one before.

I decided I had to go to Lebanon. And there I found the last pieces of the puzzle, lying in the rubble of Beirut.

20

The white buildings of Beirut embraced the blue water of St. George's Bay. After hearing for years of fractricidal war, I was deeply moved by the sight of this splendid and terrible city. Indeed, I was surprised that it was here at all, that anything had survived the endless fighting.

But life in Beirut went on in what seemed a remarkably banal way. Soldiers and militiamen with automatic weapons slung over their shoulders roamed the streets elbow to elbow with busy shoppers, while gunfire and artillery from the Green Line dividing Christian East Beirut from Moslem West Beirut thudded nearby. Once called the Paris of the Middle East, Beirut was now a ravaged beauty; rubble, craters and pocked ruins were the marks of her terrible disease. By the coast and on the Green Line the devastation was total, while other neighbourhoods were relatively unscathed.

Since the airport was closed, I had come by boat from Cyprus, along with a camerawoman from CNN. The network sent a driver to fetch us at the port. Our vehicle was an absurd, giant, white London taxi that ABC News had in its service.

Like an outlandish ghost we rolled through Beirut until we reached the Commodore. The Commodore Hotel was general headquarters for the international press corps in Beirut, much as the Intercon was in Teheran. But unlike the Intercontinental, the Commodore could not have passed for a corporate hotel anywhere in the world. It had a tacky, sweat-stained kind of individuality the Intercon lacked, and it had become a legend within a legend. Like Rick's in the classic film *Casablanca*, the Commodore had romance. To complete its cinematic atmosphere, there was even, in a cage by the pool, a talking parrot left there by one of the British journalists. Coco preened his feathered finery, sang the "Marseillaise" off-key and imitated incoming artillery to perfection.

All incoming "hacks," as journalists are often called, were greeted by the hotel's urbane manger, Fouad, who treated each to a welcoming glass of champagne in the bar, which had become an oasis for crazed journalistic frivolity in a sea of political lunacy. Following our cocktail, Fouad gave me the key to my suite, which was in the annex across the street.

I dumped my bags on the bed and surveyed the narrow streets from my rooftop balcony while I contemplated my next move. I was free-lancing again for sundry outlets so I had no mandatory agenda.

I arranged to see Nabbih Berri, now the head of Amal, the Shi'a political military organization of Lebanon. To get to Nabbih Berri, one had to pass through a series of armed sentries who guarded his home, which was also the headquarters of Amal. It was a big brick building on Barbour Street, surrounded by high sandbag barriers behind which several sentries in jeans and fatigues lounged, holding their weapons casually. They seemed to wear their violence like a comfortable old shirt.

They searched my bag and with sullen ill will sent me up the wide, bare stairway to Berri's office. Nabbih Berri, a stocky, good-looking man, wore a business suit, but despite his urbane exterior, he was a Lebanese warlord.

I wanted to discuss Sadegh privately, so at my request, Berri dismissed all but one of the people in the room. One trusted confidant, a man named Nassir, remained. Berri was open, expansive even. He told me about the early days when Sadegh used to visit.

"He used to stay with me in this very house," Berri confided. "Downstairs, where I still live."

"Sadegh worked here to reconcile Amal and the PLO," Berri confirmed. "But as an outsider. His first concern was always Iran. Always."

When I turned the discussion to Mousa Sadr and Khomeini, Berri suddenly grew circumspect. "Mousa Sadr will always be our only leader. Khomeini is our religious leader as well, but not our political leader."

Though known as a moderate in his religion and politics, Berri would go no further on the subject of Khomeini. He offered no criticism of the excesses in Teheran, only a stoic reiteration of his loyalty to Mousa Sadr. His statement that Khomeini was their religious leader and not their political leader was absurd. He knew as well as I, probably better, that for Khomeini religion and politics were one.

I wondered why Berri was taking this line. I knew that the reli-

gion and politics offered up by Khomeini were far from Mousa
Sadr's tolerant pacifism. Was Berri afraid of losing or antagonizing
the extremists among his own people if he attacked Khomeini? Or
did he seriously not object to Khomeini's behavior?

"What about Mousa Sadr, then?" I asked. Evidence aside, I
thought I would probe for his personal theory. "Do you know what
happened to him?"

By now I had information that Mousa Sadr was dead. One of
Qaddafi's diplomats had jumped the colonel's ship. When he
resigned as Libyan ambassador to Jordan, Aziz Omar Chenib had
made some interesting declarations to the press. First, he said that
Qaddafi had sent limitless funds to him at the embassy in Amman
to sow discord within the PLO. Second, he said that Qaddafi had
assassinated Mousa Sadr and his two companions in August 1978.
Sadr, he said, had refused to go along with Qaddafi's plans for
Amal to become anti-Syrian and pro-Libyan. The three Lebanese,
Chenib claimed, were shot by three of Qaddafi's personal aides in
the El Azizeh casern in Tripoli. The bodies were buried near an
agricultural project run by one of Qaddafi's relatives, south of the
city of Syrte, near El Souloul-el-Khadr. Three Libyan agents, he
went on, then traveled to Rome on the passports of the dead
Lebanese. One was disguised in the robes of a Shi'a priest.

Officially, though, Amal accepted none of this, and acted as
though Mousa Sadr were alive. When I questioned this, Berri's face
became a mask. "It is better not to ask such things. Much better for
you. Do not pursue this question."

I was astonished. Was I being warned, or threatened? It was
impossible to tell. And why should Amal object to a journalist seeking the answer to this mystery? Surely they should welcome any
inquiry. "Is Khomeini pursuing the matter?" I persisted.

"Now is not the time to ask these things," Berri said. "Do not
go into this any further."

I said no more. And as I left, Berri's confidant, Nassir, asked me
if I would care to lunch with him one day. I accepted.

Berri offered to have his own driver and one of his bodyguards
drop me off at the Commodore Hotel on their way home, so I went
downstairs with them. They were both muscular young men and
were heavily armed.

In the car, guns poked from under the front seat, a common sight
in Beirut. We chatted as we wound through Beirut's streets, and

even joked about a song on the radio which had to do with a woman who was *majnoun*, crazy for love.

Then one of Berri's bodyguards abruptly asked me what I thought of Khomeini. I said something noncommittal. For the rest of the way to the Commodore, he extolled the virtues of the fiery Ayatollah and the Islamic revolution in Iran. His words hung like an ill wind over Lebanon.

Two days later Nassir picked me up at the Commodore. As we drove along the Corniche, the seaside road, he talked idly of how nice the beaches used to be before the fighting. We passed the wretched shanties and shacks that were the refuge of the Shi'a who had fled the Israeli-occupied south.

Nassir was young and handsome, a kind of dark James Dean. We drove to a seaside restaurant, a favorite Amal haunt, I was told. From the window by our table, we looked out across the blue bay. And I wondered why he had invited me.

I was still wondering when he would get to the point as we ate olives, raw vegetables and crisply fried fish. He answered my relatively harmless questions about Mousa Sadr's background, about his own days in Amal, and about Sadegh.

"Did you know Sadegh?" I asked.

"Oh, yes. We met in 1972, at Mousa Sadr's place in Hazmieh. The big house."

"I know the house," I answered vaguely as I picked up a huge black olive.

"Sadegh used to have a thing for a girlfriend of one of my sisters. He was a very good-looking guy, very intelligent. An excellent guy. Afraid of SAVAK, though. All the Iranians were."

"What about Sadegh and Arafat?"

"Arafat and Mousa Sadr met with people like Sadegh and Yazdi in the Liberation Movement of Iran, but Arafat didn't believe in the LMI. He was more in league with the Djalalodin Farsi group."

"The Libyan faction," I concluded.

"That's right. In 1979 the PLO was with the Libyan faction in Iran. You know, Farsi, Beheshti, that bunch. All of them were against Mousa Sadr. The PLO had had it with Mousa Sadr, of course. He had said they had to leave Lebanon after the Israeli invasion. The UN decree formalized that."

I contemplated his answers and decided to take the plunge. "What about the disappearance of Mousa Sadr?"

Nassir looked around uneasily, then leaned toward me conspiratorially. "All I know," he said, "is that according to our information, Ghotbzadeh accepted something like $360,000 from Qaddafi to keep quiet about it."

I looked at Nassir through new eyes. I wondered what kind of idiot he took me for. It was Sadegh who had pushed the Italian inquiry, with no cooperation from Amal. That information was public record and relatively easy for a journalist to find out. So why try to tell me such a stupid story? It was Qaddafi's line. He couldn't possibly believe it himself.

Nassir must have known how much Sadegh hated Qaddafi. But then everyone seemed to believe rumors about everyone else. Perhaps the Amal people were not sure of Sadegh.

I smiled to myself. For that matter, Sadegh was perfectly capable of taking money from Qaddafi and then spitting in his eye. But some things were certain. Sadegh had gone to great lengths to find out about Mousa Sadr's disappearance, and he believed Qaddafi to be the culprit. And Amal must know that, so why try to shift the blame to Sadegh?

I said none of this to Nassir. Suddenly I felt very vulnerable in the savage political wilderness of Beirut. "That's an interesting idea," I said to Nassir, then shrugging, "but who knows?"

When I returned to the Commodore, I talked with an old friend, Bill Claiborne of the *Washington Post*, a veteran correspondent in the region. We draped ourselves over the bar, the nerve center of the press corps in Beirut, and I explained to him all that had happened. I needed an ally.

"Oh, God! Don't ask them any more about it, then. I don't know what they're up to, but take the warning. This is not a health resort."

* * *

As I walked along the Corniche where Sadegh had once walked, I pondered the pattern that was emerging like a photograph in a darkroom.

Sadegh was allied with Syria and Amal in Lebanon, and was the enemy of Qaddafi and Moscow and, up to a point, the PLO. Moscow and Syria were officially allies, but Syria marched to her own drum, especially where the Middle East was concerned. Qaddafi was closer to Moscow. So far it made sense.

Djalalodin Farsi, the pro-Qaddafi/PLO man in Beirut, Beheshti and their cohorts—especially Khamenei and Khoeini'a (the religious leader of the students) — were the allies of Qaddafi and Moscow inside Iran. Both Khameini and Khoeini'a had longtime links with the Soviets, and Khamenei had received part of his education in Moscow. Djalalodin Farsi and his group had burrowed like moles into the clerical camp. Farsi's two principal players were Behzad Nabawi, the small, feral translator who had appeared to control the hostage negotiations from the prime minister's office, and who treated us to gloating press conferences every day, and Hassan Ayat, a Marxist intellectual and Islamic ideologue disguised as a stylish businessman. Farsi, Nabawi and Ayat had formed their own political party, then allied it to the IRP and grew in its shadow.

This, then, was at the core of the hostage crisis: these men were maneuvering Iran into a Libyan political mode: Islamic totalitarianism "allied" with Moscow.

Immediately after Khomeini's return to Iran, Nabbih Berri and other Amal leaders had come to Teheran to ask Khomeini to pressure Qaddafi about Mousa Sadr. Khomeini cut off relations with Libya, but did little else.

Moustafa Chamran Sadegh's old friend had come to Teheran with Berri and the others, and was effusively greeted by Bazargan and, oddly, Khomeini. Bazargan had pressed him to stay on and serve in the government as defense minister, and Chamran had done so.

The hard-line clerics, Farsi and his group, looked on this with immense displeasure. One more to eliminate. These men, a bizarre alliance of clerical fascists and Middle Eastern communists, settled down to the business of destroying their moderate opponents. The hostages were the perfect tool.

The PLO and the Tudeh, then, were the powers behind the "students," as Sadegh had indicated from the outset. Khoeinia's presence in the embassy compound with his "dear students" was not accidental.

Things were further complicated, of course, by Qaddafi's rows with Arafat and Moscow, and splits within the PLO.

But just how far these mullahs would go with Moscow once they tasted their own power was unknown. Moscow, I reflected, was playing a very dangerous game indeed. The men in the Kremlin might eliminate enemies like Sadegh, only to find they had created an Islamic monster they could not control, one that would threaten to disrupt the Moslem population of the Soviet Union — all sixty million of them. Moscow was obviously counting on being able to move in if Islamic government failed, but that was by no means a certainty. Moscow, I decided, was going to be very sorry.

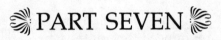

PART SEVEN

THE FINAL PATH

21

In the spring of 1981, the clerics and the Tudeh moved in for the kill. Khomeini announced that all those who deviated from his line would be declared "corrupt criminals of the earth" and punished with death. The clerics called for the execution of Bani Sadr, accusing him of fomenting riots against Islam with his speeches. *Mardom*, the Tudeh newspaper, took up the cry, urging the arrest and execution of Ghotbzadeh.

In a speech to the air force officers at Shiraz, on May 28, Bani Sadr replied that he would resist the substitution of an IRP tyranny for Pahlavi dictatorship. Thinking Khomeini would at least see the will of the people, Bani Sadr went to see the Imam before leaving again for a trip to Hamadan on the western front of the war with Iraq.

Khomeini smiled. "I wish you victory, Mr. Bani Sadr," he said warmly.

As soon as Bani Sadr left, his newspaper was closed. The commission of clerics Khomeini appointed to investigate the charges against him found him guilty of unlawful speech against Islam. Using his constitutional powers as *faghih*, Khomeini dismissed Bani Sadr from office. Then the Imam generously invited Bani Sadr to repent for his deviations so that he could be forgiven by Islam.

Dazed, Bani Sadr returned to Teheran to fight. But his enemies could now, with Khomeini's blessing, invoke the wrath of their god on his every move.

On June 20, the Mudjahedeen and Bani Sadr's smaller forces organized a mass protest march together. Five hundred thousand citizens poured into the streets. The Islamic judges declared it an uprising against Islam, and sent the Pasdaran, the Revolutionary Guards, to round up the demonstrators. Fifteen teenage girls were the first to be sent to the firing squad. "Death to Khomeini!" they cried before being silenced in a rain of bullets. Thousands followed them to the wall, nearly all young students and teachers.

Bani Sadr went underground, sheltered by the Mudjahedeen,

and hunted by the Fox and the Shark, Beheshti and Rafsanjani. The Fox and the Shark took over Bani Sadr's presidential powers and announced that they and Rajai, the prime minister, would form a three-man presidential council.

June 28. The IRP headquarters was a nondescript two-story building on a narrow street on the south side of Teheran. The entire political leadership of Iran was present, save Ayatollah Khomeini, to listen to Beheshti savor his victory over the Mudjahedeen.

Beheshti licked his lips as he began speaking. And as he opened his mouth, an apocalyptic blast ripped through the room. A wall of searing heat and solid sound wrenched bone from bone and ripped flesh from flesh, as the steel and concrete roof heaved and fell on the screaming mass of clerics.

The force of the bomb was stupendous, but from the smoke and fire some emerged clutching their wounds. Khamenei staggered out, and Rajai, too. Rafsanjani, it turned out, had left a few moments earlier. The Shark survived even out of water. But the Fox?

Beheshti's head lay in the bloody rubble, eyes and mouth gaping, severed from his cloaked body.

"How many of them?" Sadegh asked.

"Sixty-four dead, counted so far," Shin answered, as they pored over the papers and kept an eye on the television in Sadegh's office.

"Somebody had the right idea," Sadegh muttered.

"Mudjahedeen?" Shin ventured.

"Maybe. I wouldn't have thought they could pull it off, though. They probably used Tudeh expertise."

Shin shook his head. "They'll savage the Mudjahedeen now."

"The bomb was right in a garbage pail next to Beheshti. It must have been huge. People heard it all over the city."

"Agha," Shin suggested tentatively, "don't you think you should go the Imam and express your sympathy at the loss?"

"No."

"I just thought it might be politically expedient to —"

"No!" Sadegh replied with anger. "I'm glad Beheshti's dead. And to hell with the Imam!"

* * *

The internal divisions in Iran exploded now into more violence as murder begot murder.

Khamenei was preaching in a Teheran mosque when a bomb hidden in a tape recorder blew up in his face. But he was lucky. He was seriously wounded, but escaped with his life.

Hassan Ayat, Farsi's friend and now the ideologue of the IRP, was not so fortunate. Unknown assailants descended on him in the street. When they left, his body lay bloody and lifeless.

The regime pinned the blame on the Mudjahedeen, and the prisons bulged and ran blood. Hodjatoleslam Mohammed Rey-shahri, head of the special military revolutionary courts — the same official who had had Sadegh arrested in November — and Ayatollah Ladjevardi, Teheran's revolutionary prosecutor, became famous. It was Ladjevardi who announced that Bani Sadr was to be arrested. Already four hundred of Bani Sadr's men had been detained and twenty-five had been executed.

Then there was an even greater blow. Not a blow that would shake the world, but one with considerable meaning for anyone who understood the situation. Moustafa Chamran was killed at the battlefront. The second member of the truly moderate triumvirate of Beirut was dead. First Mousa Sadr, then Chamran. Sadegh was the only one left.

The official communiqué said Charman had died of wounds received in the fighting. But no one believed it.

"The Americans betrayed him," Sadegh told Shin. "He'd contacted them for help, for a coup. But the Israelis wouldn't hear of it, of course."

"So he was assassinated?"

"Of course," Sadegh insisted. "But we'll never know exactly by whom."

In Iran, Bani Sadr and Massoud Radjavi, leader of the Mudjahedeen, were the subjects of a massive manhunt. Finally, the Mudjahedeen arranged for one of its pilots in the air force to fly them out of Iran.

As their plane revved, a Pasdar guard suddenly took an interest in its passengers. The two fugitives listened with their heart's pounding, while the pilot talked his way out of danger. Then he climbed in the cockpit, and in seconds they were airborne, and Bani Sadr watched Iran disappear below him.

The IRP moved to close the gaps in its ranks. Hojatoleslam Javad Bahonar, another mullah of the IRP and Rajai was installed as president. The new president and premier were meeting with their aides in the premier's office on Sunday, August 31, when the roar of an explosion and burning tongues of flame engulfed them. It was another bomb. From the next building, Rafsanjani saw the column of smoke. Beneath the smoke, Rajai and Bahonar lay mangled in death.

But again the IRP simply reconstituted itself. Like a cancerous cell it had a reproductive life of its own. Khamenei became president, his cousin Mousavi became prime minister, and all down the line, Rafsanjani and other hard-liners smoothly slid in to fill the gaps.

Sadegh watched it all in bitter disgust. To his everlasting regret, he'd recognized too late the power of the mosque. But he saw the cracks: Rafsanjani was maneuvering now for an advantage over Khamenei. He was pulling the Pasdaran into his embrace. Sadegh also saw the ideological splits in the IRP and all the petty schemes. These mullahs were far from invulnerable. He could take them on; he could win.

As the others gathered for dinner, Sadegh sat in his armchair contemplating a photograph of Khomeini. And while he thought no one was watching, he slowly tore it into small pieces, and let the fragments fall, one by one, into the ash tray.

Sadegh now began in earnest to plan a counter-coup. He called it the Nedjat e Englaab e Islami Iran, the Salvation of the Islamic Revolution of Iran. Working closely with him were Shin and Mahdavi, a young mullah who had joined them for the ill-fated newspaper venture. The fact that Sadegh was organizing became the most open secret in Iran, if not the world. Everybody knew the Big G was up to something, though not precisely what. Unperturbed, Sadegh forged ahead. There was no point, he decided, in whispering in codes. Those in the IRP were venal, but not stupid. Since they were bound to figure it out anyway, or hear it in the dark, arched corners of the mosques, it was best to keep them nervous about it. The main thing was to keep the names and the details out of their clutches.

He sent Shin and Mahdavi to solicit the help of Saudi Arabia. The Kingdom of the House of Saud watched the new group with interest. They had been more than a little distressed at recent developments in Iran, fearing the evangelistic revolution's aggressive military posture and its effect on Saudi Arabia's devout Moslem population. To them, Sadegh represented a more acceptable brand of Islamic republic. Pro-Arab and adamantly anti-Zionist, he would, if his scheme worked, drastically reshape Iran's role in the region.

He had already tried to end the war with Iraq. He would not let himself be used by the Israelis, as the Shah had done. The idea, however, also had its drawbacks, not the least of which was that it would have a distinct lack of appeal to Washington, the House of Saud's erstwhile ally.

But for the Saudis the advantages outweighed the disadvantages. They promised Shin one hundred million dollars, but they wanted to know first that Washington had no violent objections.

Shin and Mahdavi secretly made contact with agents of the American administration. In Geneva, they met with two anonymous emissaries of the U.S. government. Shin's distress grew as the Americans interrogated them. Clearly the Americans were more concerned about Ayatollah Shariatmadari's role than about Sadegh's. For them, Shariatmadari Ayatollah was the linchpin.

Ayatollah Kazem Shariatmadari was next in stature to Khomeini. Since Khomeini's return, he had attacked the extremists. He had spoken against Khomeini himself, declaring that the position of *faghih* was unacceptable, urging people not to vote for the constitution.

The VVIR distorted his remarks to sound like support. Nevertheless, Shariatmadari's followers in Tabriz, the center of his parish province, took to the streets. They were quelled brutally, and Shariatmadari, the Grand Ayatollah who had bestowed the title of Ayatollah on Khomeini many years before, was eventually placed under house arrest.

Shariatmadari had agreed to support Sadegh if his coup succeeded.

But even though he had the support of the key religious leader, the Americans were still suspicious that Sadegh was a KGB plant. Did these people ever read the papers or pay attention to what happened in the real world? Shin wondered. Or did they only study MOSSAD reports on the Middle East? Dejectedly, he returned to Teheran.

Sadegh next sent Bourguet to Washington. The administration might have changed but the staff of the State Department was still there, and Christian knew them. All Bourguet wanted was American neutrality. He wanted no help, no money and no CIA underfoot.

But in Washington, Bourguet was met with unfamiliar coolness in the cubicles of the State Department. The shaggy lawyer did not impress the two men he met with. Having been so badly burned in the hostage negotiations, the Americans regarded Sadegh and company with limitless skepticism. "A cowboy," Hamilton Jordan had called Sadegh. Well, the American had had enough of the rodeo. And there were all those other reports saying Sadegh was a KGB or Libyan agent. Not everyone at State swallowed this information, but there was doubt.

"If Ghotbzadeh is to get Saudi help," Bourguet said, stating the situation baldly, "the Saudis need to know your government won't object."

The senior American official shook his head. "Out of the question. I don't think you realize our position in the Middle East or in Saudi Arabia. We are in no position to tell the Saudis what they can and can't do. On the contrary, any such word from us would probably be counterproductive. They're very touchy."

"But it's the Saudis who want to know! Or at least our Saudi contact."

"Out of the question."

Baffled, discouraged and angry at the Americans, Bourguet reported back to Sadegh on the failure of his mission. Undaunted, Sadegh sent Bourguet off to see other "friends" in the Middle East, to ask for financial and political support.

Following Sadegh's instructions, Bourguet began at the United Nations in New York. There, he was furnished with an airline ticket to Morocco. At Rabat airport he was met and ushered to a sleek car that whisked him to an air-conditioned hotel.

In the morning he was picked up again and taken to an isolated villa. Inside, a high Kuwaiti official greeted him and asked after Sadegh. Bourguet marveled at the elaborate response Sadegh apparently inspired.

After meeting with the Kuwaiti he reported that although they couldn't promise anything, they were sympathetic.

Whenever I called Sadegh, he was subdued, as though he could scarcely be bothered to breathe. When I asked, "How are you?" he invariably replied, with a shadowy spark of black humor, "Oh, I'm alive." This was how he responded to all familiar callers.

"But I'm bored," he added one day. "Can you send me some movies? Some videocassettes?"

"I'll see what I can do. Anything in particular?"

"No. Whatever."

"All right. I'll try to find a way to get them in. Sadegh, why don't you do what our friend did? I can help on this end."

Our "friend" was a person Sadegh had helped to escape from

Iran via Turkey, after which I had taken over responsibility for his future in the West.

"No," he replied softly. "No. It's all right."

And I understood that I could not argue. There could be no more exile for Sadegh.

Bitterly, Sadegh thought about his friends who had for so long been his comrades in arms. Where were they now?

"None of them come to visit," he told Alef. "None of them. Tabatabai came once. Ahmad came once. Terrific. But the rest? Only you and Shin."

"Sadegh, your real friends are still your friends. The others never were."

Sadegh Tabatabai, his pal from Beirut days, was firmly ensconced in Khomeini's camp. His sister, after all, was married to Ahmad Khomeini, and Tabatabai and Ahmad had begun a profitable import-export business. They each paid one visit to Sadegh, then dropped him, and went on to make a fortune dealing arms for the war with Iraq that Sadegh had tried to stop.

Khodapanahi, who had shared his flat in Paris, whom he had brought to power at the NIRT and the Foreign Ministry, now worked actively against him, serving in the prime minister's office. He became known as Khomeini's Beria.

And Habibi. That hurt. Habibi had used dirty tricks against both Sadegh and Bani Sadr in the presidential campaign, and now worked hand in glove with the clerical hard-liners. Habibi, their mild-mannered friend from Paris days.

Bani Sadr, in Paris, refused to help, when Shin went to him. "I'd rather see Sadegh stay alive," was all he said.

Bazargan did what he could, clinging to his seat in parliament. Yazdi stayed in the shadows with Bazargan; Sadegh never saw him. He still wondered what Yazdi's game was.

Karim Lahidji was different. He had always been the same, standing his ground, fighting for human rights. Once he came to Sadegh, who wanted him to join in the coup attempt. Lahidji refused, trying to persuade Sadegh to escape instead, and live to fight another day. But for Sadegh, the resistance had to be in Iran. He had no other child to live for, he told Lahidji. Later, Sadegh helped Lahidji and his family get out of Iran to France.

Alef suddenly exploded. "Blast and damn Khomeini!"

"No!" Sadegh burst in on his diatribe. "You can't blame Khomeini for what happened! We're the ones who did it.

"We had every chance to run the country. He went back to Qom to be guide, not führer. He didn't want to run things that way, he never did. And what do we do? We fight and bicker and let it all fall apart until he has to intervene, over and over. We couldn't govern so he had to. And then he found that the IRP could. And now it suits him. We gave it away!"

Alef had no reply. He didn't agree. Khomeini had aided and abetted the IRP, had sabotaged Sadegh and Bani Sadr from the start, in his opinion. But there was truth in Sadegh's words.

"And even if a father is a terrible father," Sadegh said, half to himself, "he's still your father."

Alef opened the backgammon board. "No more politics today," he said. "Your first move."

* * *

Arriving as he did every day to visit his friend, to try to divert him with tall tales and backgammon, Alef looked in vain for Sadegh in his rooms. Hearing a strange noise, he followed it to the back of the house and suddenly, quietly, he stopped.

On the balcony over the garden, he saw Sadegh bent weeping like a child, or a wounded animal, the heartrending sobs of uncomprehending pain and grief clawing the air.

"Allah," Sadegh cried suddenly in a low, broken voice, "Oh my God, let me die!"

The naked pain struck Alef to the marrow, tore the laughter out of his eyes forever in that stark moment. He went slowly forward to clothe his friend in a few sad shreds of comfort. "Sadegh, Sadegh, no, you're not alone, don't despair so . . ." and the two sat together in silence for a while.

"Sadegh, we can get you out of the country. It's all been planned. There are people willing to do their part every step of the way. South then east through Baluchistan."

"No. I won't leave."

"But they might arrest you any day."

"No. I told you. I won't. I can't. Iran doesn't need a seventeenth opposition in exile to add to Bani Sadr and the bunch in Paris. Khomeini has stolen the revolution from the people and from us, and we have to get it back. If I leave, what credibility do I have? We're responsible. I have to stay here and do what I can. And if I can't do anything, I'd rather die," he said with bitter anger. "I've had enough. Of Khomeini. Of myself. Of all of it."

"But it's no good if they just kill you! What good are you then?"

"I'll have died for what I believe in."

Alef stared bleakly at the implacable truth.

"Never mind all that," Sadegh said abruptly. "We'll pull it off."

*   *   *

Sadegh's house became his oasis. A fountain flowed in a chamber he called his Omar Khayyam room. Outside, he spent long hours planning and tending an intricate garden, as he mulled over his strategies.

Every day, he moved farther into a world of his own. His friends were used to his long, thoughtful silences, but now these withdrawals into meditation grew longer. Sadegh had begun a journey down the mystics' path toward oneness with God, the path of the Sufi. Even his garden was a Sufi metaphor.

The believer needed no mosques or mullahs. If Sadegh had only recognized before that this had always been the core of his faith. If he had only looked in the mirror and seen himself instead of Khomeini.

For this was my faith, too, the god in the flower. This I could understand.

And finally I realized that behind his veils, Sadegh had understood me, knew me better than I knew myself.

*   *   *

Women friends came and went. Many offered themselves to him and some of them he took. There were those he cared for a little and there were those he cared for dearly. There was one he helped to escape from Iran. And there was one in particular, who helped him and loved him. An employee of the French embassy, she took risks to carry his letters to Bourguet.

"Are you ever going to marry one of these flowers or are you going to garden forever?" Alef asked in exasperation.

"No. Marriage is out of the question now. There was one I would have married. . . ."

"One? Who?"

"Carole, you remember."

"Ah. The satanic journalist."

It was Alef who told me this when I next saw him. Perhaps he made it up to console me. This young woman was part of Sadegh's life and she loved him. I knew that. And knowing Sadegh, I felt he must feel deeply about her. If he didn't, he wouldn't be the man I loved. I could scarcely ask him, though, since I knew of the relationship only through Christian and Alef. I felt torn and bewildered, stung by twinges of involuntary jealousy, hoping for Sadegh's happiness, wanting to be with him, wishing I could alter the stars in the heavens. But he belonged to Iran. I never could live there.

"I came in one day," Alef told me, "and found Sadegh reading books on farming in Quebec. It was right before he made his move against the regime. He hadn't given up on that, even then. It was a dream, as the revolution had been."

"Can you imagine Sadegh and me raising cows and chickens on a little farm in Quebec?"

"Yes," Alef answered. "I can."

But these were things I learned much later. At the time I knew only what Sadegh was planning, and I feared for him. In spite of that, I shopped for the tapes and sent them to Christian. One of the films was *Apocalypse Now*.

Christian took the tapes to Iran when he went. He found a new Sadegh.

Sadegh's heart and soul had reassumed the shape of the vessel that was Iran. It was not just the long *aba* robe, the bowls of fruit and pistachios always available, the poems and the Persian language. Something had changed in Sadegh himself, as a river changes when it finishes a turbulent journey and spreads out in harmony into the sea. This was a new Sadegh, one who had emerged gradually since returning home. America and his years there, France and his time there, were as remote as songs of innocence. It was as if his heartbeat had slowed and his blood flowed to another rhythm.

*   *   *

Following my hasty departure from Teheran, I had free-lanced in London, gone to Spain and spent more time in Paris. I peddled my stories as I went and I spoke with Sadegh as often as possible. When I returned to Toronto, I was offered a job as a producer and cohost of a CBC newsmagazine show called *Worldwide*.

Not long after Christian's visit to Sadegh and our long discussion about the changes he had observed, Sadegh called me.

"*Mr. Ghotzzb . . .?*" the note from the secretary at our office read.

She had abandoned the exotic spelling of Sadegh's name, hoping I would figure it all out. It read simply, ''Message of thanks.''

I called Sadegh back immediately. His warm, tired voice assured me he was fine. Still, in that moment, I knew something was about to happen.

''I wanted to make sure our friend is okay and that you'll look after him. And thank you,'' he said. Our friend was a person he'd smuggled out through Turkey.

My heart filled the room as I struggled to answer him. ''I will. I'll take care of him. Don't worry. Everything is fine. Sadegh, can you . . . visit?'' It was a veiled way of asking if he, too, could escape. I knew he wouldn't run, but I had to ask.

''No. Not for a while. Someday,'' came his equally veiled answer.

Oh, Sadegh, no. Leave now! Get out of there! Don't do this! This is your good-bye, isn't it? You know, you know what's going to happen. And they're listening and I can't say anything. I can't say I love you. The satanic Western journalist can't say much of anything for fear of listening ears. But you know I do love you.

I felt sick inside. Iran had always held him as I never could. It was going to take him back now. I knew it absolutely.

''I understand, Sadegh. I — I think of you, I can't say so . . .'' I struggled.

''I know. Don't worry so. Good-bye, my dear.''

''Good-bye. *Khoda hafez.*''

I replaced the receiver in its cradle and stared at the message scrawled by the secretary. ''*Mr. Ghotzzb* . . .?'' I felt suddenly afraid of it, of half his name. To me, it was symbolic, something evil from the void, cutting him off in midlife.

So you try to frighten me with threats of execution?
But if I were afraid of execution,
I wouldn't be dancing in the lovers' circle.

It was Sadegh's favourite poem, by an ancient Sufi. He liked to quote it to Shin. And now he had to answer the threats.

22

The two Americans Shin had met in Geneva represented either the CIA or the National Security Council. They were still playing cat and mouse, and Sadegh was suspicious that he might be their mouse. But they had made tentative suggestions about supplying limited support. What they offered was too little too late. A new element suddenly spurred Sadegh to act sooner than he wished. That element was the Hojatieh.

Actually, the Hojatieh was an old element, an old faction of the clergy. It was a secret society with almost impenetrable veils of obscurity around it. No one actually knew who belonged, shrouded as the society was, like Freemasons, in the mists of rites and codes. In spite of their secret membership, the Hojatieh made it known that they were conservative in all senses of the word. They stood for private property and a free market, and against all clerical government control in all sectors of the society. They were opposed to clerical control in the marketplace and to the fact that certain industries had been set up by the government and others seized. The Hojatieh was becoming more overtly opposed to the regime, and was making its views known to the press, through the bazaar, inside the mosque and through its own secret channels. And the IRP was getting ready to break it.

As he did in most key organizations, Sadegh had a friend in the Hojatieh who kept him abreast of its plans.

"We're planning a coup d'état," whispered his friend. "Very soon."

"We'll have to be ready to seize their coup," Sadegh told Shin. "Let them start it, then we'll take over and save the republic from them. We'll never have another chance. The Hojatieh clerics are just as bad as the ones we've got now. If they won, they'd be practically indestructible."

"We aren't ready," Shin advised. They had major support in the regular army, the regional tribes, the bazaar, but they needed more time.

"We have no choice," Sadegh answered.

They were nearly ready. Forty-eight of them were to be in key positions ready to seize power: the VVIR, the ministries, the presidential palace, IRP headquarters and Khomeini's house.

Most wanted to eliminate Khomeini conclusively with nothing less than a rocket launched from a neighboring window. Sadegh refused to agree, but deep inside he knew Khomeini's chances were nil. Those who were willing to risk everything on a coup would never countenance sparing the head of the monster.

If they failed, the forty-eight were to eliminate those of their own followers who would be arrested and tortured for confessions. Sadegh reluctantly agreed to this brutal contingency plan.

"The rest of us are dispensable," Shin argued. "You're not. Without us, you can lead others. Without you, we are nothing anyway."

"If anything happens to me," Sadegh said grimly, "get Nabawi."

"Nabawi?"

"Nabawi. He's the worst of the lot."

It was agreed that Sadegh would go into hiding that night and remain underground until they struck.

"I'll come back at four o'clock," Shin promised. He left then to meet the others.

At four, Shin phoned just to make certain all was well.

"I don't feel well," Sadegh said. "Don't come."

Shin froze. It was the Pasdars. They had come for Sadegh. But Shin and Sadegh had foreseen that possibility and they were ready for it. The forty-eight were armed and prepared to rescue their leader.

"I'll get some medicine and come over," Shin promised.

"No! Wait awhile. I'll be all right."

The Pasdars took Sadegh to the huge police block near the Foreign Ministry where Reyshahri installed his personal prisoners. Later, he was moved to the infamous Evin prison.

The Pasdars also seized Mahdavi, and almost immediately after, forty-four of the forty-eight were rounded up. They then began to pluck from their hiding places seventy of the military officers who supported Sadegh's plot.

Shin and Alef went into hiding, meeting clandestinely to find a way to save Sadegh. Clearly they had all been betrayed.

"It was Mahdavi's wife who sent to the Pasdars and turned him in," said one of the others to Shin. "She was suspicious of all his

comings and goings and meetings. She was fed up with all his phi-
landering with other women. What an end to a coup!"

But that was not quite how it happened.

*   *   *

My clock radio had gone off and the strains of some popular tune
filled the room. I turned over, ignoring this first soft request to get
out of bed. A familiar male voice followed the song. He warned of
crowded feeder lanes on the 401 and of an accident on the Don
Valley Parkway going south. I tossed again, facing the radio as the
announcer intoned dramatically, "The World at Eight." It was the
morning CBC news broadcast.

"And from Iran . . . Attempted coup . . . Sadegh Ghotbzadeh,
former foreign minister . . . arrested."

I jolted awake, my senses suddenly alert to the voice on the radio.

I called Christian Bourguet immediately.

"This time they mean business," he confirmed. "We're trying to
get other governments to intervene — the Algerians, the Saudis—"

"What about the Syrians? The Assads are Sadegh's friends.
Khomeini might listen to them." It was the beginning of a ritual.
Every day we would speak on the phone and report to each other.
From the outset, we could hope for no better than a prison term.
Our struggle was to prevent execution, but we could not intervene
directly. We were from the satanic West.

In Iran, Shin still hid and still tried to find out what had gone
wrong. He didn't believe the whole debacle could be laid at the
feet of Mahdavi's wife. Mahdavi hadn't known enough of the
details. No. They had been penetrated. They had feared that from
the beginning. It might have been the clergy. He thought not. More
likely the Tudeh, particularly those in the Sarb e Daran, supposedly
an organization of ex-royalist officers they had contact with, which,
he learned, was thoroughly penetrated.

A week later the Pasdars came to ransack Shariatmadari's house.
They devastated his library and desecrated his theological seminary
in Qom. They interrogated the sick ayatollah for six hours and then
arrested his sons-in-law and his pregnant daughter.

Hojatoleslam Mohammed Reyshahri, prosecutor of the military
revolutionary court, announced the news: "Sadegh Ghotbzadeh
has been arrested with his accomplices for planning to kill the Imam
and all the members of the Supreme Defense Council, and carry

out a bloody purge in the responsible organs of revolutionary institutions. The plot was organized by nationalists and power-hungry elements with no aims other than to gain power. They wanted to open the way for their Western masters, including the United States."

Khomeini boiled with rage, regarding his viper son malevolently. "Such an idea," he said loftily on the radio, "would only occur to unsophisticated minds. A group of several hundred people are incapable of challenging a country such as we have here. They are misled in that they do not know the power of Islam."

Reyshahri then announced that Hector Villalon had acted as the link between the plotters and the CIA.

"Raving madness," replied Villalon to reporters in Paris. "Totally false and senseless."

And then Sadegh was put before the cameras.

He was a ravaged echo of the foreign minister he had once been. I was filled with agony watching him and listening to his toneless voice.

"I was seeking to overthrow the government, not the Islamic Republic. From the start I had expected the proposal to kill Imam Khomeini, but then I reconsidered. I wanted him saved, but I did not know how to go about it. The final decision was to have been made in the days following my arrest."

He struggled on. "Two intermediaries told me that Ayatollah Shariatmadari told them he could contribute nothing toward carrying out the plan, but if it succeeded, he would make statements in its support. He was rather frightened and took a very conservative attitude."

Sadegh did not apologize. "I am shamed before the nation," he said. "Free me, or execute me."

I leaned back and closed my eyes. Days in America must have still lingered. "Give me liberty or give me death" had been the words of the patriot Patrick Henry. And they were Sadegh's words, too. His shame was failure, not treason. It was *they* who were the traitors in his eyes.

They had questioned him savagely. Gleefully they told him of the arrest of his followers, but he gave them no names, no confirmations, no excuses, no denials. He acknowledged his plan to overthrow the government and confirmed that Ayatollah Shariatmadari had supported it. That was Iran's last chance now. If Shariatmadari would acknowledge him, it would ring the bell of revolt.

But when Shariatmadari was put before the cameras by his captors, the frail old ayatollah was a beaten man. He acknowledged that Sadegh's organization had contacted him and that he had agreed to support the coup if it was a success. He then asked Khomeini to forgive him for a stupid mistake, one that any human being could make in a lifetime.

Shariatmadari had saved his old skin and Iran would now wither and die.

* * *

I tried to bury myself in work. I was scheduled to go to Nicaragua to film a documentary, but I was reluctant to leave.

"Go," Cheron advised. "There's nothing more we can do. Sadegh has other help. You go to Nicaragua, my dear. Keep in touch with us from there."

So while Sadegh sat in the encroaching void, I flew to Nicaragua, the country where that other revolution of 1979 had occurred, a revolution that blistered in the same sun, on the other side of the world.

I returned home from Nicaragua in August, and my partner and I began the arduous task of editing the documentary we had shot there. But no matter how hard I worked, or how long the hours, part of me was in Iran with Sadegh.

I spoke daily with Bourguet, Cheron and Vallette, as the weeks dragged on. We were helpless, but we still hoped there would be some reprieve: an uprising, a change of government, a miracle. And in spite of all I knew of Khomeini, I clung to the belief that he would not actually kill a man who had in the past been his devoted son.

At last the trial of Sadegh Ghotbzadeh began.

Five months in prison had changed him. He was heavier, with a full beard and a different mien, a kind of weary intensity.

Weighty in robe and turban, the revolutionary prosecutor of the special military court, Mohammed Reyshahri, intoned a verse of the Koran to open the proceedings. Then, referring in each instance to the relevant page numbers of the huge dossier that gave the details in the case, he read the list of accusations against the accused, Sadegh Ghotbzadeh, son of Hossein, identity number 1086, bachelor, arrested April 7, 1982."

We were back in the looking-glass world, where "the King's messenger is in prison being punished, the trial doesn't even begin until next Wednesday and of course the crime comes last of all."

"Having assumed leadership of a group of individuals for the overthrow of the Islamic Republic to install a genuine Islamic Republic," read out Reyshahri in his harsh grating voice, "you are accused of collaboration with armed groups for the realization of these evil objectives; giving financial support to these armed groups; sending agents abroad with a view to obtaining money and information for carrying out the extermination plan; having taken $60,000 from the foreigner Villalon; sending Seyyed Mehdi Mahdavi as his representative to Saudi Arabia to obtain money; having relations with socialist organizations with a view to carrying out the extermination and sending agents to them; sending an agent to Ayatollah Kazem Shariatmadari to obtain his collaboration and approval; planning and command of plans to seize military centers, centers of the army, the komitehs and the radio and television; preparation of a plan to destroy the house that is the humble abode of the Imam. . . ."

The list went on and on.

"Given that we need now hear the explanations of the accused and ultimate verifications, and the canonical deliberations in this regard, the judicial dossiers on the other accused shall be presented in the next session."

Seyyed Mehdi Mahdavi, the young mullah who had helped Sadegh when he was trying to start a newspaper, and who had helped him plan the coup, was being tried along with Sadegh. He had been broken in Evin, and now sat trembling in his place, having told all he had to tell. Sadegh regarded him with detached pity.

"Inconsistencies," Reyshahri said stridently; "first you said yes, you wanted to overthrow the regime, then you said no."

Sadegh looked his accuser in the eye. "Most of the dossier is far from reality and is in fact utterly false. For me, the essential questions are constitutional. In three categories: First, according to you, it was a plot to overthrow the Islamic Republic. According to me, it was a plot to change the governing individuals. Second, the plot to sacrifice the Imam. This is more serious. Three, my ties with foreign powers. At the same time as I reply to these charges, I am surprised the worthy prosecutor had omitted others, notably the names of those who were in it. Five-sixths of the dossier is historic, old hat. Only a sixth deals with current matters.''

Reyshahri bridled angrily at the dig from his enemy in the dock.

''I accept as always,'' Sadegh went on, ''the charge of plotting to overthrow the government or regime. I have said over and over to you that our plan was based on an agreement to maintain the Islamic Republic of Iran and the Imam. My friends gave their word that they accepted these principles: to replace the government except the Imam. I fought all my life for the Islamic Republic of Iran. Therefore, I am not about to act as you accuse, or to give it away as a present to a hundred people or two thousand or two hundred thousand.''

Exasperated, the prosecutor shouted, ''Do you accept the constitution?''

Calmly, Sadegh replied. ''I accept it but not the manner in which it is applied. The constitution is a contract signed between the people and the government and so both are obliged to apply its articles. If one of the citizens fails to apply it, the apparatus of the state arrests, judges and condemns him. But if the government breaks the pledge, what must be done? *You* say, like it or lump it. If you have force and brutality before you, you just say that's how it is and that's how it will be — if you can't look, close your eyes.''

''Do you accept the constitution?''

''For the fifth time, yes.''

''Does the constitution of the Islamic Republic allow you to mount a coup d'état?''

Eye to eye, Sadegh looked at Reyshahri. ''No. But it doesn't permit the heads of state to break the constitution, either. The constitution was first broken by the authorities of the State.''

The session ended in a welter of contradictions.

At the next session they attacked Sadegh's foreign connections and returned again to the fate of the Imam. The prosecutor zeroed in on two businessmen, Habibzadeh and Kambizi, who had come to talk to Sadegh about a coup.

''They came to ask me to support their organization, and eventually I agreed. We talked of fighting to change the government and save the Islamic Republic. They talked of circling the Imam's house. One was to buy the house next door. They decided to blow

288 The Man in the Mirror

up the Imam's house, but after discussion they dropped the idea. I hadn't decided on it yet."

Then it was Mahdavi's turn. He poured forth with all that had been torn from him in Evin: trips to raise support, trips to Lebanon, trips to Germany, meetings with Villalon and encounters with the Saudis.

Sadegh watched sadly. He would not join Mahdavi's spectacle. When they turned to him, he denied everything. And on it went, with Sadegh smiling wryly. The effort they were making to put a legal patina on all this farce was almost rewarding.

Anxious to maintain the judicial stance, the court proudly published an account of the proceedings, but they did not publish everything.

I read the transcript of the trial in the Teheran papers in a daze. Alef told me about the portions of the trial that were not printed. These details were passed to him by a friend on the inside, who had witnessed Reyshahri's anger at Sadegh's often crude defiance.

Among the portions not printed for "moral reasons" were exchanges on Sadegh's moral conduct.

"Why did you never marry?" Reyshahri asked snidely.

"If I want a glass of milk, I don't need to buy the whole cow," was Sadegh's shocking reply.

They arrested a woman who had been associated with him and interrogated her in prison.

And they questioned him again on the satanic Western journalist, Jerome.

"She was your CIA contact and arranged your meetings with Hamilton Jordan," they accused. "You arranged special permission for her to come here when no journalists were allowed in the country."

"I arranged for her to come because she cared about Iran. I wanted the Western world to understand our side."

Above all, they censored Sadegh's damning arguments against the men who were trying him for his life.

"This is all backwards!" Sadegh roared. "You should be sitting here, and I should be sitting there! You should be on trial for all the crimes you have committed in the name of Islam!"

Behind the scenes, Nabawi and Farsi urged Reyshahri to execute him.

Once, long ago in Paris, when the dream of the revolution became a nightmare, Bourguet and Cheron had compared their friend to the French revolutionary Georges Danton. Danton was one of the most complex and controversial statesmen of the period. He began as a pure revolutionary and took part in the revolutionary government. But gradually he became more moderate and objected to the government's reign of terror. His opposition led to his arrest, trial and execution by his one-time partner Robespierre.

Sadegh's trial, I reflected, was eerily like Danton's. The French revolutionary had raged in the courtroom, his voice echoing across the Seine as he accused his accusers: "Yes," he cried, "I, Danton, will unmask the dictatorship that is now revealing itself in its true colors . . ." Angrily, the president of the court rang his bell. "Do you not hear my bell!" he cried. "Bell!" Danton shouted back at him, his voice now hoarse. "A man who is fighting for his life pays no attention to bells!"

Sadegh knew what Danton knew, that they had decided the verdict long before the trial. When asked by the tribunal for his address, Danton had given it as, "Soon in oblivion . . . in the future in history's pantheon."

Sadegh resorted to no such flourishes. He demanded the death penalty. Only Khomeini could save him now.

Ahmad visited Sadegh in his cell and told him that his father would pardon him if he retracted everything and begged forgiveness. Sadegh sent Ahmad away.

It was Sadegh's greatest challenge to the Imam. To save his "son," Khomeini would have to recant, to acknowledge his own sins. But Sadegh knew his "father" would not pick up the terrible gauntlet.

And in contrast to Danton, Sadegh did not beg the people to forgive him. "All I want," he told a sympathetic guard, "is for the people to know that I accept my responsibility for what has happened and that I stayed to try to change it. That's all."

Back on the silent path, Sadegh returned to his meditation and his God.

* * *

I called Bourguet on the phone from the Toronto newsroom. Someone with a contact in Khomeini's office passed the word to Christian that the death sentence would not be carried out. Sadegh would be given seven years in prison.

We breathed a painful sigh of relief and set about verifying the news. We were assured he would indeed be given a seven-year sentence.

I focused on Sadegh, on all I knew of him. I wondered if he would welcome this news, or if he would not, after all, prefer to end the action and the passion.

*   *   *

There is another Persian legend, about a magical bird called the Simurgh. It is a fabulous bird with brilliant blue and gold and green and red feathers that sweep into a long plume like a horse's tail. It lives on a mountain and can make others immortal. A sufi mystic based a poem on the legend:

One day thirty small, ordinary birds decide to go in search of the Simurgh. When they finally reach their destination, exhausted and bedraggled, they find, at last, the Simurgh.

And in her radiant face, they see—themselves. For *Simurgh* means *thirty birds*, and the Simurgh says: I am a mirror set before your eyes, and all who come before my splendor see themselves, their own unique reality.

The passionate journey ends in the cold stone of Evin, name of evil, his Bastille. It had fallen and risen up again to claim him.

But he had found the fabulous bird. He had struggled up the face of the mountain, and there he had met the dragon. And he plunged his sword into its red-gold eye, the dragon dissolved and there before him was the beautiful Simurgh.

*   *   *

They came for Sadegh in the night and walked him to the wall. They raised their guns and fired. The bullets spit into his skin, exploded into sparkling feathers of green and blue, gold and red, and his body sank to the cold stone floor of Evin. He took flight forever.

23

September 16, 1982. It was morning, the morning after we'd been assured Sadegh would not be executed. My phone rang. It was Dennis calling from the newsroom.

"Last night — The news just came over the wires. I'm sorry. I didn't want you to hear from someone, someone else . . ."

As I hung up the phone I went into a kind of trance. In the months of agonizing, I had almost wished it was over, wished for this moment. And now I would have given my own life to change it.

"We believe that a man continues to live after life . . . it's not the end of it, it's just the beginning; it's just passing by," Sadegh had said.

Sadegh was dead. The notion was strange, meaningless. "No!" I railed in the emptiness. I phoned Christian.

"We don't know exactly what happened, but they have done it," he said.

In my mind I saw the cell, the walk to the wall. I saw him standing there, wordless, and I knew absolutely that in his heart there had been no fear, no frantic regret. I knew that he went to his death and his future with more calm and fuller knowledge than those who had sent him there would go to theirs. And yet I saw the guns fire, felt the bullets sink in, felt his body falling. I fell with it into a well of pain and loss. I could not rise with his soul. Earthbound without him, I wept, marooned and angry. Angry because he hadn't saved himself, yet knowing and accepting why he hadn't.

Our whole relationship had been marked with contradiction and mixed emotions. But none were greater then those I now felt. I loved him. I admired his decision. I wept for him and for me. And I hated him for leaving me. Admiration, love and anger warred for supremacy in my thoughts. One minute I was awed by his honor; the next I cursed him for not telling a crazy old man he was sorry. It would have been so easy, and then we could have been together. He could have lived to fight another battle, perhaps save Iran from the monster he'd brought home. Who else was there? I began to

291

wonder if he had lost heart entirely, and in fact had willfully gone to his death in an elaborate suicide, a final defiant beau geste that was also a final escape.

Horribly, I found myself blaming him for leaving us all, taking the easy way out. Easy? No. It was yet another contradiction. What did I know of the courage and agony of his final days and last seconds?

I checked with my American contacts. According to them, American surveillance had picked up a phone call from Ahmad to Reyshahri immediately after the announcement of the execution. "You have done this against my father's order!" Ahmad allegedly said. "You are to go to him at Djamaran! Now!"

The Americans further claimed that Ahmad had then taken a military helicopter from Qom to Teheran, where the Ayatollah met with Reyshahri in a furious confrontation.

"If the Americans are trying to spread the word that Khomeini is innocent," Shin concluded, "then as far as I'm concerned that's one more sign that they now support this regime."

Later, when I spoke with State Department officials, they dismissed the suggestion that the Tudeh had been instrumental in Sadegh's destruction.

"Nonsense. He was betrayed by two air force officers in his plot," said the CIA informants. "Not Tudeh. He was paranoid about communists."

"That should have suited Washington. Why didn't you go along with him when Bourguet came?"

"As far as we were concerned, it was too amateur. Nothing to be taken seriously."

And since when is a coup that would have included key military leaders, major tribal chieftains, many Pasdaran and the chief religious opponent of Khomeini, nothing to be taken seriously? Since when is a group that had the support of the Saudis and other Arab nations, and other moderate liberal leaders of Iran, an "amateur" effort to be dismissed out of hand? Hardly as amateur as the contra effort in Nicaragua, I thought.

"The Americans are either so stupid they still believe everything the Israelis tell them and still think Sadegh was KGB, or they are very smart and are using this regime to wipe out all the leftists and nationalist forces in Iran. So far, that's exactly what's happening. The Tudeh will be next. Then the Americans will have Iran on its knees and at their feet. With this bunch in power, any of them could be working for the Americans now," Shin told me.

I reeled in this dizzy atmosphere of what Jon Randal of the *Washington Post* called the "perceived prevalence of plots."

But there always remained that terrible question: did the father kill the son?

"When Reyshahri asked for Khomeini's order, the Imam said, 'Do what is good for Islam,' " said one report from Iran. All the words attributed to Khomeini were ambiguous.

I thought of Sadegh's reflections on Khomeini so long ago when he'd visited him in Iraq: *"He's a real politician. Sometimes he confirms subjects without mentioning them directly. Sometimes when he hears something indirectly he doesn't say anything until the action has been taken on the matter and he knows it cannot be changed; then he rejects the action. Because by doing that he covers himself as a leader but the matter which had to be said or done is already done. So nobody can blame him for it."*

I thought of King Henry, who wished to be rid of Becket without staining his hands with blood. He cried, "Will no one rid me of this meddlesome priest?" Then he was horrified and relieved when somebody did.

Khomeini had let it be understood that he must be rid of Sadegh, his meddlesome son. As surely as if he had stood by the lines of guns and called, "Fire!" this father had killed his son.

And when I was exhausted from fighting my own emotions, I was left with simple emptiness. I was drained, but there was no respite.

Rumors began to circulate. They sprouted like mushrooms in the darkness of Iranian censorship.

"They didn't really kill him," voices whispered. "Khomeini saved him and he's in prison, but he's safe."

My phone rang incessantly. "Have you heard from him? If he's alive he'll get word to us."

"No! This is senseless. Khomeini wouldn't save his grandmother, let alone Sadegh," I cried. "Stop, please stop."

Yet some part of me clung to the rumors. I talked with Shin.

"The Tudeh started the rumors," Shin told me, "to make people believe he was a fraud, that he didn't really die a martyr and a hero true to his convictions. Even now they have to try to destroy him."

"Do you *know* then?" I pleaded. "No one saw the execution.

They didn't publish pictures the way they always do.''

"Of course not. They were afraid of the reaction. Sadegh wasn't just anyone, you know.''

"What do you *know*?''

Only then did Shin realize that I did not know.

"I was there,'' Shin replied. "At the burial. We had to look. Unless I saw I couldn't believe it, either. Later, we moved Sadegh from the Behesht Zahra to the family plot.''

"Had they shot him?'' I had to ask. "Or hanged him?''

"They shot him. His chest was full of bullet holes. I couldn't tell if they had tortured him. But in prison his beard had grown in all black. And there it was snow white.''

Then Alef called, numb with grief. "They shot him from the feet up. Slowly. It took five hours for him to die,'' he told me. "Oh, God, I shouldn't have told you. But I had to tell you. What are we going to do without him?'' Alef railed in the distance.

A young Pasdar guard who had grown fond of Sadegh in prison went mad, haunting Sadegh's cell, asking when Sadegh was coming back.

Another rumor drifted out of Iran. Sadegh, it was said, had left documents damaging to the regime somewhere in Europe. These were to be disclosed if anything happened to him.

"I haven't received any documents,'' Christian said. "But there is a story they are in Germany and will be sent to me.''

No documents appeared.

Shin admitted he'd started that rumor to try to save Sadegh's life.

But there were documents and papers in France. Christian had put them in a vault. He suggested we should go through them and through the house in Versailles Sadegh had bought to house the Imam so long ago.

I flew to Paris for a memorial service for Sadegh and while I was there, I decided, I would go to the house.

Later, I found myself in the cool shadows of the mosque in Paris. Carved sandlewood and brass lamps filled the prayer room with the aroma and light of the mysteries of life and death, as two old mullahs said a prayer for the dead one who had been named Sadegh Ghotbzadeh. We sat silently by the walls, François, Christian, Bertrand and other friends. I wore a black veil like the other women, listening as the two old voices chanted in unison the "Ya Sin'' of the Koran . . .

Surely it is we who give life to the dead, and we record that
which they send forward and that which they leave behind.
We have recorded everything in a clear book . . .
Thus Holy is He in whose hand is the kingdom over all things.
To him will you all be brought back.

Behind my veil I wept, unconsoled, finding no comfort in this
alien faith nor in any God. Wanting life, and Sadegh beside me, I
mourned for my loss, for his life, for love, truth, beauty, joy and
knowledge. I mourned for Iran.

*   *   *

Winter was approaching and the days were shorter now. The sky
was cloudy and the air damp that late afternoon when I reached
the house in Versailles. I struggled through the overgrown garden,
thorns of dead rose bushes catching my clothing. I paused at the
front door. The shutters were broken and I hesitated before entering, lest those who had broken in were still in the vicinity. The
winter light was gray, and I stood silent in the gloom trying to hear.
There was no sound. Fitting the key, I opened the door.

It was dark, musty and cold inside. Papers and books were strewn
everywhere. The desk drawers had been thrown on the floor. Boards
had been ripped up, and by the fireplace, small red candles had
been set in their own melted wax to stand on the floor.

Who were they? Who had come for a fragment of Sadegh's life?
Who of his enemies? And what did they seek? The "dangerous"
documents? I thanked heaven that Christian had removed all the
important papers and taken them to the safety of a bank vault.

I stood in the devastation, then slowly, painfully, I started picking out some of the letters and papers.

I found Sadegh's passport collection near old letters from Beheshti
and Bani Sadr. I found old press releases and yellowing back issues
of *Iran Azad*. And there were copies of Sadegh's hundreds of letters to newspapers and human rights groups harping relentlessly
over the years on the Shah's regime. Piles of Khomeini's pronouncements from Najaf and boxes of books lay about. There were four
dozen copies of a volume by Bazargan here, crates of Taleghani's
books there, and piles of Shariati's pamphlets and letters from
Habibi, from unknown Alis and Mohammads, old girlfriends and
relatives. There were Christmas cards and bank statements, phone

bills and shopping lists. The house was filled with all the flotsam of a human life. I wandered, picking up this, looking at that.

Empty rooms and peeling wallpaper and remnants of an extraordinary lifetime.

Upstairs in more bare rooms I found boxes of old clothing and worn shoes alongside new towels and blankets for the expected occupant, the wandering Imam.

As I worked through the wreckage, I thought only of Sadegh. Those last seconds. Upstairs there were more boxes. A gray coat, well-worn shoes. I picked them up, and put them down again. Inside another box I found photographs.

Kneeling, I pawed through them, too. There were snapshots of a young Sadegh with his revolutionary friends in Washington at the mosque, in Paris at the Eiffel Tower, in Beirut with Tabatabai, and, separate from the rest, pictures of a severe old man in a black turban: Khomeini at home during his exile in Iraq. I stared at the photographs and wondered if Sadegh had taken them. The black eyes seemed to scowl at me in silent evil triumph from behind the looking glass.

I threw the pictures on the floor and trembled violently, raging for the hundredth time against Sadegh's blindness, his refusal to see until too late that this was the dragon, the imposter, the negative image. Persian images of faith and father, deceit and self-deception, truth and fiction, appearance and reality.

And then, before me in the box was a picture of Sadegh as he had been in Paris. He wore the jaunty astrakhan hat and was the warm, elegant bear with the half-smile. I had a sudden image of him cold and dead in prison so far away, and just as suddenly, I felt his presence, life passing by. And in that empty house I wept and howled until I, too, was empty.

Outside it grew dark and windy. Inside, I grew quieter, subsiding, until in the candlelight, it seemed that I could see him in a Persian mirror, standing behind me. Then at last, he moved to stand, without reflection, before me.

We danced in the lovers' circle.

EPILOGUE

After Sadegh's death, those who had defeated him continued to consolidate their power.

Preeminent in Iran were Rafsanjani and Khamenei.

The two were locked in a bitter power struggle, each with his eye on eventual supremacy once Ayatollah Khomeini died.

Khoeini'a, spiritual adviser to the students, sat just below Rafsanjani as deputy speaker of the parliament, wavering between the two camps.

Mohammed Reyshahri, Sadegh's executioner, was promoted to minister of information, meaning he became in effect head of SAVAMA, working hand in glove with Rafsanjani.

Dr. Peyman, the PLO dentist, went to Moscow where he was lavishly feted. He is said to have advised his hosts they should give up Marxism and adopt Islam.

Exercising great power from behind the scenes, as ever, were Sadegh's mortal enemies, Djalalodin Farsi and Behzad Nabawi, both closely in league with Khamenei. Nabawi became Minister of Light Industry. Farsi sat in parliament and, as a powerful figure in the IRP, was on the Committee to Islamicize the University, and supervised the "reeducation" of prisoners in Evin. Farsi continued to work with Qaddafi. Khamenei restored good relations with Tripoli.

Sadegh's friends and erstwhile allies, some of whom became enemies, also continued their work.

Bani Sadr remained in exile in France writing tracts. Though he mourned Sadegh privately, his book on the story of the revolution bore no mention of Ghotbzadeh. Never once admitting any errors on his part, he continued to believe he would return to Iran as president. When I asked him if that was so, could I return to Iran without a black veil of oppression over my head, he replied that he couldn't promise that, or even fight for it.

Ibrahim Yazdi remained in Teheran, allied with Bazargan, a figure of much speculation. Though in apparent opposition to the regime, he was able to travel to the United States and was relatively free.

Mehdi Bazargan, who continued active opposition to the regime in his newsletter, was severely beaten by Pasdars on one occasion, and his offices were ransacked, but he remains at liberty, inexplicably protected by both Montazeri and Khomeini.

Ayatollah Shariatmadari was denied medical help, liberty and comfort by Khomeini to the end. He finally died in 1986.

Mansour Farhang, too, escaped into exile. He crawled on his hands and knees over the Turkish border, hiding from searchlights under the moon. He returned to teaching in the United States, his analysis of the revolution changing each time I saw him. He, also, sadly regretted his role in working against Sadegh and for Bani Sadr. "Why couldn't we see then," he said to me, "that of all of us, Sadegh was the only one that was authentic? Sadegh was for real."

Nuri Albala claims that on his last visit to Iran in 1982, he and Sadegh were reconciled. Christian Bourguet says this last part is true. Albala continues to practice law in Paris, and has officially left the French Communist party.

Hector Villalon continues his business affairs out of Paris. He keeps a photograph of Sadegh in his desk drawer.

"Alef" and "Shin," whose names I have taken from the Persian alphabet, are now in exile.

Christian Bourguet, François Cheron and Bertrand Vallette continue their law practice in Paris together. The Avenue de l'Observatoire is no longer the center of Iranian politics, though the lawyers handle some work for the opposition and some cases relating to France and the current regime. The three lawyers, their wives and their families were irrevocably altered by Sadegh and the revolution, and in them all there seems to be a permanent corner of mourning for his loss.

Iran, Israel, Libya, Syria, Lebanon, the Soviet Union and the United States all gained as well as lost.

The old lines were still drawn, between the "Libyan" faction of extremists, and the "Syrian" faction of relative moderates.

Syria had been playing with fire, backing Iran in the war against its own old enemy Iraq, and using the "Islamic Amal" extremists against the PLO and Arafat. But Assad did not want fundamentalist ideas to spread, threatening his own socialist regime.

When President Khamenei visited Damascus on September 8, 1984, Syrian president Hafez al Assad asked him to hold the line on Shi'a extremism in South Lebanon, as it became increasingly clear that Iran was backing the Hezb'ollahi and fanatic infiltrators into Amal.

Qaddafi, on the other hand, was pleased when Khamenei visited him the next day. To be sure, Amal had wiped out his own proxies in Lebanon, the Morabitoun, but the Hezb'ollahi, the pro-Libyan, anti-Syrian militants there backed by Khamenei, Farsi and his friends, were gaining ground every day. Largely thanks to resentment of the Israeli occupation.

In June 1982, when Sadegh was in prison, the Israelis had massively invaded Lebanon again. This time they went all the way to Beirut. The devastation horrified even many of Israel's friends.

Abuses under the occupation turned the Shi'a from potential friends into enemies of Israel. Nabbih Berri, responsible for the South, vowed to drive the Israelis out. The Lebanese army refused to intervene when Hezbies attacked political targets, and the Hezb'ollahi, too, grew stronger in the fertile ground of resentment for the Israeli occupation. Soon Amal and the Hezbies were rivals for control of the south.

American and European hostages were seized by the Hezbies and related "grouplets" under the direction of Khamenei, Montazeri, Farsi and their groups in Iran, while Amal and Syria tried to control them.

I watched in dismay as the twin of the Iranian beast slouched toward Lebanon to be born.

The Israelis, I reflected, might have cause to rue their efforts against Sadegh.

And what of Moscow and the Tudeh?

With the moderates destroyed and the Mudjahedeen decimated, the Iranian clergy turned its attention to the communists: their time had come. Even as the Tudeh newspaper *Mardom* proudly claimed credit for its role in helping rid the revolution of the "ambitious traitor liberals" Sadegh and Bani Sadr, the regime was purging Tudeh people from ministries and industry, having declared that the Kremlin was an "enemy of Islam."

In February 1983, the Tudeh Party was declared illegal. Members were required to declare themselves and repent. Over a thousand went to prison, and among them was the secretary general himself, Noureddine Kiannouri.

Eleven were executed. Others were pardoned after elaborate confession and recantations. But the leaders of the party, Kiannouri, Partovi and Ehsan Tabari, remained in prison without sentencing.

Moscow howled with rage. Radio broadcasts into Iran from the Soviet Union railed furiously against this treachery, which it characterized as a betrayal of the revolution. The Soviet Union, Moscow insisted, had always been a loyal supporter of the Islamic revolution.

Rafsanjani replied that the Soviet Union had the same goals as the United States, to undermine the Islamic revolution and isolate Iran. Both superpowers were satanic.

Moscow responded angrily, reminding Rafsanjani of its many joint ventures with the Islamic Republic, including the Isfahan steel mill and railways and communications links.

Iran eventually sent a delegation to Moscow, saying nothing about its mission publicly. A few weeks later, though there did not seem to be any noticeable improvement in relations, the trials of the rest of the Tudeh people were indefinitely postponed, and relations with Moscow gradually improved. The Soviet embassy expanded and diplomatic visits were exchanged.

When the dust had settled, there was Behzad Nabawi, as secure as ever and more, as Minister of Light Industry.

I pondered this. Certainly Nabawi's was the kind of post the people working for the Soviets usually go after, minister of planning being another favorite. Those two ministries are the key to planning from within, and therefore are more important than the more glamorous posts of defense or foreign minister.

But was Nabawi in the Soviet camp, or had he truly gone over to the clergy — and indeed, helped to turn the Tudeh Party in? The regime clearly had an extensive, detailed knowledge of the innards of the Tudeh. It became clear in the trials, when many were pardoned, that someone had come to the rescue, someone powerful, within the regime. Moscow was far from finished.

Wondering if the American authorities had ever realized Sadegh had never been a friend of the KGB, I went to the State Department to see those who had dealt with Christian Bourguet. They peered at me owlishly, as I theorized that Israeli disinformation on Sadegh had misled them and asked to see more of the fat file on him they had ludicrously censored. "We'll look into it," they said and a silence descended.

In November 1986, American citizens were shocked to learn that the Reagan administration, using Israel as middleman, had been selling major arms to Iran for almost two years. The scandal rocked Washington.

Those of us who had been on the beat had reported over the years on sundry Israeli arms deals and on Washington's lax attitude to illegal arms traffic to Iran. Men at the State Department admitted candidly weapons were getting to both Iran and Iraq in order to keep the pot boiling, thus preventing either side from winning. It suited all parties.

But the scope of Iranscam, as it came to be called, amazed even jaded journalists. Ronald Reagan arming Ayatollah Khomeini? Reagan and his staff claimed they had been dealing with moderates to bolster reformist elements in Iran, a country America could not afford to lose entirely for obvious geopolitical reasons. It rapidly became clear, however, that the Americans had been dealing with Rafsanjani with Khomeini's approval. And that, in spite of public statements to the contrary, they had been bartering arms for hostages held in Lebanon.

One of those involved with Rafsanjani was Sadegh Tabatabai, scarcely a moderate with his close ties to Khomeini and his business affairs with Ahmad Khomeini. He was arrested in Germany on charges of drug smuggling, but was released after much diplomatic pressure and dealing. He later continued his lucrative commerce, reportedly much of it in arms deals for the regime. When I spoke to him on the phone, he refused to confirm or deny reports he was a middleman in Iranscam, but my own sources assure me he was.

Rafsanjani, of course, was not entirely in control of the captives. Khamenei's bunch were. The Americans had been duped all round, blackmailed partly by Rafsanjani's later flirtations with Moscow, and by their worries about the pro-Moscow elements in Teheran.

I marveled at the continuing ignorance of American policy. Many agents in the State Department and the CIA had tried to warn their superiors about Rafsanjani, but the cowboys in the National Security Council galloped over their heads and straight into an ambush. Former national security council advisor, Bud McFarlane, and the redoubtable Oliver North flew into Teheran with a planeload of weapons — and left empty-handed, of course.

There were those in the American administration who were willing to support the brutal theocracy in Iran in the name of anti-communism. As usual, anti-communism was the bottom line on the morality of American foreign policy.

Rafsanjani earned points by getting weapons and Khamenei lost nothing, since he still had the hostages and his Hezbies.

Israel, it turned out, had helped lead the Americans down the garden path. David Kimche, ex-MOSSAD and Foreign Ministry officer, had assured McFarlane and others that they were dealing with moderates. It was the same pattern we had seen during the revolution and hostage crisis: American naiveté following Israeli leads. Israel, no better and no worse than other states involved, was pursuing its own self-interest in keeping an Iranian thorn in Arab sides. If need be, Israel would defeat Iran itself later, or so Rafael Eytan, former Israeli army chief of staff, predicted.

But I wondered if the Israelis would have the chance. They too had helped unleash the monster of fundamentalist Islamic revival. Such a revival is far more potent than a military force. It is a social phenomenon that could become uncontrollable and could consume much of the Moslem world. An Iranian victory in such a war would give Khomeini's Islam tremendous psychological credibility in the rest of the Moslem world, a world full of the lost, the poor and the powerless.

Sadegh was a true moderate, and Sadegh's vision of Iran would have been a true alternative for all of them, but they destroyed him. Ultimately, they all had played into Khomeini's hands.

In Iran the arrests and executions continued. Teenaged children were taken from the schoolrooms by Pasdars who roared up in their vans and stormed in shouting, ''You! And you and you! You have been denounced!'' The children were never seen again.

A young girl I knew was seized on the street by the Pasdars and taken to Evin, where they pulled out all her fingernails because she was wearing nailpolish. Another friend was dragged from her home one night and taken to prison because her boyfriend had been seen going to visit her. In prison, a powerful mullah offered to help her if she would agree to be his *sigheh*. If not, he could just as easily kill her. When he let her out of prison, she escaped the country.

The war with Iraq dragged on. By 1987, more than one million were dead, mostly Iranians. These horrendous casualties were largely due to the fact that the Iranians attacked the heavily armed Iraqi installations with wave after wave of soldiers who were mowed down by gunfire. Glorious martyrs all, some units were said to be made up of twelve-year-olds.

Prices in Iran soared, ten, twenty times over, as people queued for chickens, eggs and bread. Everything was rationed by coupons, which were oddly abundant for cadres of the IRP.

The regime continued to persecute religious minorities, especially
the Baha'i. In 1985, adding to other harassment, all Baha'is who
had worked for the government were told to refund to the regime
their life's earnings. All who didn't would be arrested.

And the Mudjahedeen and others who dared openly attack or
even speak against the regime, were treated to the same hot irons
and electrodes and whips that SAVAK had used.

Another organization called the Gasht-e Thar Allah, the Mobile
Units of the Wrath of God, sent out guards who patroled the cities
in cars, machine guns at the ready, looking for suspicious characters. They hauled off anyone who displeased them. Khomeini made
a few half-hearted efforts to curb their excesses, ordering the courts
to end unlawful imprisonment and accidental killing of children in
house raids, but he never tried to enforce them.

When the universities began to reopen, applicants were required
to pass new tests of political loyalty, and the curriculum itself, even in
such areas as medical studies, was purged of Western terms and
un-Islamic ideas, and replaced by Koranic studies. In medicine and
other sciences, this was disastrous: "I am not going to be a very
good doctor," mourned a young friend of mine who had managed
to dissemble his way through the political loyalty test to get into
medical school.

The loyalty tests were required for public service jobs and government civil service posts as well. The IRP was in full control now,
and the pragmatists such as Prime Minister Mir Hosain Mousavi
decided it was time to let up a little. They persuaded Khomeini to
issue an eight-point declaration curbing the worst excesses, particularly those of the Pasdaran, banning its freewheeling house raids
and wiretapping, and ending the loyalty tests, which continued
nonetheless, in reduced form.

Montazeri finally called for relaxation of controls, saying people
should be executed only if they were a danger to the country.
Montazeri's forces won out over Rafsanjani's in this, and Ladjevardi,
the Butcher of Teheran, Rafsanjani's ally, was removed from his
post as prosecutor general at Evin.

The relaxation did not, of course, mean the mullahs were becoming soft-hearted. The terror had established their power; they must
now settle down and consolidate it. Prime Minister Mousavi made
it clear that the regime would still strike ruthlessly if opposed, warning people that the revolutionary organizations would remain intact
and powerful. None of the architects of the terror were touched. A

committee established by the Imam to look into citizens' complaints against the repression was lost in a haze of bureaucratic shuffles. The repression continued in a million ways.

And over it all reigned the *faghih*, Ayatollah Ruhollah Khomeini. In his will, he wrote that Montazeri should replace him in matters strictly concerning religion. But he judged Montazeri insufficiently astute to run the politics of the nation. That task, he decreed, should be the shared power of Montazeri, Rafsanjani, and Khamenei.

The structures were there, and as these three kept each other on the defensive, the victor would be Khomeini's Islam. The dragon breathed and heaved and settled its great weight on the land.

One man who might have changed it all was dead.

INDEX

Abbas the Great, Shah, 222-3
AFASPI. *See* Association
    Française de l'Amitié et
    Support Pour l'Iran
Afghanistan: Soviet Union
    aggression in, 210-13
Aguilar, Andres, 178
Albala, Nuri, 67, 85, 88, 149, 168,
    198, 213-14, 298
Algerian mediation: hostage
    crisis, 241-2, 254
Ali, 21, 75, 155, 193
Amal, 255, 264, 265, 299
Amiralai, Shamseddine, 159,
    160, 162, 164, 188, 252, 253
Arafat, Yasser, 77, 81-2, 142-3,
    210, 266
Army of the Revolutionary
    Guards. *See* Sepah Pasdaran
Assad, Hafez Al, 64, 83, 84, 85,
    87, 209, 298
Assad, Rifaat Al, 64, 83, 84, 87
Association Française de l'Amitié
    et Support Pour l'Iran
    (AFASPI), 67, 121
Ayat, Hassan, 268, 272
Azadegan, 253
Azhari, Gen. Gholem Reza, 21

Baghdad, 69-70
Baha'i, 303
Bahonar, 272-3
Bahrami, Ali Akbar. *See*
    Rafsanjani, Hojatoleslam
    Hashemi
Bahrami, Mohammad Hashemi,
    239, 249
Bakhtiar, Shahpour, 26, 32, 39,
    112, 114, 201

Bakr, Hassan Al, 70
Bani Sadr, Abolhassan, 29, 30,
    34, 42, 60, 88, 106, 116, 213;
    constitution, 122-4; elections,
    154, 155, 220, 221, 228;
    escaped, 270, 272, 276, 297;
    Ghotbzadeh's arrest, 234;
    hostage crisis, 180, 181, 182,
    184, 189-90, 198, 199, 206;
    Khomeini's government, 120,
    121, 126-7; minister of foreign
    affairs, 138, 141, 143-5;
    revolution plotted in Paris,
    62-3, 67, 68, 76
Bani Sadr, Ozra, 62, 234
Bazargan, Mehdi, 2, 48-50, 52,
    69, 106, 123, 126, 220, 240, 268,
    276, 297-8; attack on U.S.
    embassy, 131-2, 133, 134, 136-7,
    138; prime minister, 112, 113,
    120-1
Beddredine, Abbas, 258-61, 265
Bedjaoui, Mohammad, 178
Beheshti, Ayatollah Mohammad,
    165, 184, 227, 240, 271; founder
    of IRP, 105-6, 116; hostage
    crisis, 142, 144, 145, 151, 180,
    181, 188, 192, 209, 241-2, 253-4;
    Jerome's interview, 108-10;
    political importance, 105-6,
    116, 121, 123-4, 136, 178, 192,
    239, 241, 267
Behzadi, Col., 244, 245
Beirut, 263
Berri, Nabbih, 81, 264-5, 268, 299
Book of Kings, 139-41, 175
Borchgrave, Arnaud de, 10, 85
Bourguet, Christian, 17, 30, 32,
    42, 67-8, 77-8, 83, 84, 88, 89,
    201, 206, 252, 258, 274-5, 279,